The Presidency of
JAMES
MADISON

AMERICAN PRESIDENCY SERIES

Donald R. McCoy, Clifford S. Griffin, Homer E. Socolofsky
General Editors

George Washington, Forrest McDonald
John Adams, Ralph Adams Brown
Thomas Jefferson, Forrest McDonald
James Madison, Robert Allen Rutland
John Quincy Adams, Mary W. M. Hargreaves
Martin Van Buren, Major L. Wilson
William Henry Harrison & John Tyler, Norma Lois Peterson
James K. Polk, Paul H. Bergeron
Zachary Taylor & Millard Fillmore, Elbert B. Smith
James Buchanan, Elbert B. Smith
Andrew Johnson, Albert Castel
Rutherford B. Hayes, Ari Hoogenboom
James A. Garfield & Chester A. Arthur, Justus D. Doenecke
Grover Cleveland, Richard E. Welch, Jr.
Benjamin Harrison, Homer E. Socolofsky & Allan B. Spetter
William McKinley, Lewis L. Gould
William Howard Taft, Paolo E. Coletta
Warren G. Harding, Eugene P. Trani & David L. Wilson
Herbert C. Hoover, Martin L. Fausold
Harry S. Truman, Donald R. McCoy
Dwight D. Eisenhower, Elmo Richardson
Lyndon B. Johnson, Vaughn Davis Bornet

The Presidency of

JAMES MADISON

Robert Allen Rutland

UNIVERSITY PRESS OF KANSAS

Published by the University Press of Kansas (Lawrence,
Kansas 66045), which was organized by the Kansas
Board of Regents and is operated and funded by Emporia
State University, Fort Hays State University,
Kansas State University, Pittsburg State University, the
University of Kansas, and Wichita State University

Library of Congress Cataloging-in-Publication Data

Rutland, Robert Allen, 1922–
The presidency of James Madison / Robert Allen Rutland.
    p.   cm. — (American presidency series)
    Includes bibliographical references.
    ISBN 0-7006-0465-0 (alk. paper)
    1. United States—Politics and government—1809–1817.   2. Madison,
    James, 1751–1836.   3. United States—History—War of 1812.
        I. Title.   II. Series.
            E341.R87   1990
    973.5'1'092 — dc20   89-70419
                    CIP
British Library Cataloguing in Publication Data is available.

Printed in the United States of America
10   9   8   7   6   5   4   3   2   1

70120

To Norman A. Graebner
Valued Friend, Outstanding Scholar

CONTENTS

FOREWORD

The aim of the American Presidency Series is to present historians and the general reading public with interesting, scholarly assessments of the various presidential administrations. These interpretive surveys are intended to cover the broad ground between biographies, specialized monographs, and journalistic accounts. As such, each will be a comprehensive, synthetic work which will draw upon the best in pertinent secondary literature, yet leave room for the author's own analysis and interpretation.

Volumes in the series will present the data essential to understanding the administration under consideration. Particularly, each book will treat the then current problems facing the United States and its people and how the president and his associates felt about, thought about, and worked to cope with these problems. Attention will be given to how the office developed and operated during the president's tenure. Equally important will be consideration of the vital relationships between the president, his staff, the executive officers, Congress, foreign representatives, the judiciary, state officials, the public, political parties, the press, and influential private citizens. The series will also be concerned with how this unique American institution — the presidency — was viewed by the presidents, and with what results.

All this will be set, insofar as possible, in the context not only of contemporary politics but also of economics, international relations, law, morals, public administration, religion, and thought. Such a broad approach is necessary to understanding, for a presidential administration is more than the elected and appointed officers composing it, since its work so often reflects the major problems, anxieties, and glories of the nation. In short, the authors in this series will strive to recount and evaluate the record of each administration and to identify its distinctiveness and relationships to the past, its own time, and the future.

The General Editors

PREFACE

The history of a presidency is fascinating to both the reader and the writer. The reader can gain information left out of conventional biographies, whereas the writer can resurrect, enshrine, or bury his or her subject with new interpretations based on fresh evidence and great powers of insight. Usually, of course, these things don't happen. Until recent times, anything scandalous concerning a president made the biographer suspect, and there are no new documents related to Madison that will radically change our interpretation of his tenure in the White House.

But as times change, so do our views of the past — and of past presidents in particular. I grew up in a small town in Oklahoma where every lawyer's office displayed a portrait of Woodrow Wilson; yet I suspect that Wilson's presidential stock has fallen fairly low in the past two or three decades. Similarly, a great deal of reappraisal is now taking place regarding Franklin D. Roosevelt. And almost twenty-five years after the assassination of John F. Kennedy, some historians are wondering aloud about his high ranking among presidents.

As the guessing game goes on, James Madison's eight years in the presidency need to be viewed from a different angle. No thinking person questions Madison's greatness, but such value judgments may be based more on his services to the nation between 1780 and 1797 than on his accomplishments in the White House. The historian Henry Adams left his mark not on one generation but on a whole century when he portrayed Madison, in his two-volume *History of the United States of America during the Administrations of Thomas Jefferson and James Madison,* as an inept, indecisive president who was out of his depth in the executive mansion. "If Madison's fame as a statesman rested on what he wrote as President," Adams contends, "he would be thought not only among the weakest of Executives, but also among the dullest of men, whose liveliest sally of feeling exhausted itself in an epithet, and whose keenest sympathy centered in the tobacco crop."[1]

Irving Brant, in his six-volume biography of Madison, leaned too far in the other direction. Harold Schultz's short biography of Madison was more balanced than either Adams's or Brant's. Schultz, Ralph Ketcham, and Marshall Smelser, in his book on the Jefferson-Madison presidencies, all set a more objective tone and asked that these Republican presidents be judged in terms of their promises and how they kept them. The ability to keep promises, it seems to me, is a good criterion for evaluating a president's effectiveness. In those terms, Jefferson and Polk stand out as among our best presidents. The names of the worst are on every tongue.

Unlike my predecessor as editor of the Madison Papers, Leonard White, I never assumed that Madison "would have been much more at home as president of the University of Virginia . . . than he was as President of the United States."[2] Madison had a clear idea of what a constitutional president ought to do and how he ought to function, particularly in relation to Congress. Madison was a strict constructionist in that regard. In this book I have attempted to portray Madison's flaws, but I confess that I have not gone out of my way to try and reaffirm Henry Adams's harsh judgment. Let the reader decide whether Madison was, as President Kennedy said, "our most underrated president," or whether Adams hit the mark when he stressed "executive weakness" in his work.

I began to take Madison seriously when I was a graduate student, working on a history of the Bill of Rights. After over thirty years of thinking and reading and writing about Madison, I can only conclude that at the end of his presidency the United States of America had at last become a full-fledged member of the community of nations. More than any man then alive, even including Jefferson, Madison deserves most of the credit for that achievement.

Old-fashioned historians — those who are chained to their manual typewriters — must pay homage to the younger, more flexible colleagues who know and can solve the mysteries of the word processor. Thus I am enormously indebted to Jeanne Kerr Sisson at the Madison Papers, University of Virginia,

1. Henry Adams, *History of the United States of America during the Administrations of Thomas Jefferson and James Madison*, vol. 2, *History of the United States of America during the Administrations of James Madison*, Earl N. Harbert, ed. (New York: Library of America, 1986), 125, 1016.

2. Leonard D. White, *The Jeffersonians: A Study in Administrative History, 1801–1829* (New York: Macmillan, 1951), 36.

and Christine Supernaw of the History Department at the University of Tulsa for their skills in eliminating most of the drudgery that writing a book entails. I am also beholden to Paul H. Smith of the Library of Congress for his supportive observations and to the editors at the University Press of Kansas for the skillful editing the manuscript received.

Robert Allen Rutland

1

★ ★ ★ ★ ★

PROLOGUE

In March 1988, as the memories of twenty-two presidential primaries faded, a Baltimore radio station commentator suggested that if James Madison had been involved in a similar nationwide popularity contest he surely would have lost, hands down. "We could probably say the same about John Adams or Thomas Jefferson," the commentator added. Undoubtedly, the roll of presidents who won office because of their political involvement or philosophy rather than their photogenic qualities could be expanded to include nearly every chief executive from Adams to Gerald Ford. When "the office sought the man," political figures often went out of their way to avoid any appearance of electioneering for the presidency. In fact, to have displayed in public a craving for White House tenure was ruinous to more than one prominent politician.

James Madison lost only one election during his political career from 1776 to 1817, and that loss was caused by his decision to take the high ground of principle. In 1777 he refused to provide a barrel of hard cider for thirsty voters and lost to a more liberal candidate who understood such matters. Madison never lost again, but he was quick to admit that he "despised" campaigning; most of the stories concerning Madison's speech making on the hustings are apocryphal. His campaigns were conducted by friends who circulated Madison's letters outlining his views on key public issues. Madison's constituents knew where he stood at all times. During his entire career of public service, including the Virginia House of Delegates (1776, 1784–87, 1800–1801), Virginia Privy Council (1777–79), Continental Congress (1779–83, 1786–88), U.S. House of Representatives (1789–97), secretary of state (1801–9), and president (1809–17), Madison's total campaign expenses could not have exceeded one hundred dollars. Most of the time, a simple franked (and thus free) letter to an active constituent was a sufficient gesture.

In Madison the voters knew what they were getting: a short, baldish, honest man whose speeches were hard to hear — but on paper those speeches made a lot of sense. Madison was a planter's son who never had to hoe a row of corn or tobacco, but he understood the feelings of those who did. Madison was so loyal to his friends that he expected steadfast support from his associates. When his cabinet officers showed signs of weakness or indecision, he was reluctant to dismiss them. When Britain and France tried to provoke a war, Madison struggled to negotiate his way around a fight.

Madison was probably the last survivor from the fading Age of Enlightenment to serve as president of the United States. He stood for something. He believed the American Revolution was an extraordinary event in human history, the harbinger of a new experience for all mankind. Madison expected the United States of America to become "a workshop of liberty" wherein the rest of the world could learn about the blessings of self-government. In terms of the great evil of his day — slavery — he was a realist. In terms of his vision for a Union of hard-working, honest people passionately devoted to the ideals of "life, liberty, and the pursuit of happiness," he was a visionary. Madison was bound to be disappointed, as all dreamers are.

2
★ ★ ★ ★ ★

STORM SIGNALS
FROM THE SENATE

There was a time in American history when presidents were elected but did not "run" for that position and hence never spent a dollar in quest of the nation's highest office. The modern presidency has blurred our historical vision of what the office was created to do and how the first presidents tried to fulfill their constitutional role. Washington's reluctance to serve beyond two terms was but one of the many precedents the first president set that would not erode until the twentieth century. Of the first five presidents, four were Virginians, and none of them ever went among a crowd with arms outstretched to shake hands and court votes. As for their public image, it is unlikely that any president between Washington and Jackson would have been recognized by most Americans. In one sense, the presidents after Washington were to be heard but not seen. Andrew Jackson changed that situation. But by the time Old Hickory took office, the presidency was on a different path than that followed by James Madison.

No president-elect of the United States ever came into office with such a close relationship to his predecessor as did James Madison. The outgoing third president, Thomas Jefferson, was Madison's closest friend. That was part of the problem. Madison learned for certain that he would become president in November 1808, but his nomination as Jefferson's successor had come ten months earlier, deftly arranged by loyal Republicans in Congress intent on squelching serious opposition. Representative John Randolph of Virginia, the enfant terrible of the Republican party, made a noisy but futile effort to prevent Madison's candidacy. As the eccentric leader of the "Tertium Quids" (a small band of congressmen usually in opposition to Jefferson's ad-

3

THE PRESIDENCY OF JAMES MADISON

ministration), Randolph may have disliked Madison because of a perceived slight. There was a rumor that Madison had turned down Randolph's request to be named as the American minister to Britain by simply saying what everybody knew to be true: Randolph, by temperament, was unfit for any diplomatic post.

The other threat to claims from Madison's supporters came from New York, where DeWitt Clinton was eager to vault from the state house to the White House. To head off Clinton, some of Madison's friends in Congress talked about renominating as vice-president DeWitt's uncle, George Clinton. This provoked Senator William Plumer to remark that George Clinton was "old, feeble, and altogether incapable of presiding over the Senate. He has no mind—no intellect—no memory." These qualities seemed, however, to make the old man an ideal vice-president, and Clinton was handily picked by the caucusing congressmen as Madison's running mate.[1]

Full of spite, Randolph spread the story that the Virginia legislature was disenchanted with Madison and favored James Monroe for the presidency. Federalists liked the idea of pushing Monroe because they believed Madison was Jefferson's pet; any candidate was preferable to the outgoing president's choice. Senator Timothy Pickering said it all when he predicted that Madison as president would be Jefferson's "monkey on a leash," with his every move dictated by the retired resident of Monticello.

Despite a straw poll of the Virginia legislators that showed Madison was favored by a 133 to 57 tally, Randolph dredged up old stories in an effort to make Madison seem cowardly and crooked. Randolph, parading his Virginia origins as proof of impartiality, engineered an anti-Madison blast bearing the signatures of seventeen congressmen and sent an address "to the People of the United States" to newspapers. In his screed Randolph claimed that Madison had retired from Congress in 1797 to avoid the slings and arrows fashioned in the Alien and Sedition Acts, and he revived an earlier charge that Madison had connived with land speculators in the notorious Yazoo land fraud.

Both charges were spurious, and knowledgeable men in Congress remembered that Randolph had declared a personal vendetta against Madison a few years earlier after a fight over a proposed purchase of Spanish Florida. In 1806, when President Jefferson wanted two million dollars to buy Florida as he had bought Louisiana, Randolph deserted his chief to denounce the appropriation on the ground that it was wrong "to bully another nation out of its property."[2] Madison's candor at the time—he thought Spanish Florida

1. Quoted in Irving Brant, "The Election of 1808," in Arthur M. Schlesinger, Jr., and Fred Israel, eds., *History of American Presidential Elections, 1789–1968*, 4 vols. (New York: Chelsea House, 1971), 1:191.
2. Quoted in Henry Adams, *History of the United States of America during*

was cheap at the price—infuriated Randolph. Thereafter, Randolph never missed an opportunity to keep Republican waters in Congress muddied by insinuations and innuendoes about Madison's honesty and fitness for office.

Federalists who had chafed under Jefferson's administration disparaged Madison as the "crown prince" but had no candidate of their own able to mount a formidable challenge. Thus, without ever having to make a single campaign speech, Madison realized that he would soon have a new career as first magistrate. Surely, because of his intimate view of the White House during the eight years Jefferson was president, Madison must have had some misgivings as the inevitability of his election became apparent. In other words, the delirium we associate with election to the modern presidency was not evident in 1808. Dolley Madison may have been overjoyed, but James Madison had his sober side. Politics had been his calling from 1776 onward, but his other public posts had been sought or filled with a sense of expectancy and a feeling that he could accomplish something important. Now Madison must have known mingled emotions, for the Republic was at a crossroads between war and peace, the economy was depressed, and his partner in statecraft for the past twenty years was retiring from public life. Knowing that he would be carrying on alone for the first time may have caused Madison to wish for a moment that he, too, was going back to his plantation.

What qualms Madison may have felt as he saw his bustling household prepare for a move to the presidential quarters are of course not known. To partisan outsiders, Jefferson's two terms appeared to have been exemplary in every field save one: foreign affairs. Despite the "Revolution of 1800," with Jefferson's kept promises of lower taxes, a reduction of the national debt, and a decent respect for the civil liberties endangered by the Alien and Sedition Acts, Jefferson and his secretary of state had been forced into a tight corner by the warring powers of Europe.

Britain and France were back at their centuries-old game of trying to destroy each other's pretensions to world dominance. Rather than risk a war with either of the great belligerents, Jefferson and his foreign policy adviser ultimately decided to place a quarantine on American ocean-going commerce late in 1807, after nearly fifteen years of being seized, harassed, and humiliated on the high seas. The quarantine, legally enacted by Congress as the Embargo Act, led to a disastrous drop in commodity prices that hurt farmers and planters and caused widespread unemployment in seaports. The self-imposed boycott on international trade was frankly an experiment in

the Administrations of Thomas Jefferson and James Madison, vol. 1, History of the United States of America during the Administrations of Thomas Jefferson, Earl N. Harbert, ed. (New York: Library of America, 1986), 695.

diplomacy, but idle shipmasters and merchants did not see it that way. Angry protests from New England were heard throughout Jefferson's final year in office. An embarrassing repeal of the experiment bewildered Jefferson and Madison, who had counted on more public support from all sections of the nation. Leading Republican newspapers chose to ignore any hostility as Jefferson prepared to quit the presidency. Instead of rebuke, the party faithful praised the outgoing president for his adherence "to the Principles of '76."

Madison, however, knew that in the last eight months or so the State Department was a slough of frustration. Only the most intimate cabinet members probably knew the whole story, but as there is usually an attempt to make a president's last year in office pleasant, if not triumphant, Jefferson's problems as he became a "lame duck" (this phrase is full of important meanings but had not yet been invented in 1808) were manifest. They ranged from the president's personal finances to the continual threat of war with Britain, and the difficulties had grown apace after passage of the Embargo Act.

Jefferson's public image was close to Washington's. Although they probably would not have recognized him on the street, every schoolboy knew how Jefferson had been the principal author of the Declaration of Independence, and even Federalist detractors acknowledged that Jefferson's tenure as the first secretary of state had been salutary. But Federalists balked at that point, for it was during the final days of Jefferson's cabinet service that a profound philosophical split appeared to shape forever the future of American politics. Cabinet infighting over the proper way to pay off the national debt, the chartering of a national bank, and the maintenance of a sizable army or navy placed Jefferson and Secretary of the Treasury Alexander Hamilton in opposite camps.

President Washington's leaning toward Hamilton's position gave Jefferson the excuse he needed to retire from public life (permanently, he insisted), but in the aftermath of the disputes Congressman Madison collaborated with Jefferson to form an opposition party. Finally, after the war of words over ratification of the Jay Treaty in 1795 the Federalist and Republican parties emerged. At the heart of the controversy, which became unusually bitter after the Alien and Sedition Acts were passed (in a brazen effort to stomp the Republican party to death), was the struggle to win the presidency. For as the constitutional powers available to the president became evident in that first decade of trial and error, the controversy centered on the proper role for the executive in a self-governing republic. In drafting the Constitution, lessons of history had been useful in handling legislative matters; but the shaping of a Republican presidency had been an inventive rather than a historical process. The strictures of Machiavelli and the examples of Pericles and Julius Caesar had not helped.

Then, for the first time in American history, a lesson became evident after Alexander Hamilton's ambition to be elected president became so blatant that he had to settle for being a power behind the scenes. Hamilton's frustrated followers, for all their conniving, were unable to hand the presidency to the secretary of the Treasury, but Hamiltonian financial policies left an indelible blueprint for the young nation. Jefferson's touted Revolution of 1800 had not dismantled the major facets of Hamilton's fiscal program (funding the national debt and the Bank of the United States) but had only slowed down the money changers. President Jefferson had a Republican Congress, which made it easier for him to get taxes repealed or to undo the harm left in the wake of the Alien and Sedition Acts; but as the Federalist party withered away (except in New England and other, local strongholds), factions grew apace in the Republican congressional majority as ambitious men jockeyed for patronage or higher office in the sleepy national capital.

The Federal City at Washington was more a blueprint than a fact, and most of the power was based at opposite ends of the newly christened Pennsylvania Avenue. Toward the Potomac was the barely finished executive mansion with a popular president in charge. Nearby, a brick structure known as the Seven Buildings housed some cabinet offices, and only a stone's throw away the James Madisons lived on F street, in leased quarters. A wooden bridge crossed Tiber Creek as one headed north up the broad, unpaved avenue. On Capitol Hill stood a cluster of boardinghouses where state delegations in Congress tended to break bread, chat incessantly, and look suspiciously on their neighbors. "Outwardly, and in certain aspects of its inner life, the Hill resembled nothing so much as an early New England community," James S. Young notes; but there the resemblance ended. The gathered congressmen were "a society of transients" who "merely wintered in Washington, spending more time each year with constituents than with each other."[3] The rustle of skirts was seldom heard in the Capitol except when Congress was in session, and even then many of the lawmakers left their ladies at home. Only the more affluent congressmen brought their families to the capital for the social season that opened after the president's annual message had been read to Congress. The British minister thought the whole spectacle amusing as vying congressional daughters and local belles turned Washington into "one of the most marrying places of the whole continent."[4]

Many congressmen found their six dollars a day inadequate and complained about the high cost of living in the capital. Apparently, the farmers who elected them to the House of Representatives believed six dollars was a princely sum, and as the lawmakers learned, tinkering with their salaries

3. James Sterling Young, *The Washington Community, 1800–1828* (New York: Columbia University Press, 1966), 87–89.
4. The British minister was Augustus John Foster. Quoted in Constance McLaughlin Green, *Washington: A History of the Capital, 1800–1950* (Princeton, N.J.: Princeton University Press, 1976), 49.

in upward fashion would not be tolerated by the voters. The lack of amenities, the half-finished aspect of the place, and the low pay resulted in a high turn-over rate that modern Congresses, with their low turnover, do not experi-ence. During Jefferson's first term, 52 percent of the lawmakers either lost their quest for reelection or voluntarily dropped out; in Jefferson's last years a third of all senators and representatives were part of the turnover. In these unsettled circumstances, regional loyalties counted more than party discipline, and after Jefferson's reelection in 1804 the atmosphere in Congress seemed to be "more anarchic than cohesive."[5]

Nobody was more aware of the turmoil behind the scenes than Madison, but, like Jefferson, the retiring secretary of state had an almost mystical belief in the ability of elected representatives to act rationally and responsibly. Had he not made a plea for quality in the legislature when he wrote *The Federalist* No. 57? "The aim of every political constitution," Madison insisted, "is or ought to be first to obtain for rulers, men who possess most wisdom to discern, and most virtue to pursue the common good of society; and in the next place, to take the most effectual precautions for keeping them virtuous, whilst they con-tinue to hold their public trust." If the men elected by the people were a disap-pointment, then republicanism was not working well. Madison was loath to ad-mit such a possibility. When he wrote in *The Federalist* No. 51 that "in framing a government which is to be administered by men over men, the great difficulty lies in this: You must first enable the government to control the governed; and in the next place, oblige it to control itself," Madison already knew how small-minded elected representatives could conduct themselves.

Nonetheless, Madison thought the linchpin of the Republic was Con-gress, where at least one branch — the House of Representatives — was elected directly by the people. Therefore, the people had to be trusted. And if the men they elected sometimes performed in strange or obstreperous ways, that was the price one had to pay for republicanism. As a profound theoretician of government, Madison decided no one had yet come up with a better idea. So he accepted Congress for what it was and hoped that as president he could guide the Republic into peaceful waters at a time when much of the world was at swords' point.

The European war heated up midway in Jefferson's first administration, bringing a boom to American farming and shipping but exacting an onerous burden in international commerce. The truth seemed to be that the United States was still Britain's foster child, a fact that the Federalists around Boston seemed to savor while Jeffersonian Republicans loathed the implications. Af-ter all, who had won the American Revolution? Then, from the summer of 1808 onward, Jefferson had relaxed his grip on the reins of government. In-

5. Young, *Washington Community*, 152.

8

stead of exerting his authority to make the transition easy for Madison, Jefferson decided to move the executive office into a neutral corner. Perhaps Jefferson thought that by adopting a do-nothing attitude, he would free Madison of any encumbrances left from the bitter wrangling in Congress during much of 1807 and 1808.

To observers, the presidency seemed tailormade for Jefferson. "We are all Federalists, we are all Republicans," Jefferson intoned in his sparkling inaugural address that helped bind the wounds created by the bitter voting in the contest with Aaron Burr. Voters judged by deeds, not words, and when Congress responded to Jefferson's call for tax reductions and frugality in the national government, the tide of Federalism ebbed. Political promises were being kept. A steady flow of dinner invitations brought influential congressmen to the executive mansion for long meals where the president made his points between courses. Party lines held together, giving Republicans a lopsided majority in the House and a comfortable one in the Senate. The president's official family seemed as congenial as any that ever served a chief executive. Jefferson's original cabinet had lasted through various storms with all the major posts still occupied by the original appointees, and for the first time in the nation's history, a president had served without once vetoing a measure passed by Congress. There was unity without pleas for united action, and Jefferson's presidency was applauded by public testimonials ranging from the gigantic cheese rolled from New England to Washington (a "mere peppercorn" compared with the citizens' affection for the president) to his reelection in 1804 without serious opposition from fretting Federalists.

This deceptive political calm was promoted by a powerful newspaper, the *National Intelligencer.* Its publisher-editor, Samuel Harrison Smith, came to Washington at Jefferson's urging, and naturally the newspaper found Jefferson's ideas and programs praiseworthy. Critics called Smith "Silky-Milky" behind his back, but to editors at the far corners of the Republic, articles from the *Intelligencer,* which was published three times a week, had the ring of gospel truth. In an era when the president's annual message to Congress was one of the biggest news stories of the year, the leading Washington newspaper set the political tone for the rest of the country's print media. Smith started the paper during the heat of the 1800 election and the *Intelligencer* became authoritative when the House of Representatives deadlocked in the presidential balloting between Jefferson and Burr. Thereafter, the news in and the views of the *Intelligencer* were widely broadcast via the mails, when only newspaper exchanges or personal letters furnished information. The Philadelphia *Aurora* and New York *Evening Post* were also Jeffersonian in their bias, and in most American cities and hamlets (Boston excepted), the newspapers tended to give Jefferson's administration the benefit of the doubt, even when the embargo tested the editors' loyalty. The Boston *Independent*

9

Chronicle had a weakness for Jeffersonian policies but was in the shadow of the *Columbian Centinel,* the voice of Federalism in New England if not the nation. Editor Benjamin Russell used the *Centinel* to flay Republicans and their idol in particular, but as time passed Russell found his influence waning. South of Washington, the Richmond *Enquirer* provided enough encomiums of Jeffersonian politics to satisfy the whole region.

The power of the *Intelligencer's* columns excepted, Washington in Jefferson's day was not the nerve center of a huge republic. Rather it was a village of 5,650 souls that was growing rapidly (like the nation itself) by about 1,200 inhabitants per year. New York, some 250 miles to the northeast, was already the financial center of the country, with Boston and Philadelphia making similar but hollow claims as their harbors silted up and commerce flowed toward the deep harbor surrounding three sides of Manhattan. The great wealth of the nation would be concentrated and to some extent created in the real-estate boom that fed New York City's speculators enormous profits. Risk takers in the 1790s who had thought the District of Columbia would be a real-estate bonanza were now either bankrupt or trying to outwit the sheriff. The most infamous example is Robert Morris, who helped finance the American Revolution, served at the Federal Convention in 1787, and became one of the first senators from Pennsylvania. Morris acquired the titles to thousands of acres of land, most of it in the wrong places, and he died in 1806 after a term in debtors' prison, a shattered, ruined man. Elsewhere, the Astors, Brookses, and Biddles amassed fortunes from investments in Manhattan or Boston real estate, international commerce, and diversified banking. Half-finished buildings, in contrast, dotted the landscape after the initial building boom in Washington had collapsed three years after the seat of the federal government was moved there from Philadelphia.[6]

Thus Washington was still a village, in a nation of villages, hamlets, and farms; the four largest American cities had a combined population of around 175,000. The U.S. population in 1800 was 5.3 million (including both whites and blacks) and largely agrarian. The voting white males numbered close to 2 million, and perhaps 85 percent were farmers. Thus when Jefferson said that yeoman farmers constituted the backbone of the Republic, he was placing the future of the United States in the hands of its overwhelming majority. The Jeffersonian Republicans' appeal was to men of the plow who had a small mortgage or none at all, who raised or grew what they ate and wore, and who probably never saw one hundred dollars in cash in their entire lives.

In these circumstances, money was not yet the ruling force in American life. Jefferson's own financial situation was strained during his last years in office and would deteriorate steadily until his death. The twenty-five thousand dollars he earned as president went to pay a host of mounting debts,

6. Ibid., 22–23.

yet in his insouciant way Jefferson never curbed his appetite for excellent wines or expensive books. On paper, Jefferson's holdings in Albemarle County, Virginia, seemed to make him wealthy. But this wealth was calculated in land and slaves, fluctuating in value and never worth in cash what plantation owners believed was their true value. Madison, as a planter, shared that same illusion; although he never indulged in wine or books to the same extent as Jefferson, Madison hated to say no to his wife. Dolley Madison enjoyed buying expensive cloth for new gowns, insisted on having a carriage for her about-town calls, and indulged other whims of fashion that strained Madison's five-thousand-dollar salary as secretary of state.

The average citizen knew nothing of the tensions that had racked Jefferson's administration during its final year in office. The nagging opposition of Congressman John Randolph and his small circle of Tertium Quids began in 1806 after Jefferson's impetuous kinsman, who had been a kind of majority leader after the euphoric days of 1801, tried to taint his own party and Madison in particular with scandals related to the infamous Yazoo land frauds. (Madison was one of three commissioners who favored an out-of-court settlement that was rejected. Randolph led the opposition.) Thereafter, Randolph quickly fell from grace to become the inveterate foe of the administration on almost every issue, small or large.

In the Senate, a willful band of nominal Republicans — the "Invincibles" — jockeyed for positions of patronage and power and were becoming more-frequent allies of the Federalist majority that never forgave Jefferson for having crushed Hamilton's ambitions. Under Jefferson's prodding the national debt was reduced fifty-three million dollars, taxes were kept low, and defense expenditures were cut drastically.[7] Inland, farmers shifted their allegiance to Jefferson as he proved Federalist alarums to be groundless — their taxes were lower, there was a market for their goods, and the hysterical campaign charge that Jefferson was "the anti-Christ" come to power had proved groundless. Internecine battles in Congress were inevitable, however, as congressmen with strong personalities or overpowering ambition dined at Jefferson's table but sometimes proved recalcitrant when votes on critical issues were counted. Adding to Jefferson's woes were his recurring migraine headaches, which sometimes lasted for weeks and in May 1808 had, by his own admission, reduced him to "a state of almost total incapacity for business."[8]

Something had to give. Seven years of adroit party leadership, easy dealings with congressional leaders, and some swallowed pride in dealing with Britain and France had made Jefferson's tenure as president seem akin to a

7. *Annual Report of the Secretary of the Treasury, Statistical Appendix, Fiscal Year 1978* (Washington, D.C.: GPO, 1979), 62.

8. Dumas Malone, *Jefferson and His Time*, 6 vols. (Boston: Little, Brown & Company, 1948–1976), 5:578.

golden era. The death struggle between Britain and France had postive effects for the United States, as the value of goods carried in American bottoms in 1807 reached one hundred eight million dollars, and imports to Yankee ports climbed to nearly sixty million dollars. The latter figure was particularly significant, for the main source of federal revenue was the duty on imports. Sea-island cotton sold for fifty-one cents a pound in 1805, and a year later 83,186 hogsheads of American tobacco were shipped abroad. Naturally, this prosperity created a renewed appetite for arable lands as the soil on the eastern seaboard suffered from destructive farming practices. Land hunger became a national phenomenon. The Louisiana Purchase in 1803 was an opportunity that grew out of the resumed Anglo-French war, and by grasping it the president was able to add much of the trans-Mississippi West to the young nation for only pennies per acre.

The first real crisis Jefferson faced came after Britain began enforcing its dreaded Orders in Council, aimed at a blockade of Napoleon's Europe and bound to harm a rising neutral commercial nation. Impressment of American sailors, seizure and condemnation of American cargo vessels, coupled with staggering losses in maritime insurance, threatened to bring American prosperity to an end. Jefferson had on several occasions considered declaring war against both Britain and France as these warring powers tried to outdo each other in insulting the American flag on the high seas; but as a classic antiwar republican Jefferson knew that the nation's economic gains would be lost if war came. For example, after the HMS *Leopard* fired on the USS *Chesapeake* in June 1807, Jefferson could easily have taken the United States into war against the British bully. Instead he huddled with his secretary of state and searched for an alternative.

Their answer, unabashedly a desperate one, was the Embargo Act of 1807, which Congress passed with lightning speed. Once in place the law forbade American ships to embark for foreign ports, in effect grounding all Yankee vessels except those plying coastal waters. New England, after a few prosperous years of shipbuilding and commercial carrying, was hit hard. Within months it was clear that the Embargo Act had been a crashing failure. Strict enforcement of the law alienated New England, impoverished the South, which was dependent on exports of tobacco and other farm products, and led to smuggling and lawlessness that shocked the patriot-president and his secretary of state.

The Invincibles, a coterie of Republicans who joined Randolph in openly defying their chieftain and his loyalists, vented their anger by often voting with the Federalists, who insisted that Jefferson was more of a monarch than George III. The triumphant days of the Louisiana Purchase had faded when Congress considered alternatives to the failed Embargo Act and eventually voted to call off the embargo on Jefferson's last day in office. As was Jefferson's habit, he did not talk about the vicious behavior of the leading Invincibles, Virginia Senator William Branch Giles and Maryland Senator Samuel Smith. But was the president so naive as to be unaware of their behind-the-scenes maneuvers intended to embarrass the administration? Dumas Malone, Jefferson's biographer, was somewhat mystified when he dealt with Jefferson's final months as president. The trouble — if that is the right word for it — began in earnest when Jefferson sent his last State of the Union message to Congress in December 1808. Earlier the president had described himself as a mere spectator of public matters, and to an old friend, he had written: "I have thought it right to take no part myself in proposing measures, the execution of which will devolve on my successor."[9] But Madison and Secretary of the Treasury Albert Gallatin, the number-two cabinet member and a trusted confidant, had urged the president to make decisions regarding the critical state of foreign affairs and reveal them to Congress. There was some talk of recalling the American ministers at both Paris and London as a diplomatic "firing over the bow" of the warring powers, and more than one Republican in Congress would have voted for stronger measures — even war — if Jefferson had asked for it. Certainly Gallatin thought war was better than the discredited embargo policy, and he was frank to say so. Both Madison and Gallatin wanted a meeting with the president to make their point, Malone noted, "but Jefferson appears to have paid no heed whatsoever to this suggestion. There may have been meetings of executive officers which were not recorded, but no 'precise and distinct course' was recommended to Congress by the President."[10] And, Malone continued, Jefferson's "'abdication' of presidential leadership seems to have occasioned little complaint or even notice at the time."

Madison did not complain, but he must have noticed what was going on in Washington boardinghouses and parlors. In mid-January 1809 Senator Smith sent Madison a note giving details of the embargo's repeal and a companion bill (later dropped) to allow American merchant vessels to arm and defend themselves on the high seas. If these strong measures were not adopted, Smith told Madison, "I fear that we Shall lose all the Spring Elections — and if not done before we rise [adjourn], Maryland will be lost."[11] Madison watched as Congress reversed itself and passed the Nonintercourse Act (forbidding all commerce with the belligerents, but giving both Britain and France an escape clause) and repealed the detested Embargo Act for good measure. Perhaps the vindictive spirit of erstwhile flatterers of the president repelled Madison. At any rate, Jefferson's final days in office were free of grating news from his cabinet. In the Senate, however, a cauldron of malice was be-

9. Ibid., 5:622.
10. Ibid., 5:623.
11. Samuel Smith to Madison, 19 January 1809, Madison Papers, Rives Collection, Library of Congress (hereafter cited as DLC).

ing stirred by William Branch Giles, the senior senator from Virginia and a ranking Republican whose dislike of President Jefferson bordered on the irrational.

By 1808 Senator Giles, who was not a humble man, was yearning to climb the ladder that led to the presidency. When Senator Stephen Bradley of Vermont presided over the January 1808 Republican caucus at which Madison had been nominated for president, Giles had sponsored a resolution recommending George Clinton as the vice-presidential candidate. Giles was probably already nurturing his dreams of placing a third Virginian in the executive mansion at some future time.[12] He was certainly capable of figuring that Clinton, who was a none-too-healthy sixty-nine, could remain as vice-president for only a few years, at which point he would conveniently die, thereby opening the way for some younger heir apparent.

How Madison reacted to all the behind-the-scenes maneuvering that took place after the January caucus is problematical. The precedent set by Washington regarding a candidate's conduct required that Madison ignore all the fuss, and he therefore never formally acknowledged his candidacy. How much Jefferson discussed the circumstances of Madison's succession to the office is also a mystery, for their correspondence is singularly silent on the subject.

Republican victories in the key states of New York, Pennsylvania, and Virginia set the tone for the presidential balloting in 1808. The electoral college was to meet in December, but the people chosen to vote then were selected by the state legislatures; thus a citizen wishing to vote for Madison had to signify his approval of the local candidate committed to support a Madison elector. The system was not so complicated as it sounds, and most voters knew what they were expected to do when they walked up to the polls and gave their preference audibly and unmistakably. By the middle of November, the presidential race was settled.

Congressman Randolph, still harboring hopes only he fully understood, tried to embarrass his fellow Republicans by making a great noise on behalf of the governor of Virginia, James Monroe. Possibly without Monroe's prior approval, Randolph attacked the caucus system of nomination and in the next breath asserted that James Monroe was a more capable and deserving Republican than Madison. Years earlier, in the election campaign for the First Congress, Patrick Henry had tried to keep Madison out of the House of Representatives by talking Monroe into running against his old friend. In 1789 that ruse had failed, and Randolph's manipulation in 1808 was no more successful, although Randolph kept insisting (contrary to the facts) that Madison was implicated in the Yazoo land fraud.[13] At the January 1808 caucus, Madison had 83 votes, Clinton 3, and Monroe 3.

12. William G. Morgan, "Presidential Nominations in the Federal Era, 1788–1818" (Ph.D. dissertation, University of Southern California, 1969), 97–98.

13. Marshall Smelser, *The Democratic Republic, 1801–1815* (New York: Harper & Row, 1968), 181.

In fact, Monroe could have put a stop to his wildcat candidacy by disavowing the whole scheme; but Monroe nursed a wounded pride and was tempted by the opportunity to settle an old score. Madison stood apart from the whole proceeding and allowed friends to fight his battle in the time-honored Virginia tradition. When the fall elections were in full swing, Thomas Ritchie (editor of the Richmond *Enquirer*) wrote friends around the state that they should publicize the fact that Federalists in Virginia intended "to throw all their Weight into the Scale of James Monroe. . . . It is the duty, therefore, of the friends of Madison, to turn out to a Man." And turn out they did, so that when returns from the populated counties were tallied they showed that in his home state Madison received 14,655 votes to Monroe's 3,408.[14] Most of New England went for Federalist Charles Cotesworth Pinckney and 6 votes were cast for Clinton in New York; elsewhere, however, Republicans tended to stay in line.

Madison gave no public sign that he knew what was going on, but by the time Congress was set to convene it was clear that 106 electors pledged to Madison had been chosen—17 more than were needed for a majority.[15] Just when and where Madison and his lady first celebrated the news is only conjecture, but by the middle of November 1808 Dolley Madison knew that she was going to be moving to a new address on 4 March 1809. As Mrs. Madison made her plans, misgivings were heard from a few Yankee congressmen as the cant about a "Virginia dynasty" began; these rumblings carried to Boston parlors out of resentment that three of the first four presidents were born in the Old Dominion.

While Jefferson's servants nailed the packing crates at the president's house, Madison surveyed the political scene in Washington with anxiety. On his desk lay a letter from Senator Giles warning Madison not to appoint Gallatin as his successor in the State Department. If Madison had served as Jefferson's right arm, surely the able secretary of the Treasury had been the president's left arm. This was no secret to Giles, but the Virginia senator apparently wanted to test Madison's mettle. Madison was so open in his dealings, public and private, that he was slow to discern the devious methods of men who called themselves Republicans. Madison had known Giles since the Second Congress, when the young politician from Tidewater Virginia had promised to abet any plan to enbarrass Alexander Hamilton's fiscal

14. Ritchie to the Madison Electors Committee, 21 October 1808, James Monroe Museum, Fredericksburg, Va.: *National Intelligencer,* 25 November and 2 December 1808.

15. Irving Brant, *James Madison,* 6 vols. (Indianapolis: Bobbs-Merrill Company, 1941–1961), 4:466.

schemes. Now Giles was a political ally of Senator Samuel Smith from Maryland and Senator Michael Leib from Pennsylvania.

This trio of Invincible Republican senators matched in arrogance anything the Federalist party could point to as determined opponents of the incumbent president. Their sense of self-importance and ambition had been nurtured in the halcyon days of republicanism, during Jefferson's first term, when Congress with alacrity had passed the president's campaign-promised program into law. Once the Invincibles saw that when the voting was close, their three votes could make all the difference, they made no secret of their enmity toward Gallatin, who was far to clever (and foreign-born to boot) to admire their schemes for patronage and power. Along with Representative John Randolph, they worked overtime to make Jefferson's life miserable during his final year in the White House.

Like the jackals they were, those in the Giles-Leib-Smith crowd determined to make a small mistake of Jefferson's into a major blunder just as the president was preparing to step down. Jefferson had decided to send his young friend and confidant from the Paris ministry days, William Short of Virginia, to St. Petersburg as the American minister. Confident the appointment would go through the Senate, Jefferson instructed Short to prepare for the mission, packed him off to Europe, and in due course the president made the required nomination. Giles pounced on it. Who was this stranger (Short had been in Europe most of the time since 1785) that pretended to be an American? Why, said Giles, Short was nothing but "a denationalized Monarchist . . . who is generally deemed a miserable miser, and misanthrope, and as far as he is known in Virginia, is, I believe, only known to be despised."[16] Giles connived with Leib and Smith to get the nomination rejected during Jefferson's last week in office by a humiliating vote, 0 for the nomination, 31 against. Now Giles and his cohorts were going to tame Madison.

Giles was so eager to intimidate Madison — as he believed he had embarrassed Jefferson — that he wrote Madison a threatening letter less than a week before the inauguration. Perhaps Giles was testing the waters, but it is more likely that he was warning Madison that the Senate was ready to turn its hostility on Jefferson's successor, if necessary. Not only had the senators of Jefferson's own party repudiated the Embargo Act by repealing it, but they had rubbed salt in the wound by unanimously rejecting the president's nomination of Short. Take heed, Giles seemed to say:

> Such is the unfortunate state of the intercourse between Mr. Jefferson and
> the senate at this moment respecting appointments, that a nomination
> from him, is rather a signal of distrust than of confidence in the person

16. William Branch Giles to Madison, 27 February 1809, Madison Papers, Rives Collection, DLC.

nominated. . . . Since the conversation, which last passed between us [regarding Gallatin's appointment as secretary of state] . . . I shall be compelled to vote against the nomination for the following reasons.

And what were Giles's compelling reasons? First, he thought Gallatin untrustworthy; second, his nomination would "disgust a very great portion of the Republican party, in my opinion the most respectable"; and third, such a nomination would "increase the shade of distrust now cast over the measures of the administration, respecting our foreign relations, at a time when not a doubt ought to exist upon that subject." And so on until his ninth reason, which was that senators would assume Gallatin's nomination meant that Madison was cut from the same cloth as Jefferson. Giles implied that Jefferson had turned his back on true Republicans by appointing men known for their "eccentricities . . . and favoritism." Basically Giles was hinting as strongly as he could, without being insulting, that Gallatin must go.

Although ultimately Gallatin did not go (he simply held onto his Treasury post), Madison's reaction to the dark hints from the Giles-Smith-Leib faction showed astute congressmen and senators who knew of this Republican infighting that Madison was being cowed, that he did not want a fight to establish at the outset his control of the party and his office. With hindsight it is easy to see that Madison should have ignored Giles and his troublesome friends and taken his chances with the Senate. In all likelihood, Gallatin would have been confirmed as secretary of state, although the vote might have been close.

Madison was willing to pay a high price so that he might begin his presidency in calm waters. Whether he asked for Jefferson's advice on cabinet appointments is not known, but they probably discussed Gallatin's status. Somehow Madison would keep the clear-thinking immigrant in the cabinet but not where he wanted him. Instead of hard talk, Madison and the outgoing president kept their conversations free of discord and apparently nonpolitical.

During the last days of Jefferson's administration, Madison seems to have busied himself with State Department business and tried to stay out of the president's way. At least that was the impression created by Washington gossips. Federalist Congressman Samuel Taggart told a friend: "Madison our new President [-elect] it is thought is cautiously reserving himself for events. It is said that he takes very little part in the affairs of the Cabinet and that in many cases he is hardly consulted. Some of the warmest Jeffersonians are beginning to be jealous of him and to call him a trimmer."[17] Madison was too kind a man, and too old a friend, to make Jefferson's final days in Washington difficult.

17. Samuel Taggart to the Rev. John Taylor, 19 February 1809, in George H. Haynes, ed., "The Letters of Samuel Taggart," *American Antiquarian Society Proceedings* 33 (1923): 334–35.

Many people in the raucous twentieth century might have difficulty understanding the placid Jefferson-Madison relationship. Historian Adrienne Koch in her masterly way told of their fifty-year association and its impact on American history. Parallelling their great political collaboration was a deep friendship.[18] This friendship had ripened after they both served in the Continental Congress, yet Madison always seemed willing to be the junior partner. For one thing, Jefferson, born in 1743, was Madison's senior by eight years. For another, Madison was short, Jefferson was tall. Jefferson was outgoing and enjoyed large dinner parties with plenty of good Madeira afterward. Madison, on the other hand, was painfully shy, although he did share Jefferson's appetite for good wine, good books, and a pure brand of republicanism. Their commitment from 1776 onward to the ideals of the American Revolution also helped to cement their friendship, and we have no record that they ever had a disagreement during their public life or thereafter. Why, even when Jefferson sold Madison a sick horse and the poor creature soon died they outdid each other in apologizing and regretting the incident. When one Virginian sold another Virginian a "critter" that died within a few days, that was grounds for all kinds of trouble. With Madison and Jefferson, the matter was settled quickly and amicably.

All their past dealings, including the splendid visits exchanged between Monticello and Montpelier and the help Martha Jefferson Randolph received from Dolley Madison when Martha acted as the president's hostess, were part of the background as the Jefferson-Madison team prepared to separate. No record exists of their farewell conversation in Washington during the spring of 1809; there was probably more small talk than discussion of key issues, for Jefferson had the good sense to realize that from now on Madison would make it his business to keep the Revolution of 1800 alive. Jefferson was giving up his "splendid misery," and Madison, whom Jefferson once described as "the greatest man in the world," was trustworthy.

Although Madison must have been aware of the shambles left by Jefferson, he kept any misgivings to himself. Madison began preparing for the presidency in Williamsburg in the spring of 1776; thus he brought more experience as a public man to the office than any of his predecessors. Could he keep the United States out of war? Could he also keep the Republicans in Congress at peace with each other? Those were the major challenges Madison faced as he blew out the candles on his bedstand on 3 March 1809. How well he slept that night is not recorded.

18. Adrienne Koch, *Jefferson and Madison: The Great Collaboration* (New York: Alfred Knopf, 1950).

3

★ ★ ★ ★ ★

THE VIRGINIA DYNASTY CONTINUES

The air was so stifling in the ballroom of Long's Hotel on the night of 4 March 1809 that somebody had to break the window. A few hours earlier President James Madison, inaugurated at noon that day, had walked into the room with Dolley Madison on his arm. The president looked a bit weary, but his buxom wife was enjoying every minute of the finale for her husband's first day in office. Proud and perky, Mrs. Madison wore "a pale buff colored velvet [dress], made plain, with a very long train. . . . Her head dress was a turban of the same colored velvet and white satin (from Paris), with two superb plumes, the bird of paradise feathers." The witness added: "She looked a queen."[1]

Dolley Madison's attire told the assembled ladies that the president's wife was not going to follow her husband's habits of plain dress. The president came bedecked in his usual black smallclothes, proudly announcing that the dark garment was cut from cloth produced on American looms from wool shorn from American sheep. The band played "Madison's March" as the couple entered the room shortly after Thomas Jefferson had politely made his appearance. Jefferson soon took his leave, and Madison would have joined him but for the circumstances. "I would much rather be in bed," the president confided to a friend as the air became fetid and the jostling guests pushed their way toward the punch bowl. Another observer, John

1. Margaret Bayard Smith, *The First Forty Years in Washington Society*, Gaillard Hunt, ed. (New York: G. P. Putnam's Sons, 1906), 62–63.

Quincy Adams, curtly noted that "the crowd was excessive, the heat oppressive, and the entertainment bad."[2]

All in all, it had been quite a day, enough to tire the most rugged of men. But Madison was not rugged; in fact, he had taken pills and purges for most of his life, and his small frame surprised most observers because it was in such contrast to the intellectual strength of its possessor. Madison had tried to keep up appearances that day, however. He had started with the carriage ride up Pennsylvania Avenue early in the morning, surrounded by the dashing cavalry escort. The procession stopped at the Capitol, where Madison alighted to join the congressional committee of greeting. They conducted the president-elect to the Senate chamber, where the president pro tem gave Madison his seat. The room was packed with Supreme Court justices, congressmen and their wives, members of the diplomatic corps in their flashy uniforms and useless swords, and a host of wellwishers.

Madison began his speech before he had taken the oath of office. The president-elect was, an observer noted, "extremely pale and trembled excessively when he first began to speak."[3] Madison's voice rose as he gained confidence and composure, and the crowd settled back. "The present situation of the world is indeed without parallel," Madison said, "and that of our own country full of difficulties." Americans had known unprecedented prosperity until the vagaries of war had caught up with the country and made it go from boom to bust, Madison seemed to say as he laid the blame for recent depressed times on Britain and France. Americans were suffering from the pressures exerted by "the injustice and violence of the belligerent powers," whose arbitrary edicts came in the face of the proclaimed neutrality of the United States. In his short speech, Madison repeated the message often heard from his predecessor: Let Americans cherish peace and friendly intercourse with all nations and "hold to the union of the States as the basis of their peace and happiness."

He repeated the Republican litany of low taxes, civil rights for all, and a prudent reduction of the national debt and threw in a clause concerning the Indians. Let the government undertake benevolent plans to convert the Indians "to a participation of the improvements of which the human mind and manners are susceptible in a civilized state." As for Jefferson, Madison said he could not suppress an expression of sympathy for the man who had left office with "the benedictions of a beloved country." Admitting his own

2. John Quincy Adams, *Diary*, Allan Nevins, ed. (New York: Longman's, Green & Company, 1929), 58.

3. Irving Brant, *James Madison*, 6 vols. (Indianapolis: Bobbs-Merrill Company, 1941–1961), 5:12–13.

deficiencies, Madison said he would rely for his strength on "the well-tried intelligence and virtue of my fellow-citizens" and their elected representatives. He concluded his speech by dutifully recognizing that the nation's destiny ultimately lay in the keeping "of that Almighty Being whose power regulates the destiny of nations."

Madison then turned to place his hand on the Bible, and we can only guess at the thoughts going through his head as he glanced up at the administerer of the oath, Chief Justice John Marshall. The two Virginians who had fought political battles together and then turned on each other philosophically, together performed their constitutional duty as Madison swore to defend the Constitution against all enemies, foreign and domestic.[4] Next came the handshakings and obligatory courtesies to the diplomats and, finally, an exit to the carriage. Madison was probably tired before the clock struck noon, and twelve more hours of ceremonies, dining, and handshaking lay ahead. At last the clock face showed midnight, and the president was able to excuse himself.

If they drove down Pennsylvania Avenue on their return that night, the Madisons would have noticed that the candles in the White House had been put out hours earlier, casting darkness over the packing cases marked for a Monticello destination. Jefferson had been assured that he could take all the time he needed; Dolley Madison was a patient woman. She was also regarded by a segment of the Washington community as a power in her own right. Louisa Catherine Adams, John Quincy's wife, said it all when she later recalled how things had been in the White House during Jefferson's tenure. She noted that the Madisons had attended presidential dinner parties as a matter of course.

> Mr. Madison was a *very* small man in his *person*, with a *very* large *head* — his manners were peculiarly unassuming; and his conversation lively, often playful. . . . His language was chaste, well suited to occasion, and the simple expression of the passing thought : . . in harmony with the taste of his hearers.
>
> Mrs. Madison [on the other hand] was tall, large and rather masculine in personal dimensions; her complexion was so fair and brilliant as to redeem this objection, in its perfectly feminine beauty. . . . There was a frankness and ease in her deportment, that won golden opinions from all, and she possessed an influence so decided with her little Man.[5]

4. Gaillard Hunt, ed., *The Writings of James Madison*, 9 vols. (New York: G. P. Putnam's Sons, 1900-1910), 8:47-50.
5. Louisa Catherine Adams, "Autobiographical Sketch," *Miscellany*, Adams Family Papers, microfilm, reel 269, Massachusetts Historical Society.

Certainly Dolley Madison knew how to have a good time and how to make everyone feel at ease that day in March 1809. Fifteen years earlier, she had been a young widow facing the world with an empty house and a baby boy who had survived the yellow fever epidemic. Now she was the first lady and probably too excited to fall asleep.

This American Republic that the new president had sworn to serve and protect was a union of seventeen states and a vast territory stretching from the Ohio River to the Rockies; it contained nearly seven million citizens and "others not taxed" (blacks and Indians). Nearly 85 percent of the population lived on farms or plantations, which meant that the yeoman farmer honored by Jeffersonian rhetoric dominated the young nation statistically, if not in practice. Voting was limited to white males, and records were spotty. In New England towns, voters turned out dutifully, but in the South an election took several days and turnout was low if rain muddied the roads or if the candidates were dull men. In the 1808 presidential campaign in Virginia, for example, fewer than twenty thousand souls out of a total population of eight hundred thousand had bothered to vote. Such statistics never troubled Madison, for he shared Jefferson's view that what counted in a Republican society was the participation of educated, informed citizens.

Most Americans in 1809 were not well educated, although a good proportion (particularly in New England) could write and read. European visitors were struck by the reading habits of American farmers, tradesmen, sailors, and seamstresses — in short, those people who acknowledged no class barriers such as those confronting their illiterate counterparts in Europe. Few Americans attended public schools once they were old enough to plow a straight furrow or make a quilt, but their reading habits did not stop after formal training ended. Proof was found in the rise of American weekly newspapers, whose numbers more than doubled between 1801 and Madison's inauguration. Moreover, regional newspapers such as the Boston *Columbian Centinel* or the Richmond *Enquirer* passed through dozens of hands before tattered copies were used for secondary purposes in kitchens and barns. Books also captured the public imagination. Parson Mason Weems's *Life of George Washington* was popular in American parlors and reached a ninth edition in 1809, the same year Washington Irving's *Knickerbocker's History of New York* created a mild sensation. The small number of novels by American authors gave ground to the pirated editions of British writers, notably, Defoe, Fielding, Richardson, and Swift.

Americans in 1809 may have been the best-read people on earth, but what concerned them more than romantic novels or politics was the everyday business of life. Risk-taking merchants and shippers sought huge profits from cargoes bearing trademarks from China, Spain, Denmark, Portugal, and the Sandwich Islands. American wheat, cotton, corn, fish, furs, ship bread, and bacon were traded in world markets for silks, calicoes, lace, sugars, spices, and delicate wines — or had been, until the 1807 embargo halted international trade through legitimate channels. Sea-island cotton exports fell from 8.9 million pounds in 1807 to fewer than 1 million pounds in 1808, and other commodity exports suffered similar drastic declines. The depression in shipping hit New England early in 1808, and as Madison took office restless merchants and seamen from Portsmouth to Charleston were eager to resume the ocean trade that had brought close to sixty million dollars to American pockets before the clampdown.

Commerce in the United States was not at a standstill as Madison took office, but farm prices were depressed. Corn, the southern staple, fell from its high of 94 cents a bushel in 1804 to 71 cents in 1809. Wheat, from what was then the American breadbasket in Pennsylvania and New Jersey, sold for $1.10 a bushel in 1809, a 46-cent drop from the 1804 boom price.[6] Some luxuries also came to the table at depressed prices. The Madeira that pleased President Madison's palate cost less than 70 cents a bottle, and the champagne served at the White House cost only 25 cents more. Sugar was available for every table at 11 cents a pound. No one ever spoke of a hungry American, for even the meanest home had access to cheap pork, molasses, corn meal, hominy, roasting ears, greens, beans, and fresh milk.

All of these necessaries were bought with cash in the cities or on credit in villages or towns. Rural communities operated on long-term credit, with settlements once or twice a year as crops came to market. Cash might be paper notes from the Bank of the United States or (after 1811) mushrooming state banks. Coins often came from a Spanish or British mint, for an act of Congress outlawing foreign coinage as legal tender was more than forty years away. Copper pennies, half-dimes, dimes, quarters, and dollars were also used by small traders, and bankers lent money at 6 percent to most borrowers or at 4 percent to the better risks. Much of the country's trade was carried on by barter — parcels of land were swapped for herds of cattle, or droves of hogs were traded for hides, bulk cotton, or other less perishable items. Soap, candles, yarn for looms, basic furniture, rugs, and bedding were often homemade by men and women whose workday began with dawn and ended ten, twelve, or fourteen hours later. After supper families talked, read aloud, whittled, knitted, or went to bed early to save firewood and candles. Itinerant peddlers brought needles, ribbons, thread, bonnets, Bibles, knives, scissors, iron pots and skillets, spices, and basic primers to remote markets.

6. Lewis C. Gray, *History of Agriculture in the Southern United States to 1860*, 2 vols. (Washington, D.C.: Carnegie Institution, 1933), 2:744, 1039.

Only city dwellers had a choice of theatrical entertainment as well as a variety of museums where paintings, stuffed animals, curiosities of nature, and an occasional live elephant might be seen.

This was the United States of James Madison's day—a country on the move but uncertain as to the next stopping place. What happened at the local blacksmith's shop was of far more concern to the average American than Napoleon's maneuvers or the whims of Whitehall ministers. The United States was a big country even in 1809, with a small man in the White House whose business it was to keep the economy surging, the citizenry busy, and the cost of government low. Congressmen were paid to pass laws that would help farmers, plantation owners, merchants, and shippers to operate at a profit. And President Madison, the average American probably surmised, was paid to worry about Britain and France.

Nobody knew how much more the presidency involved than Madison. He saw himself as the keeper of the flame as the torch of republicanism was passed from Jefferson's grasp to his. Before either of them became key figures in the emerging Republic, Jefferson told Madison that the new nation must maintain a predominant interest in farming and planting: "I think our governments will remain virtuous for many centuries; as long as they are chiefly agricultural; and this will be as long as there shall be vacant lands in any part of America. When they get piled upon one another in large cities, as in Europe, they will become corrupt as in Europe."[7] Early on, Jefferson had tied his destiny and that of the United States to an alliance between government and the tillers of the soil. Madison agreed, but he was never as vociferous as Jefferson in describing the opposition as "monocrats" who wished to Anglicize the Constitution. Still, Madison was wary of Federalists' intentions. The footdragging, not to mention the outright hostility, of Federalist leaders in Massachusetts and Connecticut during the difficult days of the embargo had mystified Madison as much as it had infuriated Jefferson. When Jefferson looked back on his last months in office, he saw the High Federalists flirting with treason when they spoke of either a separatist movement or forcible opposition to Republican policies. Madison, on the other hand, was loath to admit that the "eastern," or New England, men willfully stretched their dissent beyond constitutional limits. (In Madison's time, the region east of the Hudson River valley was regarded as "eastern." As the country expanded, the term was applied to all east-coast areas, and the "old" East became the more familiar New England.) While in office, Jefferson avoided name calling and instead pursued policies that made recalcitrant governors appear

7. William T. Hutchinson et al., eds., *The Papers of James Madison*, 16 vols. (Chicago and Charlottesville: University of Chicago Press and University Press of Virginia, 1962–), 10:338 (hereafter cited as *Madison Papers*).

to be extremists. And now that Madison was at the helm, he may have assumed that if he gave the Pickerings and the Quincys enough rope, they would hang themselves.

The great challenge facing Madison as he took over from Jefferson was to keep the United States out of war; but he realized that he ought also to guide the country back to the prosperity that had existed a few years earlier. Taking advantage of Jefferson's popularity, his supporters had won a majority in Congress, which they enlarged by matching words with deeds. Taxes had been cut, the public debt was being diminished each year, civil liberties were exercised in the marketplace and newspaper offices, and frugality was the watchword in those tiny bureaus where the business of government was transacted. This was Republican theory blended with Republican practice.

Theories and their effect on real practice fascinated Madison. In 1786 he studied ancient and modern confederacies in search of clues for strengthening American confederation, and then only a month before the Federal Convention, when Madison outlined the "Vices of the Political System of the United States," he concluded that although Republican theory exalted majority rule as the proper source of "Rule and power," reckless legislative majorities since 1776 had often threatened liberty and property in nearly all of the thirteen states. He had paid little attention to executive performance in the past, but when Madison was at Washington's elbow in 1789 and for a few years thereafter he witnessed the evolution of a Republican presidency, and time and again he saw greed, ambition, and misused power in Congress but rarely if ever in the presidential conduct of Washington, Adams, or Jefferson. We do not know if Madison was a praying man, but surely he must have hoped that the Congress elected in 1808 would share his dreams of moderation in domestic matters and a united front in foreign affairs.

As a realist who had served in the State Department for eight years, Madison recognized that the nation's foreign policy needed a new direction. His own pet theory of economic coercion as an instrument with which to threaten the warring powers had failed, though Madison was reluctant to admit it. Repeal of the Embargo Act and the frantic search for a viable world-trade solution through half-baked legislation revealed the administration's confusion in the face of haughty Englishmen and double-dealing Frenchmen. Yet, if a peaceful solution could be found, what an opportunity to show the world that Republican virtue and patience could triumph! It only the nation could be piloted through the reefs and shoals created by the belligerent powers, Britain and France.

As Madison shouldered his presidential duties, he, like Jefferson, was committed to the idea that the United States of America was proof that men, for all their faults, were capable of self-government. Madison also shared Jefferson's belief that American prosperity depended on laissez-faire policies that would permit self-reliant farmers and planters to send their products to the West Indies, Europe, and the Orient at a fair profit. National expansion became part of this program when Louisiana was purchased, and Madison's greatest strength lay in the South where the leading public men assumed that East and West (Spanish) Florida and possibly Cuba and Mexico might someday become part of the American empire. The Louisiana Purchase proved that territory could be acquired without bloodshed. As a Republican and a planter, Madison seems to have assumed that American expansion was inevitable and an undisguised blessing, for the alternative was (as Jefferson had warned) an Anglicized nation where city dwellers were cursed with extremes of poverty and wealth and where a privileged few owned most of the land.

But whereas Jefferson spoke of the farmer-citizen as the chief source and beneficiary of republicanism in action, Madison knew that prosperity had to have a broader base than farms and plantations. Madison opposed artificial privileges such as those conferred on owners of stock in the Bank of the United States, and in his congressional days he had denounced stockjobbers and the paper profits made by speculators. But Madison was sophisticated enough to realize that an expanding national prosperity necessarily involved shipping, commerce, manufacturing, and even banking, and it required free usage of the world's waterways to market the nation's commodity surpluses. Perhaps one reason for his early break with the Federalists was Madison's patience in the face of their intensity. Nobody had to tell Madison that in the field of foreign affairs, for example, the machinery provided by the Constitution was cumbersome; but in an era dependent for transportation on sails and wooden wheels, speed was not a top priority at the State Department. And as for Congress, Madison saw on several occasions that Jefferson's policy recommendations had been implemented with a heady sense of urgency. When public opinion moved in a certain direction, Congress sometimes hurried to catch up. Madison must have believed that he could lead public opinion as well as follow it—and he had no clearer message for the nation than his belief that the survival of republicanism and the Republican party depended on the continued existence and growth of the Union.

To some degree, Jefferson had taken the union of all the states for granted. Madison, in March 1809, was not so sure that the Union was strong. To the other shibboleths of the Republican party Madison added his own first priority: Preserve the Union. Since his days in the Continental Congress, Madison had known how fragile the bonds of union became when sectional interests for fisheries or river navigation clashed, and he must have considered the blustering language and sub-rosa resistance to the embargo as a worrisome signal flag hoisted during Jefferson's last year in office. The immediate question was, Would the scrapping of the embargo policy mean that New

England might be wooed away from the belligerent Federalists? To some degree, the implied threat of sectional disunity was the most serious problem facing Madison as he took office.

To be sure, there were other issues on Madison's mind, for he had more to worry about during his first weeks as president than the Federalists' rancor, Napoleon's duplicity, or George Canning's arrogance. He had been besieged for the past three months by advice from congressmen, senators, office seekers, relatives, and expectant well-wishers. And nobody understood better than Madison the accidents of history that had brought him to the office he had helped to create.

Nine years earlier, gazing across the meadow at his home in Orange County, Virginia, Madison had thought that he was going to spend the rest of his life at Montpelier. His father was dying, and the plantation that James Madison, Sr., had created—with its twenty-six hundred acres of red clay soil, dozens of outbuildings, numerous slave quarters, some forty slaves and their children, and main house with its two stories and broad porch—would become his. Thomas Jefferson was then vice-president, and if the Republican party succeeded in the fall elections and Jefferson was elected president, Madison knew he would be pressed to serve in the cabinet. Aaron Burr, his friend from Princeton days and the man who had introduced Madison to his future wife, was to become, according to party plan, the vice-president, in line to succeed Jefferson after a decent interval.

But two elements upset this plan: embittered Federalists and Burr's overwhelming ambition. The Federalists, smarting under Alexander Hamilton's vindictive lash, threw enough electoral votes to Burr to keep the nation in suspense for several weeks. The House of Representatives voted, and voted, and voted; a tie continued to keep Burr in contention for the first office. Furthermore, Burr had reneged on earlier promises to stand aside. Thus a motley alliance of Jefferson haters kept the people's choice from the clear victory their votes had signaled. Switched votes and abstentions finally gave Jefferson the presidency, but the damage to Burr's future within the Republican party was done. He would be the vice-president for four years and then he must go.

Jefferson's disgust over Burr's apparent treachery cleared the way for James Madison to break the vice-presidential hold on the main office by succeeding Jefferson. No deal was made because none was needed—Burr's ambition had destroyed him politically. Madison would not return to private life for sixteen years.

Madison's second term as president ended in 1817, and he retired to Montpelier. There Madison pondered his "notes" on the Federal Convention some forty years after he had first recorded them; the former president must have also reflected on the tumultuous events of 1787 following the compromise over representation. Although that "Connecticut compromise" did keep the Convention from dissolving, it also had caused Madison to discard his ideas about national government. In his disappointment Madison had tried to strengthen the executive office at the expense of Congress. On 17 July, the day after the dramatic vote, Madison told the delegates that the real dangers in American state governments must not become obstacles to the framework they were seeking. "Experience had proved a tendency in our governments to throw all power into the Legislative vortex," Madison warned as he veered toward a stronger presidency. Before the Philadelphia meeting broke up after completing its work on 17 September, Madison had become the champion of a president empowered to appoint with Senate approval Supreme Court justices, cabinet officers, and ambassadors. When some delegates favored selection of the president by Congress, Madison balked, saying that "the people at large was in [his] opinion the fittest" method of selection, and so he approved the electoral college system as an indirect means of a popular ballot.[8]

Madison viewed the role of Congress with an increasingly jaundiced eye as the Constitution took its final shape. He favored a motion to give the president power to revise bills before they took the force of law (after consulting "the Judiciary departmt."). The motion lost and was replaced by the president's power to veto bills he considers unacceptable. But Madison still hoped for some affinity between the president and the justices that might take the sting out of unwise legislation. Speaking for his motion to allow the president to appoint Supreme Court justices, Madison said the president "would in general be more capable & likely to select fit characters than the Legislature, or even the 2d. b[ranch] of it, who might hide their selfish motives."[9] Madison's proposition was at first rejected, so that justices were to be chosen by the Senate. Eventually, of course, Madison's idea prevailed, and he probably would have preferred even further checks on the congressional powers if the delegates had been more encouraging.

Thus the office Madison helped to create was the epitome in 1787 of a Republican chief magistrate: a man over thirty-five, native-born or a long-time resident, who was responsible to the people for his four-year term and bound to observe the laws while protecting and defending the Constitution

8. Max Farrand, ed., *The Records of the Federal Convention of 1787,* 4 vols. (New Haven, Conn.: Yale University Press, 1986), 2:35, 56.

9. Ibid., 2:80.

itself. Much presidential responsibility was unspecified. He would be commander in chief but only as a civilian; he could veto laws but was limited
to recommending "such Measures as he shall judge necessary and expedient";
and he could direct foreign policy but only with the advice and consent of
the Senate. In addition, he could be impeached for misconduct, and his salary was set by a Congress that could be hostile or niggardly. The contradic-
tions abounded, but because Washington was to be the first holder of this
office, and time was slipping away, the convention delegates saw no need
to dot every *i* and cross every *t*.

Madison must have pondered all these facts far more in the fall of 1808
than he had twenty-one years earlier when the Constitution was finished.
After Washington's tenure, who could have guessed the course the presidency—and for that matter, the whole nation—might take. Even while he
was acting as a majority leader in the First Congress, Madison helped shape
the ceremonial side of the office and struck a few blows on behalf of a Republican conception rather than a kingly one. When some Federalists, for
example, wanted to have Washington's profile on all coins, Madison thought
it smacked too much of monarchy, and he led the opposition in squelching
the proposal by "substituting an emblematic figure of Liberty."

Whether Madison avoided President Washington's weekly levees because he thought they were too much like a royal tea party is not certain;
but he was inclined to go to the president's quarters only when asked. As
Alexander Hamilton's stock went up in the presidential precincts, Madison's
went down. Madison maintained his friendship with Washington, but after
1791 much of its tone changed. From that time until March 1801, Madison
was outside the executive office, looking in occasionally but never part of
the policy-making process. After the fight over the Jay Treaty in 1795, Madison helped to create a political party that was, if anything, meant to curb
the discretionary powers of the president. Madison's tenuous friendship with
Hamilton was the first casualty of this political realignment, and after the
Jay Treaty battle, "Federalists said Lucifer Jefferson seduced Madison: thus,
his [Madison's] reputation was that of a man irresolute and submissive."[10]
Professional Jefferson haters thereafter insisted that Madison was simply a
puppet manipulated by the master of Monticello.

The story is true only to the extent that when Jefferson thought he was
stepping aside and leaving the arena of public affairs forever, he told Madison to set his sights on the presidency and implicitly offered to help. When
Jefferson surveyed the political situation late in 1794 he told Madison to be
ready for the day when he might be called to the presidency, and Madison

10. Marshall Smelser, *The Democratic Republic, 1801–1815* (New York: Harper
& Row, 1968), 187.

replied: "Reasons of *every* kind, and some of them, of the most *insuperable* as well as *obvious* kind, shut my mind against the admission of any idea such as you seem to glance at."[11] Whether Madison was alluding to his frequent illnesses or simply thought he was ill-fitted for the presidency is not clear. At any rate, Jefferson seems to have accepted Madison's judgment, as his younger friend then slipped into retirement. But in 1801 Madison was called back to public service and spent the next eight years at Jeffersons's side as his most trusted friend and staunchest ally.

As secretary of state, Madison saw the presidency change radically from what the delegates had discussed in 1787. The political parties then held to be fatal to republics had sprung into being, and Jefferson's election was based on a reactionary approach, the main feature being a total dismantling of several Federalist programs that were considered the antithesis of republicanism: higher taxes, a large federal budget for armaments, an expanding diplomatic corps, and a permanent national debt. Once in office, Jefferson had strained the constitutional limits of his powers by authorizing the Louisiana Purchase and had sought on more than one occasion to add to the continental Union through dollar diplomacy. Faced with a devastating European war, Madison worked with Jefferson on a program to maintain American neutrality that clashed with the war aims of Britain and France. Constantly insulted by both powers, the Jefferson administration finally threw up its hands and opted for the all-embracing Embargo Act, which withdrew American ships from the lanes of international commerce. In reaction, New England shippers and merchants excoriated the embargo and countenanced smuggling and defiance of the laws. Convinced that Jefferson could do no wrong, most of the South sent to Washington repeated testimonials of its approval of the embargo despite the plunge in farm commodity prices that the policy entailed. The president and secretary of state were mystified by the northern reaction and bound to believe that the southern position was in fact the majority view.

Before these sectional tensions could be exacerbated, President Jefferson in 1808 let it be known that he approved of the precedent set by Washington and would not seek a third term. Immediately speculation began as to Jefferson's successor; but almost as soon as the question was asked, it answered itself. The strong personal bond between the president and Madison was not based on friendship alone, but on their similar political philosophies, which had been nurtured for thirty years. Since their first association when Jefferson was governor of Virginia and Madison was on the council of state, the two planters had agreed on nearly every political question. Even when Jefferson was the American minister in France, Madison had filled in the gap

11. *Madison Papers,* 15:428, 493.

by promoting Jefferson's 1779 bills for establishing religious freedom in their home state. They also were closer for the common enemies they had faced; nothing was more remarkable than their shared contempt (if that is the right word) for Patrick Henry. In a moment of frustration, Jefferson had once suggested that because Henry was too politically powerful to be bested in a legislative hall, they ought to pray for his early death.[12]

Henry had long been in his grave by the time Madison became president, but there were other Virginian Republicans who contributed to the discord that made the Tenth Congress (in Jefferson's last two years in office) notable for its ineptitude. Madison knew where Randolph stood, and although John Taylor of Caroline (who had broken ideologically with Madison and Jefferson) was no longer in the Senate, Giles was no improvement. Fortunately, Virginia was still the most populous state in the Union, and its twenty-four seats in the House of Representatives were held mainly by friendly Republicans, including John Dawson (who now represented Madison's old district), longtime friend Dr. Walter Jones, and Madison's erstwhile brother-in-law John G. Jackson, who came from a hardscrabble western district.

The trouble was that none of the administration's friends could intellectually match either Taylor or Randolph, and thus the Eleventh Congress, which Madison had to deal with, was led by inferior talents and honeycombed with recusants. The most exciting new face belonged to a Kentuckian, Henry Clay, who came into Congress in the middle of the session and impressed colleagues with his confident air and personal charm. As Madison read the congressional roster of these mediocre men he must have sighed with regret. At least it needs to be said that Madison was overly sensitive to the dry rot that had set into the congressional leadership during Jefferson's last six months in office and which was still there in 1809.

In short, Madison was a spectator to this political downhill slide without being able to do much about it. Like Jefferson, Madison disliked argumentation and unpleasantness within the official family. The falling-out of Randolph and Jefferson had been so traumatic, nobody in the cabinet wanted to go through it again with Giles or any of his Senate pals. Aware that Gallatin was intellectually superior to his enemies, Madison took comfort in the fact that he was not losing his best cabinet member, and he may have consoled himself by assuming that in discussions on foreign affairs and finance — the greatest problems facing the country — Gallatin would be on call.

12. Ibid., 8:178.

Gallatin was not only superior to the available Republicans, he was also spared from the presidential virus that had caused William Branch Giles and Aaron Burr to destroy their characters on the altar of unbridled ambition. The Constitution would not have stood in the Swiss-born Gallatin's way because a saving clause allowed "a Citizen of the United States, at the time of Adoption of this Constitution," to be eligible for the presidency. But Gallatin was far too shrewd to become a victim of the lust for power that had trapped so many Republicans running through the Capitol's corridors around the House and Senate chambers. Gallatin seems to have possessed more sense than most public men ever exhibit, and he also had a clearer understanding of human nature than even Jefferson or Madison. To these inestimable traits, Gallatin added skill in intricate financial matters and a clear notion of how practical politics works.

Perhaps more than any other man in Washington during Madison's two terms as president, Gallatin understood the limits of political power. Madison recognized Gallatin's acumen and deferred to his judgment more than the records show. Gallatin's work in Jefferson's cabinet had impressed Madison, for the secretary of state had recognized his colleague's ability to handle the administrative details that President Jefferson had tended to overlook. Gallatin also taught Madison an important lesson: Government programs cost more money than the original estimates indicate.

In short, Gallatin was the Gibraltar in the Madison cabinet, a pillar that would not surrender to petty politics or to bigotry. His foreign birth and slight accent made him a target for men who wanted to harm the president politically, but Gallatin was so far ahead of them in ability that Madison came to depend on his secretary of the Treasury as a confidant, policy planner, and liaison with congressional leaders. If Madison had a second-in-command, it was Gallatin. In an era when drunkenness, debauchery, and womanizing were a recognized but hidden side of a public man's Washington career, Gallatin's exemplary personal life and devotion to his wife also made him stand out, although it won him no respect from the backbiters lurking on Capitol Hill. Because Gallatin was already in the cabinet as secretary of the Treasury, Madison had only to urge him to stay on, thereby avoiding any confirmation battle in the Senate.

So Madison ducked a fight and instead sent to the Senate a nomination as secretary of state for Robert Smith, who had been secretary of the navy in Jefferson's cabinet and had the added advantage of being the brother of Senator Samuel Smith of Maryland (he of the Invincibles). Then Madison tried a geographical balancing act for the rest of his executive inner circle. As secretary of war he picked Dr. William Eustis, a onetime congressman from Massachusetts with limited military experience (he was a surgeon during the Revolutionary War) but good Republican credentials. As secretary of the navy he chose a South Carolina Republican, Paul Hamilton, who espoused military preparedness and had a fondness for ardent spirits. Neither the postmaster general nor the attorney general were part of the official cabinet in 1808; for those places Madison simply settled for Jefferson's appointees, Postmaster Gideon Granger and Attorney General Caesar Rodney. The truth was that Madison opted for harmony and the appearance of a broadly based national cabinet rather than a collection of the best minds in the Republican party. As Madison later learned to his dismay, he had not really avoided a fight and his cabinet included only one first-rate administrator. In his quest of moderation, Madison ended up with mediocrity.

Part of Madison's problem grew out of his philosophical approach to the presidency. The presidential model created at Philadelphia in 1787 was not supposed to be a heavy-handed version of Charles I, Louis XIV, or Frederick the Great. Instead, the president was to execute laws passed by Congress, adopt policies that benefited American prosperity, and ensure that the American flag was honored—in short, duties performed by a president during peacetime.[13] Jefferson had embodied this presidential model perfectly during his first term by setting the country on a Republican course of reduced national debt, lowered taxes, and restored civil liberties in the aftermath of the Alien and Sedition Acts. It was now Madison's job to preserve the gains made by the Jefferson presidency and to avoid war.

As president, Madison retained much—but not all—of the executive-branch machinery installed by his three predecessors. Washington, Adams, and Jefferson had relied on their cabinets through meetings, through full but private discussions of public issues, and through the occasional call for written opinions. Madison, in contrast, appears to have substituted frequent personal visits to the various offices for systematic, regularly scheduled cabinet meetings. Gallatin was a frequent caller at the White House and their conferences often may have been a practical substitute for full cabinet meetings. Madison's relationship with Robert Smith was far different from the one he had with Gallatin; for although Madison knew the State Department clerks and felt at home in the modest offices, Madison never gave Smith his full confidence. There was a lack of rapport between the two that spelled trouble, even though Madison probably exhibited great politeness in their official dealings. Gallatin, on the other hand, was as close to Madison as he had been to Jefferson, sometimes making a suggested change on a speech draft or preparing major legislation for a congressional committee on ways and means.

As in Jefferson's time, Madison's cabinet officers worked with Congress

13. Ralph Ketcham, *Presidents above Party: The First American Presidency, 1789-1829* (Chapel Hill: University of North Carolina Press, 1984), 120.

by holding informal conferences with lawmakers, drafting bills or recommending legislative changes in pending measures, and making reports requested from House committees. If Congress wanted to know the condition of the navy, a resolution requesting information on costs, equipment, and manpower was sent to the secretary; his clerks would compile an answer and the secretary would forward it to the proper office or committee as a formal report. This system worked because Congress knew where the taxes it levied were spent and the cabinet reports at the end of a session constituted a working history of how the federal government operated. There was even a periodic report on all salaries paid to federal officials, from the president down to the lowest paid postmaster. In Madison's last year in office, Postmaster John Junkins of White Eyes Plains, Ohio, was paid $1.09 for his labors. Madison's $25,000 salary never varied in his eight-year tenure; the chief justice received $4,000; and customs collectors at Boston, New York, Norfolk, and Philadelphia took home $5,000. Next to the president, one of the highest paid federal employees was Archibald Bullock, customs collector at Savannah, Georgia, who made $7,263 in 1816. Understandably, congressmen came and went after a term or two, but customs collectors stayed on as long as their political base was safe.

Most of the cabinet officers had about six clerks working for them. The Treasury, in contrast, usually had over fifty. Gallatin's offices had desks for sixty-seven of the one hundred twenty-three government employees working in the last year of Jefferson's administration, and the situation was little changed by 1809. Outside the capital, mainly in seaports, the Treasury had a payroll of over seven hundred for duty collectors, inspectors, and crewmen of vessels used to intercept smugglers. Congress placed the General Land Office under the Treasury in 1812; after that the office expanded as did patronage for registrars and surveyors in the field. The State Department was also the home of the Patent Office, carried on the paper work for the 1810 census, and was the administrative base for the federal mint, but even so a handful of clerks and messengers kept the office functioning efficiently, although the growth of correspondence with the territorial governors may have caused greater use of the quills and candles budgeted in the department's contingency fund.

The War Department was scaled down during Jefferson's first administration in compliance with Republican ideology, but it did take on added duties for the superintendency of Indian trade in 1806. By 1809 the War Department's staff consisted of a chief clerk, thirteen regular clerks, and two messengers. There was no army general staff, and the only important officer stationed in Washington was the paymaster, who drew a $120-a-month salary and kept two clerks busy. When the army expanded as war clouds loomed after 1808 and officers were commissioned in droves, Secretary Dearborn dropped the policy of recommending men with some military experience and "gave decided preference to Republicans."[14] In contrast, the United States Navy was contracting, as Jefferson had cut naval appropriations to the bone in his first year in office. With fewer ships or shipyards to oversee, the secretary of the navy needed only a few clerks to keep accounts and maintain correspondence with the scattered naval agents at various ports who purchased stores and timber for government use. Robert Smith was regarded second only to Gallatin in administering a tight—in Smith's case a light—ship. (The two secretaries detested each other—a good reason for avoiding full cabinet meetings.)

The attorney general was still considered the counsel for the executive branch, practically the president's personal lawyer, and did not become a cabinet officer until the law was changed during Madison's tenure. As chief counsel, the attorney general did not have to reside in the capital to earn his three thousand dollar salary and was permitted a private law practice on the side. At times cabinet members consulted Caesar Rodney and requested written opinions, but he was not invited to cabinet meetings unless legal problems were discussed. Congress could also seek his opinion and ask for reports. The settlement of the Yazoo claims, for example, involved the attorney general in efforts to close that dispute, which dragged through both Jefferson's and Madison's presidencies.

The postmaster general was not an official member of the cabinet either, but he was at times heavily burdened with affairs that affected the national well-being. With over two thousand post offices under his charge, his was the federal agency most familiar to the average American. Although Madison was never as interested in the "mailbox" arm of government as Jefferson had been, he expected Gideon Granger to see that available patronage was not wasted on critics of the administration. Usually Granger consulted a congressman when a vacancy occurred in his district, but in one notable incident—Michael Leib's appointment to the Philadelphia postmastership—Granger ignored both local politicians and Madison's best interests in awarding a sensitive and lucrative position. Running the Washington end of the vast postal network required only a dozen clerks.

Publishing the salaries of these public servants was a device Congress used to let the public know how tax money was being spent and to give taxpayers the opportunity to compare wages earned by government employees with those earned by private workers in related fields. The clerks themselves

14. Most of the information on the workings of the civil service in Washington during the Madison presidency is based on information found in Noble E. Cunningham, Jr., *The Process of Government under Jefferson* (Princeton, N.J.: Princeton University Press, 1978), 87–164.

were anonymous, or nearly so. As Noble Cunningham noted, "Little is known about most of the men who held the clerkships in the government offices in Washington," even when their numbers were relatively small. Many had moved to Washington from Philadelphia around 1800 and kept their places when the Republicans came to power, despite Federalists' charges to the contrary. Policy decisions were made at cabinet meetings, in the president's office, or in the secretary's place of business; the bureaucracy that was slowly created to implement decisions was to remain small until the middle of the nineteenth century, when federal land and military policies underwent significant change. (The distribution of federal lands would be greatly affected by the Homestead Act, and the army would be enlarged to handle the Indian problem as territory expanded.) During Madison's years in the White House, pressures for Republican frugality and hence little expansion of government services kept the federal payroll low and the number of bookkeepers and clerks in the hundreds, not the thousands.

Somewhat spellbound by Henry Adams's judgment of Madison, the late Leonard D. White in his book *The Jeffersonians* (1951) found little good to say about Madison's presidential tenure in terms of administrative abilities. "Madison's Cabinet was a failure from the outset," White wrote, and he gave short shrift to Madison's presidency by implying that it was an administrative disaster. Although White often overstated his observations, he did concede that departmental staffs between 1801 and 1821 performed well and were essentially unchanged in size or performance over two decades.

When Madison's lieutenants filled a vacancy in the post offices or customs houses, they took the advice of local Republican leaders. The turnover was not wholesale, but every seaport community had a Republican who thought he was better than any Federalist holding a place in the customs house, and much of the mail coming to the White House concerned applications for jobs that the writers believed were filled by incompetents of a different political persuasion. Madison followed Jefferson's policy of not answering such personal appeals, although he may have turned many such pleas over to cabinet members for final action.

On balance, Madison was a good administrator in that he did not try to do everything himself, knew how to delegate power, and realized that party loyalty had to be rewarded as a matter of political expediency. His reasons for the higher level appointments of Eustis and Hamilton are not clear; surely Madison was disappointed in their performance and yet he was patient to the point of recklessness. Although it is not fair to say Madison sought geographical balance in his cabinet officers rather than competence, he showed a tendency in that direction, and he was loath to make changes until circumstances forced him to do so. No president enjoys admitting that he has made a mistake in cabinet selection, but with Madison the problem became more chronic as the likelihood of war increased.

Because Madison did not keep a diary, we know little of his personal feelings regarding cabinet meetings, their frequency, or how much weight the cabinet's advice played in his decision-making process. We are spared the records that James K. Polk kept, detailing his boredom with the diplomatic niceties surrounding the births of royal nephews and nieces, but we also do not know whether Madison ever imitated Lincoln by asking for a show of hands and then deciding the president's lone vote outweighed cabinet unanimity.

Polk saw Indian chiefs in droves; Madison met several from the western and southern tribes, although we can only guess at the frequency of these meetings and the exact numbers involved. Madison alluded to Indians in his annual messages and may have shared, probably did share, Jefferson's attitude toward federal paternalism as a means of converting Indians into yeoman farmers. But we cannot be sure that he frequently greeted solemn Creeks or Osages bedecked in beads and feathers on a White House portico. Of course the silver and bronze "peace medals" that government agents brought to tribal powwows carried Madison's profile, but all they prove is that the Indian recipients had a better chance of knowing how Madison looked than the average white citizen.

In an age when portraiture on the grand or on the small scale was the chief means of conveying visual impressions, Madison did not differ from other Americans of his time. A miniature he had commissioned for his fiancé in 1783 shows Madison as bright-eyed, wistful, and beginning to show a trace of baldness. The best Madison portrait was painted by Charles Willson Peale around 1793, when Madison was forty-two or forty-three, and already he was showing the wrinkles and hair loss of an older man. Later portraits, some done during the White House years and several others after Madison had retired from public life, reveal a man of prim countenance, his hair combed forward, his small frame clothed in his usual black jacket, light vest, and smallclothes (knee breeches), with a white scarf and stockings completing the ensemble. Madison, unlike Jefferson, never received a foreign diplomat wearing his house slippers; but, on the other hand, the well-tailored presence of a Chester Arthur or a John F. Kennedy was beyond both Madison's means and his personal lifestyle. As president, Madison had more on his mind than a fashionable wardrobe.

Keeping the United States out of a fight with either France or Britain had consumed much of Madison's energy since 1806 as first French and then

.icy made his work as secretary of state difficult. Neither of the warers seemed to care about the rights of neutral nations, and the weaker cral the more contemptuous their policies. As president, Madison now ne brunt of the British crackdown on Napoleon.[15] When Napoleon re- .ed with a blockade (mostly on paper) of Britain that made American ships fair game if they touched a British port en route to Europe, only trouble for the United States could ensue. What Napoleon's decrees meant almost required a lawyer's skill for clarification, but his point was that a neutral ship touching a British port lost its neutrality and thus became fair game for French privateers or naval vessels. This concept flew in the face of the American claim that "neutral flags make neutral goods" and therefore their cargoes and ships were protected (not very well, as it turned out) under international law. After the battle of Trafalgar (1805) had established British naval supremacy, however, the French edicts were less troublesome than the British omnipresence.

For three years Jefferson sought Madison's advice on how to avoid war with the major powers and keep American ships plying the oceans, and in desperation the two Virginians decided on a hands-off policy (the Embargo Act of 1807) that revealed sectional differences that were almost as deep as those slavery would expose. Although Gallatin had never wanted to cut off all commerce with the outside world, which is what the Embargo Act did, he went along with his president and cabinet colleagues in the hope of finding an alternative to war.

Madison was more troubled by the failure of the Embargo Act than any other cabinet member, probably because it was his idea in the first place. Since his earliest days in Congress, Madison had sought ways to curb British high-handedness in world commerce, and always he had failed because of the New England Federalists' votes, which the Virginian had interpreted as pro-British. Early on (1803–05), Madison was optimistic that in a trade war with Britain, the United States would eventually triumph. "Her dependence on us being greater than ours on her," he told Jefferson, "the supplies of the United States are necessary to the [British] existence," whereas the goods sent from Britain to the United States "are either superfluities or poisons."[16] But time proved Madison wrong. Repeatedly rebuffed in efforts to force Britain into a commercial treaty based on mutual advantages, Madison became more and more Anglophobic as he saw the "monocrats" triumph with the Jay Treaty, and he intensified efforts to break away from the old Franco-American alliance of 1778. Madison also seemed distressed by the plain truth that the United States was Britain's best customer.

15. Bradford Perkins, *Prologue to War: England and the United States, 1805–1812* (Berkeley: University of California Press, 1968), 223–60.
16. *Madison Papers*, 12:269–70.

British discrimination against the U.S. commerce after 1783 was a major factor in Madison's growing antagonism toward Britain. Increasingly, Madison came to agree with Jefferson's view that only blows to British pocketbooks would win John Bull's respect. "England is still our enemy," as Jefferson once observed and never forgot. "Her hatred is deep-rooted and cordial, and nothing is wanting with her but the power to wipe us and the land we live on out of existence. Her interest however is her ruling passion, [and] when they shall see decidedly that without [some treaty arrangement] we shall suppress their commerce with us, they will be agitated by their avarice on one hand, and their hatred and their fear of us on the other."[17] Jefferson never changed his mind about Britain, and in time Madison agreed wholeheartedly with him. The continued impressment of American seamen, the dastardly *Leopard* incident, and the hovering of Royal Navy sails within sight of the American capes were further proof that Britain still regarded the United States as an upstart pseudo-nation.

Madison had little time to fret over his cabinet choices, for a change in the British diplomatic mission in Washington heralded alterations in the standing orders to interdict American commerce. In dumping the embargo policy, Congress had enacted a nonintercourse law that was a carrot-and-stick approach to the problems of international commerce. The new law opened to American ships all of the world's sea lanes except those to France and Britain; however, it allowed the president to renew commerce with either belligerent power if it would call off its restrictions on American shipping. The law caught the eye of George Canning, the British foreign secretary, who was always looking for a way to expand Britain's overseas markets.

Canning's timing was propitious because David Erskine, son of a Scottish peer and married to a pretty American girl, had just been name minister to the United States, replacing a haughty predecessor's stiffness with an effusive goodwill that had caught most of Washington off guard. Erskine received orders from the British foreign office allowing him to negotiate under the new American law for cancellation of the detested Orders in Council (which authorized seizure of American sailors and cargoes). Erskine held back until Madison was settled in office; he then laid out his instructions and awaited the reaction of the new president and his cabinet. Canning conceded that the United States was troublesome, so with the new act in mind he offered to cancel the Orders in Council provided that the Americans would allow the Royal Navy to enforce American laws on Yankee ships that might try to cheat and head for a French port. Madison heard what he

17. Jefferson to John Langdon, 11 September 1785, in Julian Boyd et al., eds., *The Papers of Thomas Jefferson*, 24 vols. (Princeton, N.J.: Princeton University Press, 1950–), 8:512.

wanted to hear, that the British would modify their restrictive orders and pay for the damages inflicted by the *Leopard*; but he rejected as "insulting" the notion that the British navy might intercept American ships illegally bound for France. How could a sovereign nation allow another power to enforce its laws? Madison did not need a crystal ball to see how American public opinion would react to this British scheme.

Eager to succeed, Erskine downplayed Canning's sine qua non on the boarding of American ships and ignored the matter of British enforcement of American contraband laws. To Madison, Erskine's willingness to sign a pact provided that the Orders in Council would be revoked seemed to vindicate Republican patience and foreign policy stretching back eight years. What did it matter that the United States would be even more firmly attached to Britain commercially so long as American products reached British markets rather than French ones. A whirlwind of discussions and negotiations came to a climax on 19 April 1809, after Madison had been in office fewer than seven weeks. He issued a presidential proclamation as authorized by the Nonintercourse Act. The proclamation set 10 June as the magical day when Britain's obnoxious orders would be withdrawn.[18]

Express riders hurried the news to seaports clogged with idle men and ships, and farmers who had been selling their corn and wheat at rock-bottom prices exulted at the prospect of eager grain buyers. In New England, Federalist newspapers admitted that they might have been wrong about Madison — perhaps he had been right to be stubborn. Long a critic of Madison and Jefferson, the arch-Federalist *Connecticut Courant* almost apologized for its past diatribes as it acknowledged the speed and outcome of the Erskine-Madison negotiations: "We owe it to president Madison and his cabinet to say (and we do it with pride and with pleasure) that they have come forward with a degree of promptness and manliness which reflects much honor on them and the country. . . . Mr. Madison is now effectually resisting the French decrees by a total non-intercourse with that country; and this nation will thank him for it to the latest generation."[19] In Boston countinghouses, where invectives against Jefferson and Madison had been a morning ritual, there was a sudden awareness that Madison was probably not so bad after all.

In the halcyon days following the president's 19 April proclamation, Madison expressed the hope that Napoleon would be shocked by the Anglo-American declaration once it was confirmed at Whitehall. Madison's mail brought a nasty British tract—*War in Disguise; or The Frauds of Neutral Flags*—that blatantly attacked the American claim that "free ships make free

18. *Madison Papers* [Presidential Series], 1:125–26.
19. Hartford *Connecticut Courant*, 3 May 1809.

goods"; it had sold so well in London that it was into its fifth edition. Madison first saw it in 1805 and had written a turgid rebuttal that fell flat. Now he seemed to dismiss the pamphlet and in the euphoria of the day failed to realize that it touched on a delicate British nerve — that neutral flags made a contraband cargo neutral made no sense at the Admiralty. Regarding the bitter attack as merely a harmless anti-American screed, Madison absentmindedly thanked the envoy who sent it. His mind was more on a vacation at Montpelier, now that the British had backtracked on the Orders in Council. And from Monticello came a congratulatory message. "The British ministry has been driven from it's Algerine system," Jefferson exulted. The agreement with Erskine came "as the triumph of our forbearing & yet persevering system. . . . It will lighten your anxieties, take from cabal it's most fertile ground of war, [and] will give us peace during your time."[20]

It all seemed too good to be true, and to Madison's dismay, it was too good to last. When Canning read the preliminary draft he was quick to note that Erskine had dropped the demand for the right of interception for the Royal Navy. Without that provision, Canning would have none of the agreement, and in short order he drafted a cabinet disavowal of the pact and ordered Erskine back home. On 25 May the American envoy in London learned of Canning's denunciation. In Paris John Armstrong, the American minister, read one day of the proclamation and on the next saw Canning's rebuff in Parisian newspapers.[21] Armstrong did not realize the hopes Madison had placed on the pact and simply passed the incident off as "a true specimen of modern diplomacy."

Six weeks passed before the bad news reached Washington, catching Madison off guard at Montpelier and leaving his cabinet in a quandary as to the next move. Madison delayed a return to the capital, even after he read Gallatin's message confirming the impression that Erskine had never insisted on the boarding rights of the British navy as a key part of the deal. "To propose as an indispensable condition what they knew we must reject is a proof of their insincerity," Gallatin told the dismayed president.

The Erskine agreement and Canning's rejection of it caused Madison to turn to his cabinet for advice. Like all presidents, Madison knew that he had the final say, but all his predecessors had consulted the cabinet in times of urgency so he was only following precedent. Moreover, Madison never gave his cabinet members equal weight when their opinions clashed. Gallatin's ideas swayed Madison on many key decisions, perhaps because Madison so often discounted Robert Smith's judgment. Madison rarely conferred with Attorney General Rodney because he was not required to be in the capi-

20. *Madison Papers* [Presidential Series], 1:139.
21. Ibid., 1:228.

tal and so he stayed in Delaware most of the time. (His successor, William Pinkney, avoided Washington completely during his two-year tenure.) At any rate, Madison often asked his cabinet for advice but never felt constrained to accept it. In this first crisis of his administration, however, the four cabinet members apparently thought Madison wanted to see them, and they expected to be called to an emergency meeting. But initially Madison delegated to Gallatin the responsibility for relaying opinions that would help him reach a decision. "I venture to hope that my return [to Washington] will not be found necessary," the president wrote Gallatin, "the less so as you will be able to bring with you so full a view of the state of things, and the sentiments of your colleagues, that my decision as far as necessary, may be made here as at Washington.[22]

But Gallatin did not think the matter could be handled so easily. Given that Congress had adjourned, only a special session could be called to sound out legislators; moreover, Gallatin was worried about the status of American ships bound for Europe, vessels that Britain might now seize under the pretext that the whole affair was an American trick. Meanwhile, Rodney was not to be found, and Gallatin hoped that Erskine's successor might soon appear with a plausible explanation for Canning's harsh repudiation.

One thing really stuck in Madison's craw. Along with the official dispatches, he read of a rumor that in the diplomatic correspondence with Erskine there was a jab (inserted by the president) that reportedly offended George III to the point that he instructed Canning not to approve the Erskine agreement. The offensive remark appeared to be an allusion to the British admiral who was responsibile for the *Leopard* incident. The American position had all along been that Admiral George C. Berkeley ought to be reprimanded and relieved of his command. What had apparently rattled George III was the statement that "while he [Madison] forbears to insist on further punishment of the offending officer, he is not the less sensible of the justice and utility of such an example, nor the less persuaded that it would best comport with what is due from His Britannic Majesty to his own honor." An American living in London told Madison that Canning had been on the verge of accepting Erskine's agreement when the king read the correspondence, pounced on that one sentence, and told his foreign secretary that "he would not ratify anything in which he was so personally insulted."[23] Thus if the story is true, Madison's little dig at George III caused the agreement to be blown sky-high. Eight years of forbearance and negotiation were lost.

Whether this rumor was true or not, the official reprimand of Erskine and his subsequent recall were facts that Madison had to deal with reluc-

22. Ibid., 1:309.
23. Ibid., 1:205.

tantly but promptly. "I find myself under the mortifying necessit out tomorrow morning for Washington," a sad Madison wrote J 3 August. "The intricate state of our affairs with England prodt mixture of fraud & folly in her late conduct" made a cabinet meeting essen-tial.[24] Could the president acting alone undo the damage of his proclama-tion, or would Congress have to legislate a humilating retreat from the Er-skine agreement? After hearing the cabinet argue the matter, Madison de-cided that he had the power to rescind the proclamation on his own. On 9 August Madison's proclamation acknowledged "that the said Orders in Council have not been withdrawn" and therefore the legal trade with Britain was again suspended to conform to the nonintercourse law.[25]

After three days in Washington, Madison headed back for Montpelier a chastened man. To Jefferson he confided his belief that the real cause for Canning's conduct was pressure exerted by "the London smugglers of Sugar & Coffee," who wanted to keep American ships out of continental harbors. Disillusionment swept the country as the brunt of Canning's reprimand struck at shippers and merchants loading cargoes for Europe. A friend in Congress wrote frankly to Madison: "My blood boils at the recital of Mr. Canning's intolerable insults," and he lamented the cowardice of his fellow legislators. "So debased have the Congress become that without some fresh & monstrous outrage, its courage will never be screwed up to the sticking place — depend on it blows blows, blows alone will make them substitute war for words."[26]

If Madison had wanted an excuse for saber rattling, he now had it. Re-publican meetings called for a break of diplomatic relations with Britain and the arming of American merchant vessels. "It would be derogatory to the Character of America as a Free, Sovereign, and independant Nation, to hold any intercourse (under the existing circumstances) with a Nation so far lost to Moral Rectitude, & resorting to disgraceful pretexts to evade the fulfill-ment of National and Solemn Contracts," Kentucky Republicans assured Madison.[27]

Madison was not looking for a war, however. His Republican philoso-phy was based on the notion that war was to be avoided at almost any cost. "War contains so much folly, as well as wickedness," he had written in 1792, "that much is to be hoped from the progress of reason; and if any thing is to be hoped, every thing [to preserve peace] ought to be tried." Madison had not changed his mind seventeen years later. So Madison took heart from the

24. Ibid., 1:317.
25. Ibid., 1:321.
26. Ibid., 1:330.
27. Ibid., 1:343.

laudatory, prowar resolutions stuffed in the presidential mailbag but never took seriously the suggestion that Erskine's downfall was sufficient provocation for war. Besides, he had other, unfinished problems growing out of that recent mess.

In announcing Erskine's recall, Canning had served notice that His Majesty's government was sending Francis James Jackson as Erskine's successor. Jackson was notorious in international circles as the British diplomat who had delivered an ultimatum to Denmark shortly before the Royal Navy had bombarded Copenhagen into submission. The impression was that Jackson's diplomatic ploy was akin to a sneak attack, for it led to a destructive onslaught before the Danes had a chance to reply. The incident left the further impression that Jackson was a British "hatchet man"—wherever he went, trouble was bound to follow. Republicans argued over whether Jackson ought to be received or sent packing, and Madison must have thought about his alternatives after hearing that Jackson and his extensive retinue had reached a Virginia port in late August. On the other hand, perhaps Jackson was bringing a logical explanation for Canning's conduct.

Madison decided to let Jackson wait in Washington while he stayed at Montpelier. When the Madisons finally returned to Washington, Jackson had already told the secretary of state that he was not authorized to add to Canning's official statements. On 3 October Jackson handed the president his credentials and after a short and desultory conversation they parted. Jackson was not impressed by Madison. The president, he observed, was "a plain and rather mean-looking little man." The feeling appears to have been mutual, for Madison sensed that their first meeting had been a diplomatic farce.[28]

Before many days had passed it was clear that Jackson had nothing new to say, and this was confirmed when the British envoy started his talks with Robert Smith. Diplomatic niceties were soon abandoned as Jackson hinted that Madison and Smith knew all along that Erskine had exceeded his instructions. The president knew that the Royal Navy had to able to intercept American ships, Jackson insisted, otherwise Canning could not approve any recision of the Orders in Council. In short, Erskine and Madison had shared a little private joke, Jackson seemed to say, by trying to trick His Britannic Majesty's government.

At first, to keep things in hand, Madison asked that Jackson stop coming to the State Department and henceforth to communicate only on paper. But Jackson repeated his charges of double-dealing, and a furious Madison instructed Robert Smith to stop the useless dialogue. Smith wrote Jackson that his letters continued to repeat "the same gross insinuation" so that there was nothing left to discuss except "to inform you that no further communica-

28. Quoted in Brant, *Madison*, 5:89.

tions will be received from you." In other words, Jackson had become persona non grata to the Madison administration.[29] Thus as his king's minister at Washington, Jackson was finished.

The Englishman took his dismissal with assurance from Madison's political enemies that the president was, once again, making a fool of himself. Told by vindictive Federalists that Madison was a weakling who was out of touch with the American people, Jackson continued to pepper the London foreign office with negative observations on Madison. He informed his brother that all of the sound and fury in the United States amounted to nothing because "dogs that bark don't bite." As for the president, Jackson said, "Madison is now as obstinate as a mule, and takes his stand upon Erskine's arrangement, which he half denies our right to disavow, and in the next breath says, we have not explained the cause of our disavowal."[30] In leisurely fashion, Jackson packed his belongings and headed north with his German-born wife, wined and dined along the way by Federalists, who continued to heap scorn on Madison as an Anglophobe bent on ruining American commerce. At Boston, Jackson was treated as a celebrity and not unnaturally his head was so turned that he told superiors in London that Madison's administration was discredited, forlorn, and following a foreign policy line dictated by Napoleon.

Considering the tone of dispatches sent to London by the British ministers (Erskine excepted), there is a discernible unreality in their estimations of American public opinion. Obviously they placed great store in the whisperings of Federalists, ignored the pro-Madison press, and thought of Republicans as just so many country bumpkins. Clearly the British envoys listened too much to the enemies of Jefferson and Madison and believed most of what they heard. In fact, even Federalist newspaper editors were generally supportive of the final act in the Erskine-Jackson drama, and New England Republican Congressman Ezekiel Bacon confirmed a widespread approbation of Madison's conduct. "In truth," Bacon observed, "I think James Madison's administration is now as strongly entrenched in the public confidence as Thomas Jefferson's ever was at its fullest tide."[31] A Boston lawyer, Bacon was closer to the people than any of the Federalists who attended the public dinner for Francis James Jackson.

Madison's mail revealed that Republicans in all corners of the Union

29. *American State Papers: Documents, Legislative and Executive*, 38 vols. [Foreign Relations] (Washington, D.C.: Gales & Seaton, 1832–1861), 3:314–19.

30. Francis James Jackson to George Jackson, 20 October 1809, in Lady Jackson, ed., *The Bath Archives: The Diaries and Letters of Sir George Jackson*, 2 vols. (London: R. Bentley & Sons, 1873), 1:24, 28.

31. Quoted in Brant, *Madison*, 5:108.

were behind him. A partisan audience in Washington County, New York, sent a message to Madison, assuring him of their support. "We feel a Just indignation at the crooked, faithless and Jesuitical policy, which has so long marked the conduct of the present Ministry of Great Britain," these Republicans told him, and they promised "that we will Support our Government in whatever measures Shall be necessary to redress those injuries we have already Sustained, to redeem our national honor."[32] Other Republican groups in Nashville, New York City, Georgia's McIntosh County, and Kentucky's Washington County pledged the president their full backing in what seemed to them a confrontation between righteous Republicans and arrogant Englishmen. Madison appears to have savored these messages, and he took the trouble to personally answer them with long notes of appreciation.

Congressmen knew from talks with their constituents while in recess that Madison had the country behind him. But did Madison have Congress behind him? Overall the answer was a qualified "yes," but there was always the problem of handling John Randolph, distant cousin, and the excessively ambitious Senator William Branch Giles. Both Randolph and Giles were hard to ingore. After the Erskine agreement and the Jackson fiasco, Randolph withheld his criticism of Madison for a time. In his first State of the Union address in November 1809 Madison reviewed the two Anglo-American gaffes and concluded that Britain was prepared to offer nothing of substance regarding the Orders in Council, the *Chesapeake* affair, or other American grievances. Trying to steer between Scylla and Charybdis, Madison appealed to Congress for guidance: "In the state which has been presented of our affairs with the great parties to a disastrous and protracted war, carried on in a mode equally injurious and unjust to the United States as a neutral nation, the wisdom of the National Legislature will be again summoned to the important decision on the alternatives before them."[33] Madison seemed to be asking Congress to vote more funds for preparedness and to figure out a way to move American shipping back into international waters. But he made no specific recommendations, which seemed to suit Randolph. Randolph listened to the message and then told a friend, "To say the truth it is more to my taste than Jefferson's productions on the same occasion. There is some cant to be sure; but politicians, priests, and even judges . . . must cant, 'more or less.'"[34]

32. *Madison Papers* [Presidential Series], 1:376-77.
33. Hunt, *Writings of Madison*, 8:80-83.
34. Quoted in Henry Adams, *History of the United States of America during the Administrations of Thomas Jefferson and James Madison*, vol. 2, *History of the United States during the Administrations of James Madison*, Earl. N. Harbert, ed. (New York: Library of America, 1986), 125, 177 (hereafter cited as Adams, *History*).

Illness kept Randolph out of action during most of the winter, but in the spring of 1810 he was back on the floor of the House, whip in hand and hunting dogs beside him as he resumed the attack. The administration's program was now specific. Madison wanted more money spent for the army and navy, a reasonable request in view of the war clouds hovering over Washington. Randolph, however, thought that the modest rearmament program was a blatant waste of money. Those war clouds were simply an optical illusion, Randolph seemed to say, for both Britain and France "know as well as we feel that war is out of the question." The Atlantic Ocean was "wide and deep enough to keep off any immediate danger to our territory." Instead of spending money for armaments, Randolph insisted, it was time to cut back on defense appropriations; "we have been enbargoed and non-intercoursed almost into a consumption, and this is not the time for battle."[35] Moreover, money for guns and ships meant more taxes, and Randolph was not voting for any new taxes. Joined by other House members, Randolph claimed to be the true disciple of Republican economy as he went on record against increasing the size of the army. Randolph spearheaded the effort to curb the administration's preparedness program, and Madison's plan for Congress to approve modest increases in the military budget was abandoned. "We talk a great deal about war, and do nothing," Congressman William Macon, a leading Republican, confessed.[36]

Meanwhile, Anglo-American relations had gone from bad to worse, with both governments playing cat and mouse because neither had a minister accredited to serve in the other nation's capital. An American chargé d' affaires in London was running the diplomatic business of the United States without guidance from Washington, and minor British officials did the same in Washington. This appeared to some Americans as a deliberate courting of war, and Madison's decision to risk a rupture with Britain upset some members of his own party. George Logan, a wealthy Quaker and good Republican, told Madison his policy seemed to be headed for war. Would the president consider a more forthright effort to maintain peace?

Logan's yearning for peace was of long-standing, for he had tried in 1798 to deal with the French directory as a well-intentioned private citizen. Logan's self-financed peace mission then had drawn Federalists' ire to the point an act of Congress was passed, and is still on the books (the Logan Act), forbidding citizens from taking diplomatic assignments on their own. Still, Madison regarded Logan as well-meaning rather than meddlesome. To Logan's plea for a peaceable approach to Anglo-American relations, Madison replied that he shared Logan's anxiety to avoid "the vortex of war. . . .

35. Ibid., 141.
36. *Annals of Congress*, 11th Cong., 1st and 2d sess., 1829.

But the question may be decided for us, by actual hostilities against us, or by proceedings, leaving no choice but between absolute disgrace & resistance by force."[37] Jackson's mission had only aggravated the situation, Madison explained, providing "a source of fresh difficulties & animosities." What should Britain do? "Let reparation be made for the acknowledged wrong committed in the case of the *Chesapeak[e]*, a reparation so cheap to the wrong-doer, yet so material to the honor of the injured party; & let the orders in Council . . . be repealed also as an expedient for substituting an illicit commerce, in place of that to which neutrals have, as such, an incontestable right." Madison also wanted to set the record straight on the rejected Monroe-Pinkney treaty of 1806, which Britain had approved but Jefferson had turned down. "You are under a mistake in supposing that the Treaty . . . was rejected because it did not provide that free ships should make free goods. It never was required nor expected that such a stipulation should be inserted."

We can only lament that Madison never was able to talk to any British diplomat as frankly as he wrote to Logan early in 1810. In his candid review of past policies and mistakes, Madison told his Philadelphia friend that the way was still open to averting war. Even the grievance of impressed seamen could be worked out, Madison said, by a mutual agreement, "which most certainly would be better for the British Navy, than that offensive resource & which might be so managed as to leave both parties at liberty to retain their own ideas of right." But that rejected treaty had left untouched the Orders in Council, and the British cabinet's insistence that it had the right to impose those edicts in international law was intolerable to the United States. In fact, to admit their validity was to surrender American sovereignty. Madison had no desire to be the first American president to confess in public that the United States of America was a third-rate power.

Logan, a vainglorious pursuer of peace, decided that he would take his mission to London. Madison made no effort to dissuade Logan and ignored the 1799 statute that could have been invoked to prevent Logan's voyage. Ready to grasp any straw that might bring a peaceful solution to the Anglo-

---

37. Madison to George Logan, 19 January 1819, Madison Papers, DLC. Madison had told Monroe and Pinkney in 1806 that they could negotiate for a stipulation that a neutral flag covers the property of neutral goods but not "the property of an enemy." Madison explained to the American envoys that the claim "free ships, free goods" was being set aside "as a means of obtaining from Great Britain the recognition of a principle now become of more importance to neutral Nations possessing mercantile Capital." In other words, American cargoes were as important as the ships that carried them and needed protection from warring powers. Madison to Monroe and Pinkney, 17 May 1806, quoted in Merrill D. Peterson, ed., *James Madison: A Biography in His Own Words*, 2 vols. (New York: Newsweek Books, 1974), 256.

American crisis, Madison wrote Logan his assessment of the situation. "If unfortunately, the calamity you so benevolently dread, should visit this hitherto favored Country, the fault will not lie where you would wish it not to lie," the president wrote. This was Madison's way of saying, "Don't blame America if war comes. Blame bullheaded England."

4

★ ★ ★ ★ ★

MORE "SPLENDID MISERY"

Madison's predecessor in the White House called his days as president a time of "splendid misery." Madison had already learned, after less than a year in office, that he would probably experience more misery than splendor before his foreign policy problems were solved. To the average American, however, the problems with Britain and France seemed too remote for much bother. Since 1765 Americans had been taught that the main difficulties facing a government were matters of finance. Yankee upbringing included the notion that the government that was best was the one that taxed least.

Jefferson adopted this idea as a basic tenet of the republicanism he shared with Madison. Whenever President Jefferson saw Gallatin—and they probably had daily conferences when both men were in Washington—a part of their conversation must have related to government spending. Jefferson had pledged his administration to reduce the national debt, and under Gallatin's watchful eye this campaign promise was duly kept. By 1809 the debt had been whittled down to a manageable size and there was a $9.5 million surplus in the Treasury. Before the embargo sent revenues from import duties plummeting, Gallatin had made the down payment for Louisiana and reduced the national debt by $27.5 million.[1] In Madison's first full year in office, the federal budget for all civilian departments, including the post office

1. Marshall Smelser, *The Democratic Republic, 1801–1815* (New York: Harper & Row, 1968), 230; Curtis P. Nettels, *The Emergence of a National Economy, 1775–1815* (New York: Holt, Rinehart & Winston, 1962), 330.

and revenue service, was $1.5 million; even so, red ink was needed unless a $3 million military appropriation could be avoided. These economies had been achieved at a cost to the nation's defense forces and diplomatic corps. The army was reduced to manning a string of frontier forts, and the navy placed most of its fighting ships in dry dock. The American minister at The Hague had been recalled to save on the expenses of foreign missions, and the post at St. Petersburg remained unfilled. One of the few American ministers still serving, John Armstrong at Paris, had the unpleasant duty of reporting that Napoleon (in answer to the Nonintercourse Act) had issued a decree from Rambouillet barring American ships from any port controlled by France. Violators would be seized, and cargoes would be confiscated. Now American shippers were doomed to condemnation by both warring powers.

There had been some troublesome squabbles in the president's official and unofficial family, too. Isaac Coles, a distant relative of Dolley Madison's, had moved into the executive mansion and served as the president's secretary until he was provoked into horsewhipping a Federalist congressman within the Capitol's confines. Coles apologized and was let off with a twenty-dollar fine, but everybody in Washington seemed a bit on edge. Coles resigned. Then John G. Jackson, a congressman from western Virginia lately widowed by the death of Dolley Madison's sister Mary, found his honor impugned when he tried to defend the Madison administration. Federalists were better shots than Republicans, some pundits noted, and were taking their frustrations out by issuing challenges. At any rate, in July fellow Representative Joseph Pearson, a North Carolina Federalist, backed Jackson into a verbal corner and drew a pistol on him. Jackson was dangerously wounded, and although he slowly recovered, he remained partially disabled. A clergyman who was Madison's acquaintance from Princeton days thought a federal law to stop such carryings-on was needed as the dueling contagion spread. "We are in danger hereby of loossing [sic] some of our most Valuable Republican members of Congress & Assembly in this state," the Maryland preacher told Madison.[2]

Less troublesome for the new president was the domestic staff that kept the White House functioning. To do the cooking, caretaking, laundering, grooming of horses, and other household chores, the Madisons had increased the number of laborers (some free, some slaves) from fourteen in Jefferson's tenure to sixteen. Papers were shuffled in the president's office by Madison himself or his secretary, and messages to and from Congress or cabinet of-

2. William T. Hutchinson et al., eds., *The Papers of James Madison*, 16 vols. [Presidential Series] (Chicago and Charlottesville: University of Chicago Press and University Press of Virginia, 1962–), 1:243 (hereafter cited as *Madison Papers*).

ficers were carried by messengers who rode back and forth on Pennsylvania Avenue throughout the day. In short, about eighteen people kept the White House going. Comparisons of efficiency would be improper, but in 1989 President Reagan had a White House staff of 3,366 to keep his presidency functioning.

An unpaid member of the staff was Madison's indispensable partner, Dolley. Washington's social gossips confessed that they found the ebullient First Lady almost without flaw. During the aftermath of the Erskine and Jackson fiascoes, Madison's one solace was the commanding presence in Washington of his wife. Dolley enjoyed being surrounded by family and friends, and after her sister Mary died, she invited her youngest sister, Anna, and her new husband, Richard Cutts, a Massachusetts Republican, to live in the executive mansion. Edward Coles, the presidential secretary who had replaced his hot-tempered brother, also was induced to take up lodgings in a wing of the White House. In addition, the front door of the presidential mansion opened to a constant stream of guests for tea parties, dinners, and special levees for the Fourth of July and New Year's Day. Usually, the congressmen and senators who lived in boardinghouses on Capitol Hill rarely socialized, but Dolley Madison's guest list brought together Republicans and Federalists, who were civil (if not friendly) when under the First Lady's roof.

After the Erskine agreement had turned into an embarrassment for the administration, most Federalists in Congress resumed their old chant that Madison was a mere shadow president and that the real chief executive was a committee of wirepullers hiding behind the White House draperies. Samuel Taggart, a Federalist representative from Massachusetts, probably spoke for a majority of his party when he compared Jefferson and Madison as presidents. "There is I believe this difference between the last and the present President," Taggart told an old friend. "Jefferson by a system of intrigue and low cunning managed the party. M——n is a mere puppet or a cypher managed by some chief of faction who are behind the curtain."[3]

Factions did plague Madison, but he knew how to juggle hot issues until they cooled. Madison's first real factional imbroglio, which came to his attention just before the Erskine affair completely absorbed him, involved key Republican leaders in Pennsylvania. Litigation stemming from a capture-at-sea prize action during the Revolution had been bobbing up in the Pennsylvania courts since 1778. The case — *Olmstead v. the Executrices of the Late David Rittenhouse* — took on a comic aspect when the aging, widowed daughters of the original impounder were sued for prize money plus accrued in-

3. George H. Haynes, ed., "The Letters of Samuel Taggart," American Antiquarian Society *Proceedings* 33 (1923): 347.

terest, and a federal court ordered the payment. A Republican governor cajoled the state legislature into intervening, with a promise of protection and indemnity to the beleaguered siblings. Following still more litigation, Chief Justice John Marshall himself ordered the district judge to enforce his 1803 decision against the daughters. Now more than fifteen thousand dollars was involved, and a federal marshal was sent to arrest the defenseless old ladies; but he was thwarted when Governor Simon Snyder called out the state militia to defend the Rittenhouse heiresses. After several futile attempts to arrest the sisters, the federal marshal threatened to call out a posse to confront the militia force raised "in opposition to the constitution."

Federalists enjoyed the ugly situation with high amusement, for here was a Republican governor defying the Supreme Court and by implication the Constitution that Madison was sworn to uphold. The Pennsylvania legislature passed a bill approving use of the militia but also provided eighteen thousand dollars to settle the dispute. In the midst of this crisis, Governor Snyder appealed to Madison "to adjust the present unhappy collision of the two governments in such a manner as will be equally honorable to them both." Snyder wanted a solution that would leave the state's damaged pride intact.

Madison hoped to avoid antagonizing the Pennsylvania Republicans, but he also wanted to place limits on the rights of states to oppose federal jurisdictions. "It is sufficient, in the actual posture of the case, to remark that the Executive of the U. States, is not only unauthorized to prevent the execution of the Decree sanctioned by the Supreme Court . . . but is expressly enjoined by Statute, to carry into effect any such decree, where opposition may be made to it," Madison told the governor. A federal indictment of General Michael Bright, commanding officer of the militia, and seven of his men had in the meantime exacerbated the tempest, causing William Duane, editor of the Philadelphia *Aurora* and the would-be Republican boss of the state, great uneasiness. Duane blamed Snyder for allowing the matter to get out of hand and embarrass the party. "Never did *imbecility*, combined with *folly*, and egged on by *ignorance*, exhibit any thing in which the serious and ludicrous were so strongly intermixed," Duane bellowed in the *Aurora*.[4]

Eager to provide Snyder with an escape route and soothe the ruffled factional feathers, Madison took Duane's advice and pardoned Bright and the forlorn militiamen. To celebrate, Philadelphia Republicans held a public dinner honoring the pardoned eight, and politics in the City of Brotherly Love resumed its usual serpentine channels.

4. Editorial note and Snyder to Madison, 6 April 1809, and Duane to Madison, 3 May 1809, in *Madison Papers* [Presidential Series], 1:102–5, 157–59.

Federalists enjoyed Governor Snyder's contretemps, but the love feast that followed left them without a foothold in the Keystone State or any other important geographic bloc below the Mason-Dixon line.

Unwilling to admit their own failings as a national party, the Federalists tended to blame their decline upon the conspiratorial conduct of Republicans. But voters, even in parts of New England, seemed unimpressed by the Federalists' declamations when invective was weighed against campaign promises made and kept. Taxes in 1810 were lower than in 1799, and the national debt had been reduced; thus after the worst of the embargo malaise was over, voters placed their trust in candidates who pledged their allegiance to republicanism and in Jefferson's successor. Only one branch of government, isolated from the voters, proved troublesome.

Although we now see the Supreme Court decision in *Marbury v. Madison* as a setback for the Jefferson administration, one should remember that in 1810 the high court was still moving through judicial thickets with difficulty. In the famous *Marbury* case, decided in 1803 when Jefferson's popularity had probably peaked, Marshall delivered the opinion that made the Supreme Court what it is today: the final arbiter on all constitutional matters. The case centered around John Adams's "midnight appointments" (as Jefferson called them) of some minor judicial figures. An obscure Federalist, William Marbury, was designated a justice of the peace in the District of Columbia, but before his commission was delivered President Jefferson ordered all of Adams's last-minute awards to the Federalist faithful placed in a deep pigeonhole. In this test case, Marbury sued to force Secretary of State Madison to deliver the papers necessary for his employment. Aware that Jefferson was upset about the forty-two Federalists named in the final hours of Adams's presidency, Marshall could have sidestepped a confrontation by simply persuading his brother justices that they lacked jurisdiction in the matter.

Instead, Marshall and his Court chose to lecture Jefferson and Madison for having ignored their duties, but in the next breath the jurists held that Congress had erred in granting the high court jurisdiction in the case. Thus, the justices said, for the first time in American history Congress had passed a law that was unconstitutional (the 1789 Judiciary Act), and they asserted the Court's right to declare such laws passed by Congress as null and void. This startling exercise of "judicial review" was at the time hardly noticed by most citizens. Jefferson and Madison noticed because Marshall and his Court had slapped their wrists; but then the Court said that Marbury was out of luck because he had no legal rights under an unconstitutional law.

The decision upset Jefferson and he placed another black mark against Marshall's name; six years later Jefferson was still muttering about Marshall's distortion of the judicial process. The only remedy, it seemed, was to appoint solid Republicans to the Supreme Court and wait for Marshall to die. Vacancies on the Court were viewed by Republicans as opportunities to dilute the strength Marshall had summoned when on 16 April 1810 the Federalist chief justice had dropped a bombshell into the enemy camp with the *Fletcher v. Peck* decision. Even today, the findings of John Marshall's Court in this case appear to the layman as a travesty of justice because the "crooks" appear to have thwarted the honest intentions of a reform-minded Georgia legislature.

Fletcher v. Peck concerned the fraudulent sale of western lands by a venal set of predators in the Georgia legislature; the case had tortuously wound its way to the high court after over a decade of litigation. Everybody acknowledged that the original sale was manipulated by fraud and deception, but the holders of cloudy titles in New England had brought suit to recover their investments. In 1810 Marshall delivered the opinion that upheld the northerners' contention that a fraud could not be perpetrated on innocent third parties — the Yazoo land scheme was a travesty of the law, but a contract had been made that was now sanctioned by the Supreme Court. Madison was so preoccupied with foreign affairs that he failed to mention the alarming decision when he wrote Jefferson, but the reaction from Monticello was predictable. Marshall's "twistifications in the case of Marbury, in that of Burr, & the late Yazoo case, shew how dexterously he can reconcile law to his personal biasses," Jefferson insisted.[5]

Packed with Federalists, the high court appeared to Madison and Jefferson as the last bastion of a repudiated philosophy; but judges are mortal, and in the fall of 1810 the death of William Cushing gave Republicans hope that a wedge could be entered in Marshall's court. Indeed, while Madison pondered his choice for the vacancy, Jefferson told Gallatin that the death of Federalist Cushing was "a Godsend."[6]

Madison believed he must appoint a New England man to the high court to preserve the geographical balance deemed essential by party protocol. Levi Lincoln, the first attorney general in Jefferson's cabinet, was Madison's first choice, but the Massachusetts stalwart was almost blind, so he respectfully declined. The president then turned to Alexander Wolcott of Connecticut, but the Senate jackals — Giles, Leib, and Smith — joined the Federalists in rejecting the nomination, 9 to 24.[7] Madison decided to let matters slide

5. Jefferson to Madison, 25 May 1810, Madison Papers, Rives Collection, Library of Congress (hereafter cited as DLC).

6. Dumas Malone, *Jefferson and His Time*, 6 vols. (Boston: Little, Brown & Company, 1948–1976), 6:66.

7. *Senate Executive Proceedings*, 3 vols. (Washington, D.C.: Duff Green, 1828), 2:167.

and finally was confronted with a second vacancy when crusty old Samuel Chase died while Congress was not in session. Chase was from Maryland, so Madison was faced with finding a jurist from the mid-Atlantic region that would not antagonize Senator Smith. Ultimately, Madison decided to appoint the comptroller of the Treasury, Gabriel Duvall, who was the president's good friend and also was on speaking terms with the Smith family. But, having been burned on the Wolcott choice, Madison took his time to send any name forward.

For the seat requiring a New England Republican, Madison leaned toward John Quincy Adams. But Adams wanted no part of the Supreme Court, which seemed to be a low rung on the political ladder, and Adams was too ambitious to settle for a black robe. From his ministerial post at St. Petersburg, Adams sent his note of refusal. Almost in desperation, Madison turned to Joseph Story, a Massachusetts congressman said to be learned in the law. Jefferson advised Madison to forget Story, confessing that he held a grudge against the young congressman for having deserted his party in the fight over the embargo. The former president urged Madison not to appoint "a pseudo-Republican and Tory." Madison decided to delay the nominations and hope for a better Senate lineup when Congress reassembled in November 1811.

In the quiet of his study, Madison must have looked back to his own experience as a congressman and wondered how differently men now viewed their party allegiances. In the 1790s, when their republicanism was manifest but the party was weak, loyalty created strength. The embargo battle, however, had left so many bruises, in and out of Congress that there were now factions within the Republican "faction." Only when he looked at his official family did Madison find solace. Gallatin was his confidant, trusted counselor, and close friend—a valued legacy from happier times when Jefferson was president.

Not all of the legacies from Jefferson's presidency were salutary, however. Out of his zeal to convict Aaron Burr for treason Jefferson had been hoodwinked by one of the ranking generals in the tiny American army, James Wilkinson. This bad penny from Jefferson's second administration turned up again early in Madison's tenure. General Wilkinson, after joining the pack that had tried to make Aaron Burr into a traitor and then finding himself accused of taking foreign gold, had been whitewashed by a court of inquiry in 1808. Loud accusations of Wilkinson's duplicity were heard, but nothing was proved. Exonerated, Wilkinson was left with his command, and during the transition from one administration to another he was placed in charge of an American force that was to be stationed near New Orleans to ward off any foreign invasion. Wilkinson selected a camp site at Terre aux Boeufs, below New Orleans, where recruits pitched leaky tents to await an undesignated enemy in the spring of 1809, just as Madison was settling into the presidency. The only enemies the mixture of raw recruits and veteran cadre met were mosquitoes, malaria, dysentery, scurvy, and constant rainfall. By August the place was a morass of misery, with 960 men on sick call and dozens dying daily. American soldiers knew early that they did not have to suffer in silence. They wrote their congressmen, complaining of the food, the rotten tents, and, worst of all, their ineffectual leader. Madison's secretary of war professed no knowledge of the situation but promised to look into the matter and did in fact twice order Wilkinson to move the men to higher, healthier ground. Wilkinson made excuse after excuse as his men buried makeshift coffins near the Terre aux Boeufs charnel house. Finally in September the camp was moved, after 816 officers and men had died and 745 were still hospitalized.[8]

Congress reacted by demanding an investigation, which resulted in a report that questioned Wilkinson's competence. Vain as a peacock, Wilkinson was outraged and demanded another court of inquiry to clear his name. Meanwhile, in Washington a pamphlet — *Proofs of the Corruption of General James Wilkinson* — was circulated, claiming that "if the president does not drop Wilkinson, the people will drop him." The pamphlet was embraced by Federalist newspapers as a device to link Jefferson with his "pet general."[9] Thus the problem facing Madison was compounded, for it appeared that if Wilkinson was guilty of misfeasance, why had he been promoted under President Jefferson?

The investigative mills of Congress, as always, ground slowly. Over two years passed from the time a resolution calling for an inquiry into the Terre aux Boeufs scandal was approved and a court-martial made its report. Here was Madison's chance to rid his administration and the country of this grossly incompetent officer — if, of course, the court findings showed evidence of Wilkinson's culpability. But Jefferson's feelings had to be considered, as well as the political implications of admitting that Wilkinson was an embarrassment to the nation. Wilkinson's home base was in Maryland, where he had many Republican friends.

The court-martial proceedings dragged on interminably, and when the court's report was finally issued, it was filled with so much ambivalent word-

8. Noble E. Cunningham, Jr., ed., *Circular Letters of Congressmen to Their Constituents*, 3 vols. (Chapel Hill: University of North Carolina Press, 1978), 2:722–23.

9. Royal O. Shreve, *The Finished Scoundrel* (Indianapolis: Bobbs-Merrill Company, 1933), 256; Thomas R. Hay and M. R. Werner, *The Admirable Trumpeter: A Biography of General James Wilkinson* (Garden City, N.Y.: Doubleday, Doran & Company, 1941), 300–307.

ing that the court was accused of covering up Wilkinson's ineptness. Like so many military men, once in command, the court just could not make up its collective mind. It hemmed and hawed for months after the first charges had been made by Wilkinson's peers until finally it asked the president to decide the case. The final report Madison received held that the charges against Wilkinson had not been supported by hard evidence and that it "appeared" the general had "performed his various and complicated duties with zeal and fidelity."

Madison took the court's bulky transcript and tried to assess the evidence fairly. Should he cashier Wilkinson or leave him with a command? The decision seemed to be his alone, for the military men had balked at ending the career of a brother officer. Reporting on the affair to Jefferson, Madison admitted that his patience was tried: "Among other jobbs on my hands is the case of Wilkersons [sic]. His defence fills 6 or 700 pages of the most collossal paper. The minutes of the Court, oral, written & printed testimony, are all of proportion. A month has not yet carried me thro' the whole."[10] After doing his homework, Madison could have followed the dictates of common sense and sacked Wilkinson without the slightest risk to the nation's defenses. Instead, Madison chose not to pass judgment on Wilkinson. The "hero" of Terre aux Boeufs was given still another whitewash and restored to his command. The incident not only left its scars on the War Department, it also left Madison surrounded by senior military incompetents at a time when leading congressmen were talking about a war on two fronts. From the Terre aux Boeufs incident onward, Madison was clearly on unsteady ground whenever hostilities seemed imminent.

Madison's handling of the Wilkinson case was damaging to his presidency and was probably the worst mistake he made while in the White House. Not only did he saddle the country with an incompetent soldier, he also kept alive the whitewash started by Jefferson with a military decision made for political reasons. Once Wilkinson was permitted to keep his command, he was an albatross the Republican presidents thought they had to protect. This was a bad precedent, leading to further politicalization of the army and navy with disastrous consequences that would keep cropping up during the Mexican War and would get completely out of hand during the Civil War, when commands were dispersed not for ability but to safeguard party control of the White House. Some of this would undoubtedly have happened even if Madison had done the right thing and sacked Wilkinson when he had the chance. But by dodging his responsibility, Madison harmed the war effort, hurt the army's morale, and in effect became a buck-passer instead of a courageous leader.

10. Madison to Jefferson, 7 February 1812, Madison Papers, DLC.

During the summer of 1810, while the injustice of Canning's disavowal was sinking in, Madison learned that a band of Americans living in West Florida was eager to seize the area from a weak Spanish force and declare it ready for American annexation. Jefferson had hoped to buy Florida for cash, but French innuendoes had led to nothing. Portions of the Floridas were being used as bases by smugglers or as refuges for escaped slaves and marauding Indians. Jefferson's position had been that Florida west of the Perdido River had been a part of the Louisiana Purchase, and now Madison inherited this claim.

Initially, President Madison took the same line that he had held as a cabinet member: When the war in Europe ended, the business of acquiring Florida could proceed. The French minister serving in Washington told his Paris-based chieftain that when Madison was secretary of state, he had maintained that "when the [Florida] pear is ready to drop, it will fall." Madison must have been reminded of his metaphor when he was told early in 1809 that the Floridas were "as ripe fruit waiting the hand that dares to pluck them."[11]

Events seemed to crowd on Madison when he learned in the summer of 1810 that American settlers around Baton Rouge were anxious to end Spanish rule and beg for American annexation. "I feel more alarmed at our situation than I ever did since I lived in West Florida," an American expatriate wrote to a friend, and the letter was relayed to Madison. "I have lost all hope of the U. States taking possession of us," the forlorn Floridian lamented.[12] Madison received conflicting advice from the territorial governor, from a judge of known veracity, and from other settlers who wanted to enjoy the privileges of citizenship at no cost, financial or otherwise, to them. Some Americans had received Spanish land grants, for example, and wondered about the status of their titles if the American flag flew over Florida.

Madison's main problem was that he did not want to appear as a usurper willing to flaunt international law. Embroiled in Napoleonic troubles at home, Spain's grasp on its American empire was slipping, but if American forces invaded Florida capriciously the international repercussions might force a humiliating retreat. In July 1810 a diverse group of American settlers convened at St. John's Plains in West Florida to debate the future status of the region. Some of the Americans wanted to oust the Spaniards and turn the area over to the United States Army, arguing that if they delayed, Britain would seize the territory. Others wanted a separate state, which meant mili-

11. Clifford L. Egan, "The United States, France, and West Florida, 1803–1807," *Florida Historical Quarterly* 47 (1968–69): 235; John Adair to Madison, 9 January 1809, Madison Papers, DLC.
12. J. R. Bedford to Madison, 4 July 1810, Madison Papers, DLC.

tary action against the garrison at Baton Rouge; their opinion prevailed. Baton Rouge was stormed, the weak garrison overwhelmed, and the governor seized. Immediately the insurgents claimed that West Florida was a sovereign state; but they instructed their president to negotiate terms of annexation with the United States.[13] Part of their deal included confirmation of existing land titles and a "loan" of one hundred thousand dollars.

Madison would have none of the brash freebooters. Resolution of this business required regular American troops, Madison decided. He realized, as he told Jefferson, that an American occupation of West Florida "would be resented by Spain, England, & by France," but the president knew that only Britain was powerful enough to cause trouble.[14] Madison decided that the risk was worth it, and before the British could protest Madison issued a proclamation on 27 October 1810, citing the 1803 treaty with France as the basis for an occupation. Never mind that the action was slow in coming; Madison instructed the governor of the Orleans Territory to occupy the area to the Perdido River to forestall "the confusions and contingencies which threaten it." Further delay in exercising American rights to annex the region, Madison's proclamation added, "might be construed into a dereliction of their [the United States'] title, or an insensibility to the importance of the stake."[15] As expected, the British chargé d'affaires in Washington soon protested the American action as made under the cover of "a title which is manifestly doubtful." Despite the diplomatic protest, the Americans did not withdraw. But for a time it appeared that Madison might have moved too fast.

Madison's itch to bring Spanish Florida into the Union was not the beginning of an imperialist policy, but rather a continuation of Jefferson's vision that republicanism could only flourish in an expanding nation. Jefferson first implemented the policy with the purchase and annexation of Louisiana, as historian Drew McCoy noted, for his brand of Republicanism "was predicated on on unobstructed access to an ample supply of open land and a relatively liberal international commercial order that provided adequate foreign markets for America's flourishing agricultural surplus."[16] Thus Madison was in an unfamiliar role as a saber rattler, not because he wanted to flex the nation's military muscles, but because he shared with Jefferson and other leading Republicans the belief that territory adjacent to the United States

13. Hubert B. Fuller, *The Purchase of Florida: Its History and Diplomacy* (Cleveland: Burrows Company, 1906), 183–84.

14. Madison to Jefferson, 19 October 1810, Madison Papers, DLC.

15. *American State Papers: Documents, Legislative and Executive*, 38 vols. [Foreign Relations] (Washington, D.C.: Gales & Seaton, 1832–1861), 3:397–98.

16. Drew McCoy, "Political Economy," in Merrill Peterson, ed., *Thomas Jefferson: A Reference Biography* (New York: Scribner, 1986), 113.

must be annexed to provide the vital growing areas required by a nation of farmers and planters. Spanish Florida was not regarded by Madison as a pawn in an international poker game, as Canada might be; rather, Madison viewed the region as another permanent addition to the United States, not a diplomatic bargaining chip.

Some months before Madison acted on the Florida situation Congress had adjourned after passage in May 1810 of the much-maligned Macon's bill no. 2. Now American merchantmen could come and go, anywhere, as they pleased. A warmed-over version of the stop-gap nonintercourse law, the new legislation was drafted by Gallatin, and unlike the earlier act it allowed American ships to bring French or British goods into Yankee harbors while closing American seaports to the warships of the belligerent powers. As a modern historian has said, the reasoning behind Macon's bill no. 2 was hard to fathom: "It was assumed . . . that if one nation so allowed itself to be blackmailed the other would soon be compelled to follow suit."[17] And like the older law, the new one's provisions would not be applied to any power that canceled its restrictive decrees against American commerce. For Gallatin, Macon's law offered hope that sagging customs revenues might be revived, and there was always the chance that the warring nations might come to their senses and honor the revived American claim that "free ships make free goods," thus allowing ships under the American flag to roam the seas unmolested.

There was that chance, but not a good one. And because the British navy was now (after polishing off the French navy at Trafalgar) the uncontested master of the major oceanways, the law seemed to favor Britain. Federalists looking for an ulterior motive thought that the Republicans expected a clash with the British to inevitably ensue once American ships tried to reach France, and therefore a war with Britain would be unavoidable.[18]

Madison was not a visible supporter of the bill, and in private he thought it a legislative hodge-podge. But after it passed Congress, Madison, his eye sharpened for international duplicity by years of foreign office experience, thought he saw an opening for Napoleon. Macon's bill no. 2, Madison told Jefferson, "puts our trade on the worst possible footing for France but at the same time puts it in the option of her, to revive the non-intercourse agst. England."[19] There was no reason for Britain to call off its Orders in Council because the new law virtually invited the British to resume trade by using American ships and reexporting American goods to French-held Europe

17. Fred L. Engelman, *The Peace of Christmas Eve* (New York: Harcourt, Brace & World, 1962), 72.
18. Bradford Perkins, *Prologue to War: England and the United States, 1805–1812* (Berkeley: University of California Press, 1968), 240.
19. Madison to Jefferson, 25 May 1810, Madison Papers, DLC.

through a licensing system. But the wording of the new act left an escape hatch, if Napoleon could find it.

Thus the summer of 1810 saw Anglo-American ocean trade revived. One negative result, however, was a glutting of the tobacco market in British ports. Madison's own pocketbook suffered, as the tobacco he consigned to Liverpool brought a mere threepence a pound, about a third of what the president probably expected. What made Americans scratch their heads in wonderment was the disingenuous British licensing system, which allowed British citizens to trade with their enemies if they had a license while neutral Americans were denied any direct trade at all with Europe. As Madison and other frustrated Americans watched, the British naval enforcers transformed the detested Orders in Council "from an anti-French to an anti-American policy."[20]

If the British could play with loopholes, so could the French. Napoleon saw the escape hatch, as Madison thought he might, and showed again his great skill in the international chess game that Britain hoped to end with a checkmate for the French leader. Although the French foreign minister passed off Macon's bill no. 2 as an unconfirmed newspaper report when he first saw it, Napoleon read the journal more carefully. Moreover, the American minister at Paris, John Armstrong, insisted that the newspaper version was authentic. Napoleon's reaction shows that his genius was not confined to military matters. The first consul–turned-emperor discerned a diplomatic opportunity of the first order. After mulling over the unofficial report of Macon's bill no. 2, Napoleon came to a decision that changed the course of American history. "I should have liked to have a more official communication, but," Napoleon instructed the Duc de Cadore, "since he [Armstrong] assures me we may regard this as official, he can consider my Decrees of Berlin and Milan will have no effect, dating from November 1." Then Napoleon threw his curve: Withdrawal of the French decrees would be hinged on the pledge of the United States Congress to punish any nation that kept its anti-American maritime edicts in force. To make sure that Britain would become the target of American restrictions, Napoleon added, "If the British council does not withdraw its Orders of 1807," the American government was pledged to enforce strict "prohibitions on British commerce." On 2 August Napoleon dictated a letter explaining all this to the American minister, and Cadore signed it.[21] Thus the "Cadore letter" became part of history. Henry Adams,

20. Norman Graebner, Gilbert Fite, and Philip White, *A History of the United States*, 2 vols. (New York: McGraw-Hill, 1970), 1:371; Perkins, *Prologue to War*, 244.

21. Henry Adams, *History of the United States of America during the Administrations of Thomas Jefferson and James Madison*, vol. 2, *History of the United States of America during the Administrations of James Madison*, Earl N. Harbert, ed. (New York: Library of America, 1986), 179 (hereafter cited as Adams, *History*).

not one to overstate diplomatic maneuverings, called Napoleon's directive "the most important document he ever sent to the United States government."

Thereafter Cadore moved so swiftly that he must have shocked Armstrong. In the first week of August 1810 Napoleon's foreign minister gave to the American diplomat in Paris this letter (dated 5 August 1810), which promised that all punitive French decrees aimed at American commerce would be recalled by the emperor after 1 November, provided that the British withdrew their Orders in Council. The implication was that if the British did nothing, the rest was up to President Madison and Congress. Napoleon's final draft poured it on by adding, "His Majesty loves the Americans. Their prosperity and their commerce are within the scope of his policy. The independence of America is one of the principal titles of glory to France."[22]

Napoleon must have clasped his hands gleefully as he contemplated the prospect of a ban on British-American trade, for he knew American foodstuffs were needed by the red-coated armies opposing his chasseurs. The Cadore letter left Napoleon's options open, for the foreign minister hinted that the emperor would await proof of American intentions in case the Orders in Council were not rescinded.

The cunning French emperor had called the American bluff, and Madison was so desperate for a positive response that he put the best possible interpretation on Cadore's letter. Strange to say, the missive reached Madison's desk through unofficial channels on 25 September. Armstrong's view of the whole matter was still unknown, but Madison decided not to wait, particularly given the 1 November deadline that Napoleon had mentioned. To say that Madison jumped the gun is too mild. The president threw away all caution and issued a proclamation accepting Napoleon's claims at face value. Unless the British made a similar promise to call off the Orders in Council, a clamp-down on American commerce with Britain would begin in February 1811.

To the American minister at Paris, Madison sent a dispatch exuding confidence: "Altho' no direct authentication of the repeal of the French decrees has been received from you, a proclamation issues on the ground furnished by your correspondence with Mr. Pinkney. . . . It is to be hoped that France will do what she is understood to be pledged for, and in a manner that will produce no jealousy or embarrassment here." Madison confessed that he was not sure of Britain's next move, but added, "It is not improbable that the orders in Council will be revoked and the sham blockades be so managed

22. Ibid., 179, 181.

if possible, as to irritate France against our non-resistance without irritating this Country to the resisting point."[23]

Instead of giving Madison an easy way out of his quandary, Napoleon made matters worse by saying one thing and doing another. The long interval created by the Atlantic crossing sometimes meant that while Washington was headed in one direction, the course of events in Europe was going in another. In fact, John Armstrong had deserted Paris on 12 September 1810 and was headed home. While the Cadore letter was being read by Madison's cabinet (it was not made public at the time), Napoleon gave orders for the sale of seized American ships tied up in French ports; Yankee vessels and their cargoes were to be auctioned off, with the proceeds (estimated at six million dollars) marked for Napoleon's treasury.

The delay of such bad news probably was a lucky break for Madison. If the public had known of Napoleon's duplicity following the president's proclamation, the embarrassed chief executive might have been forced to seek a declaration of war. Madison's secret fear of a French double-cross was thus realized, for in his otherwise optimistic note to John Armstrong, Madison had voiced a suspicion that Napoleon might not restore the seized vessels, although he had said nothing about the next step should the French emperor have broken his pledge.

Weeks before his departure, the skeptical American minister at Paris had read the official decree and then had heard about underhanded dealings that seemed to make Napoleon into a hypocrite. At that time, Armstrong had reported a rumor from London that Congress was about to declare war on Britain, which he knew to be false, and in the next breath Armstrong had speculated that Napoleon's odd actions proved two things. First, France wanted no war with the United States, and second, it would continue to seize ships as circumstances dictated. Thus, "she will content herself by coming within the mere letter of your late trade Instructions, that is, that she will revoke her decrees, and make her seizures a subject of future Negociation."[24] "It will be for you to decide," Armstrong added, "how far good faith will [provide?] an obedience to the injunctions of the Act of Congress, should England refuse to annul, or so to modify her orders in Council, as to leave your Maritime Rights unmolested." Soon after, Armstrong took off for the United States, leaving a confused American chargé d'affaires to marvel at French duplicity.

Madison hardly needed reminding that he was flirting again with a diplomatic time bomb, a reprise of the Erskine affair. By choosing to take

23. Madison to John Armstrong, 29 October 1810, Madison Papers, Rives Collection, DLC.
24. John Armstrong to Madison, 5 August 1810, Madison Papers, DLC.

Cadore's letter as a statement of honest intentions, Madison at least was justified in calling on Britain to rescind the Orders in Council. After agonizing over his choices, Madison finally gave the British three months to join Napoleon in canceling all their restrictions. If Britain refused, American ships would trade with that nation only at their peril, but they could carry on legal commerce with Napoleon.

Earlier, while still unaware of Napoleon's machinations, Madison told William Pinkney in London that the new law patently favored Britain because by implication its domination of the seas was acknowledged. "She has now a compleat interest in perpetuating the actual state of things, which gives her the full enjoyment of our trade and enables her to cut it off with every other part of the World."[25] The only hitch for the British, Madison suggested, was that Napoleon might "turn the tables." Sure enough, Napoleon had caught the hint that he could use a paper decree to force the American hand. Madison now stalled to see how the ministers at Whitehall would react.

Hardheaded men in the British foreign office looked at the Napoleonic gesture, read Madison's statement, and asked a simple question: Where is the proof that France is calling off its decrees? Madison appeared to have fallen into a trap of his own making, for when no news came of a British act recalling the Orders in Council, the president felt the pressure and issued another proclamation cutting off all legal trade with Britain. Reports that France was not acting in good faith shook Madison's confidence, but after struggling with Britain over commercial rights during most of his public life, it seems clear that Madison grasped the French straw as an act of desperation.

To some degree, Madison's optimism was ill-founded, for despite the odds mounted by the Royal Navy's omnipresence on the world's oceans, Madison continued to see the root of America's problem in Britain's persistent roughshod treatment of neutral commerce. "The public attention is beginning to fix itself on the proof it affords that the *original sin* agst. Neutrals lies with G. B. & that whilst she acknowledges it, she persists in it," Madison told Jefferson months before he read Cadore's letter.[26] By holding to that conviction, Madison managed to excuse the French from most of their shady dealings.

Not that Madison was the Francophile that his enemies tried to portray, for the president stood aloof from the Gallomania that his New England detractors accused him of harboring. On the other hand, if the United States had to fight someone, as more and more seemed the case, Madison preferred a war with Britain. And considering the dual declarations of war against

25. Madison to William Pinkney, 23 May 1810, Madison Papers, DLC.
26. Madison to Jefferson, 22 June 1810, Madison Papers, DLC. Italics added.

both Britain and France once discussed by the Jefferson cabinet, there was now the consolation that if the United States had to go to war, it would have to face only one enemy.

Before the second proclamation was issued, Madison explained his motives to Jefferson, stressing that the olive branch from Paris provided "the advantage at least of having but one contest on our hands at a time." But in the next breath, Madison considered the situation in West Florida and indicated a further excuse — the threat "of its passing into the hands of a third & dangerous party," specifically Britain — for allowing American troops to occupy the territory "if it can be done without violence."[27] That the British had intervened in Venezuela to quell civil rioting there, Madison said, "gives notice of her propensity to fish in troubled waters." Madison's 27 October proclamation regarding West Florida had been his way of saying, "Hands off," to Britain, but after the British chargé d'affaires had protested, the situation ended in an easy American coup.[28] Moreover, circumstances in East Florida remained unsettled.

Federalists had reacted predictably to Madison's proclamation and the ensuing occupation of West Florida in early December 1810. They denounced the move by American troops as an "invasion" and questioned the power of the president to take such a drastic step without congressional approval. To Americans on the scene, however, the occupation of territory to either the Perdido or the Pearl rivers was only half a loaf, for they wanted all of Spanish Florida. Loud complaints were heard in Washington of smuggling from Amelia Island, and slaveowners were bitter about the refuge offered to runaway blacks once they crossed the St. Mary's River into East Florida. Another source of pressure was the planters upstream and east of Mobile, who needed closer ports as outlets for their crops. Sensitive to the suggestion that he had ignored Congress with his earlier proclamation, Madison sent a secret message to congressmen in January 1811, asking for a free hand to occupy East Florida. If the Spanish would cooperate, so much the better. (The distraught Spanish governor had offered to turn the territory over to the United States if he did not receive reinforcements by 1 January 1811.) But if they would not, the occupation could be justified as a means of precluding any other nation from creating a stronghold in the region.

Congress finally backed Madison in the Florida gamble after a bitter debate in which the Federalists claimed that the president sought unconstitutional powers. The Federalists' implication was that Madison was playing the

---

27. Madison to Jefferson, 19 October 1810, Madison Papers, DLC.

28. Bernard Mayo, ed., "Instructions to the British Ministers to the United States, 1791–1812," *American Historical Association Annual Report for 1936*, 3 vols. (Washington, D.C.: Da Capo, 1971), 3:318.

American bully, jumping on a Spanish pushover; but Republicans defended the president's request on the ground that the United States had a right to claim what it had paid for in 1803. Republicans also pointed out the British threat to the Floridas and the law's provision for dealing with such a situation: Madison was authorized to spend up to one hundred thousand dollars and to move American troops into East Florida "if the local authorities were willing to deliver it up or if any foreign power attempted to occupy it."[29]

In January 1811 two American officers were instructed to proceed to the area and lead a task force into East Florida for an "amicable surrender" by the Spanish and to thwart any threat of occupation by any other foreign power. Once on the scene the American commander, General George Mathews, ruled out an easy surrender by Spain and told Senator William H. Crawford that it would take cold steel and hot lead to actually occupy and hold the coveted territory. Crawford passed this message along to Madison, who decided to give priority to other urgent matters and so left the Forida fuse sputtering with near anarchy prevailing along the Georgia-Florida border. Meanwhile, Congress was not idle. Legislation passed early in 1811 and signed by Madison placed the disputed West Florida area under Orleans Territory jurisdiction. Actual statehood for Louisiana was still a year away.

Although Federalists denounced Madison for loosely interpreting his power to use troops in support of a questionable foray in the Floridas, they were eager to convince Republicans that the Bank of the United States was a constitutionally sound institution. The issue arose in 1811 because the bank charter, which had been issued in 1791, was due to expire and renewal legislation was needed. Gallatin, practical when it came to money matters, did not share Madison's earlier doubts concerning the validity of the Bank; he needed loans so that the government could pay its bills, and the Bank of the United States was a convenient source of funds for federal purposes.

Conventional Republican doctrine held that the Bank was greedy, foreign-owned (most of its stock was owned by Englishmen, although they had no voting rights), and controlled by city-bred financiers who were unresponsive to the farmer-planter belief that banks existed to lend them money. Gallatin, eschewing party slogans, looked at the Bank as a safe place to deposit government funds, an efficient clearinghouse for tax revenues from the several port collectors' receipts, and a ready source of capital when the government issued bonds to fill gaps between income and payments. More than any other Republican, Gallatin was willing to overlook the Bank officers' shoddy lobbying practices and the critics who took potshots at the national organization

29. Fuller, *Purchase of Florida*, 188.

because they favored a looser (and riskier) state-chartered banking system.[30] As usual, Gallatin was right on every count except the one that mattered most: the need for Republican support. Hard-core Republicans like Senator Samuel Smith of Maryland winced every time the Bank was mentioned; this Invincible could hardly wait to vote for its demise.

Weighing the old arguments, Madison was inclined to agree with Gallatin. Some economic distress ensued in the summer of 1810 when the Bank had called in loans for other banks. Senator Smith, who had investments in several areas, told Madison that the Bank call was an attempt to squeeze local banks and create pressure on Congress to renew the 1791 charter. Gallatin assured Madison that this was not the case, but both men probably realized that Smith and his Senate allies were determined to embarrass the administration by refusing to pass a recharter bill. The tip-off came when William Duane, editor of the Philadelphia *Aurora* and longtime friend of the Giles-Leib-Smith branch of Senate Republicans, published a broadside attack on the Bank late in 1810.[31]

Adding to the din against the Bank was the Richmond *Enquirer*, edited by Thomas Ritchie. Ritchie was a Republican warhorse, dedicated to the program set forth during the 1800 campaign and ready to do battle with the moneyed forces in Philadelphia and Boston, which held much of the Bank's stock (what they did not possess was mainly in foreign hands). Ritchie's opposition added to Gallatin's woes and made the financial picture for fiscal 1811/12 dismal, particularly with the constant talk of war in the air. In the House of Representatives the rancor of Smith and his Senate pals was less evident, and a rumor circulated that Madison stood pat on his 1791 anti-charter arguments. By a single vote the House pigeonholed the charter renewal bill, leaving it "indefinitely postponed" but hardly a dead issue. Skeptics in the Senate thought that the Bank's charter was linked to early shuffling for the 1812 presidential campaign. If Gallatin lost on the Bank issue, the administration might suffer and be forced to make a deal with the senators who had schemed for Gallatin's downfall in 1809.

Madison played his cards so close to his vest that discipline within Republican ranks collapsed. A president's buttonholing of congressmen to win votes was a method unknown in Madison's time, so that instead of making his position clear Madison apparently stood above the battle. The president might have prevented the crisis by sending a strongly worded message to Congress, asking for charter renewal. But, biographer Irving Brant argues, Madi-

30. Bray Hammond, *Banks and Politics in America: From the Revolution to the Civil War* (Princeton, N.J.: Princeton University Press, 1957), 211–26.
31. Irving Brant, *James Madison*, 6 vols. (Indianapolis: Bobbs-Merrill Company, 1941–1961), 5:266–67.

son was afraid to admit that he had changed his mind, so he kept mum in public and only let the word pass quietly that he favored recharter. "Madison's lifelong unwillingness to make a public display of political inconsistency" thus left Republicans unsure of where the president stood.[32] The battle shifted to the Senate, where a 17 to 17 tie was broken by Vice-President George Clinton's negative vote. Jubilant anti-Madison Republicans were elated, for they appeared to have made Gallatin's removal from the cabinet inevitable.

The Bank's charter was to expire on 3 March 1811, and somebody had to pay the piper. Gallatin was willing. Conscious of the hatred showered on him by the Smiths — Robert in the cabinet and Samuel in the Senate — Gallatin said cabinet harmony required his resignation. All Washington knew that Robert Smith and Gallatin were hardly on speaking terms, and perhaps even worse, their wives had quarreled in public.[33] "The embarrassments of Government, great as from foreign causes they already are, are unnecessarily increased" by the internecine battles within the cabinet, Gallatin told Madison. "Such a state of things cannot last . . . and I clearly perceive that my continuing [as] a member of the present administration . . . invigorates the opposition against yourself, and must necessarily be attended with an increased loss of reputation to myself."[34]

Madison talked Gallatin out of resigning, but in their conference surely they discussed the other dissatisfied cabinet member, Robert Smith. Washington hallways and drawingrooms had buzzed with rumors of Smith's shaky status ever since the secretary of state had agreed with the British chargé d'affaires that the French were pulling a fast one with their Cadore letter. In many ways, Smith gave the impression to those outside the cabinet that Madison was moving from one mishandled situation to another, and Smith's cutting remarks in private conversations reinforced a rumor that Madison was going to drop Smith after Congress adjourned so that an interim appointment could be made. The state office was still regarded as a means for the party in power to avoid clashes by elevating the secretary to the presidency, as Jefferson had done so quietly. And increasingly, the man spoken of as Smith's successor was — *mirable dictu!* — another Virginian. James Monroe, so the rumor ran, was about to join Madison's cabinet.

32. Ibid., 5:269.
33. Draft letter, Gallatin to Madison, undated, Gallatin Papers, New York Historical Society.
34. Ibid.

5

★ ★ ★ ★ ★

A TIME TO HEAL,
A TIME TO WOUND

Madison's magnanimous search for a comfortable way to renew his friendship with James Monroe tells us something important about the president's character. Had he been enmeshed in the vindictive code of the day, Madison would have ignored Monroe and scorned his rival to boot. Apart from their common devotion to Jefferson, with whom they both were friends, Madison and Monroe had run into a few sharp encounters through the years. Unlike many Virginians of his day, however, Madison rarely held a grudge. (The notable exception was Patrick Henry, whom Madison detested.)

Madison had won his seat in the First Congress by outsmarting Patrick Henry after his old nemesis had persuaded Monroe to run in the congressional district that just happened to include Madison's home turf. In what may have been the most gentlemanly congressional contest in history, Madison defeated Monroe early in 1789, with several hundred votes to spare. Instead of treating Monroe as an also-ran, Madison took pains to assure his friend that their relationship stood on its former ground; in the decade that followed the two Virginians worked together in and out of Congress for the Republican programs they deemed essential. (Monroe, still Henry's pet, had filled a Senate vacancy in 1790.) The cordiality of earlier times was restored.

Then, when Jefferson came under fire from Hamilton's newspaper batteries in 1796, Monroe worked with Madison on position papers for county political meetings that were used as propaganda weapons in Republican counterattacks. Their friendship extended into domestic affairs when Madison married and turned to Monroe and his lady for help in acquiring the

French furniture and objets d'art that Dolley Madison coveted. Even when the Monroes overstepped Madison's spending limits, he paid cheerfully. During Madison's tenure as secretary of state, Monroe was a floating emissary for the Jefferson administration and often corresponded with the president and his chief cabinet officer concerning the tense negotiations with the British. The first strain in their friendship probably was felt after Monroe was rebuked by Jefferson in uncustomary fashion. In 1806 Monroe was part of the diplomatic team working in London for relief from British arrogance on the high seas. The renewed Anglo-French war had seen a resumption of Britain's age-old practice of impressing seamen from foreign vessels on the ground that the sailors were British deserters or at least came from an English parish. The hard-pressed Royal Navy sent boarding parties onto American ships to remove Yankee sailors if they had the merest Yorkshire accent or lacked proof of their American birth. Working with William Pinkney, Monroe almost obtained a British promise to stop the practice. But the Whitehall cabinet finally turned down a policy of relaxation, and the American envoys ended up signing the Pinkney-Monroe Treaty of 1806 anyway.[1] By avoiding the impressment problem the envoys had killed any chance that Jefferson or Madison would argue for their version of the pact, for the Senate was in no mood to compromise on the issue.

Jefferson read the Pinkney-Monroe treaty in a gloomy mood because he knew that the treaty was doomed without some concession on impressment; he had no stomach for a fight with the Senate. Thus the president and Madison ignored the relaxing of restraints on commerce and decided that impressment was a sine qua non. The treaty was pigeonholed, and there was no Senate fight because the treaty was never submitted for ratification.

Monroe was frustrated by Jefferson's action (or inaction) and must have thought that Madison approved of this refutation of his diplomatic skills. Added to this indignity was the coolness in Washington after John Randolph had used Monroe's name in a futile effort to stop the congressional caucus from nominating Madison for president in 1808. Among other reasons, Randolph claimed that he could not support Madison because the secretary of state was tainted by the Yazoo land scandal. It was a lie, of course, but Randolph used the incident to go for Madison's political jugular. In the ensuing debacle, Monroe appeared to be a willing pawn in Randolph's game of political chess, and yet the ineptness of the whole maneuver was apparent after Monroe received only a token vote from the Virginia electorate in the presidential balloting that fall.

Those who knew Monroe and Madison realized that the situation was

1. Bradford Perkins, *Prologue to War: England and the United States, 1805–1812* (Berkeley: University of California Press, 1968), 126–28.

simply a trumped-up scheme to embarrass the president. Jefferson himself wrote Monroe a friendly note when the spurious presidential "boomlet" was attempted and tried to tell the younger Virginian that he regarded him and Madison as his two closest friends and was pained by any semblance of rivalry between them.

> I see with infinite grief a contest arising between yourself and another, who have been very dear to each other, and equally so to me. . . . My longings for retirement are so strong that I with difficulty encounter the daily drudgeries of my duty. . . . I have ever viewed Mr. Madison and yourself as two [of the] principal pillars of my happiness. Were either to be withdrawn, I should consider it as among the greatest calamaties which could assail my future peace of mind.[2]

Madison viewed matters in the same light and was relieved when Monroe, whose income from a law practice proved disappointing, was elected governor of Virginia in January 1811 to succeed the resigned John Tyler. When official business brought Governor Monroe to Washington early that year, President Madison conveniently used a social occasion to bring his longtime comrade to the White House to heal the old wound. Madison learned that Monroe was willing to forgive and forget past differences, but he was not going to take a lesser post in the Madison administration. He would not serve as a territorial judge or governor; however, a place in Madison's cabinet would be acceptable.

Madison hoped to patch up his friendship with Monroe, as the president's proclamation under Macon's bill no. 2 (allowing ninety days for proof of French good intentions) had expired and he needed cabinet solidarity if a crisis was brewing. Lacking proof that France had actually revoked its decrees, bullheaded Republicans in Congress nevertheless passed a bill extending the ban on commerce with Britain under presidential authority and "required American courts to accept Madison's proclamation as conclusive evidence of French repeal."[3] The new law allowed British imports on American ships only, continued to ban ships flying the Union Jack from entering American harbors, and would last until the detested Orders in Council were repealed. The law, giving Madison almost carte blanche in deciding which nation the United States would attempt to coerce, created a point of no return. A complete Anglo-American embargo required ironclad proof that

---

2. Jefferson to Monroe, 10 March and 11 April 1808, quoted in Dumas Malone, *Jefferson and His Time*, 6 vols. (Boston: Little, Brown & Company, 1948-1976), 5:551-52.

3. Perkins, *Prologue to War*, 255-578.

France had stopped harassing Americans on the high seas. When the new French minister arrived unable to offer assurances that France was releasing American vessels seized by Napoleon, Madison's earlier actions seemed all the more suspicious.

Madison faced the mounting evidence of French double-dealing without a strong "hole" card. Rumors reached the White House that Robert Smith was making indiscreet remarks to the British chargé d'affaires that undercut Madison's efforts to negotiate with assurance. Smith apparently told the Englishman that the president was bluffing and that if Britain persevered the sanctions imposed by the United States after the Cadore letter fiasco would collapse because Madison knew that the Napoleonic edicts were still in force.

Madison's reaction to this news is not known, but a second rumor began to circulate in Capitol hallways: Robert Smith was leaving the cabinet, and James Monroe was joining it. Soon Madison called Smith to account, explained his discomfort over allegations that his policy pronouncements lacked Smith's support, and told the secretary of state that his resignation would be acceptable to the president. Smith's reaction was predictable. He pretended to be greatly injured by malicious gossip, protested that he was the soul of loyalty, and refused to resign. To save face for Smith, Madison suggested that he might appoint him the American minister at St. Petersburg so that the move would be interpreted as a transfer rather than a dismissal.

At first Smith agreed, but after thinking it over he had a tantrum. Madison stood his ground, for he remembered that as a congressman he had supported President Washington's right to fire an appointee without Senate approval and that precedent was firmly in place. Senator Samuel Smith could seethe, but he was no more than a fair-weather friend to Madison anyway. So Smith left the State Department in a huff, and during the summer of 1811 Madison served as his own secretary of state. In the fall he sent Monroe's nomination to the Senate and watched anxiously as the inscrutable William Branch Giles was appointed chairman of the committee chosen to study Monroe's qualifications. Now Giles was on the hot seat, and in short order his committee reported that there was nothing in Monroe's background "to justify the rejection of the nomination." Despite this faint praise, Monroe was confirmed by a 30 to 0 vote in the Senate on 25 November 1811.[4] Meanwhile the nation's attention was focused elsewhere as newspapers speculated on the British reaction to Madison's threat to cut off all commerce with Britain.

Monroe's confirmation as secretary of state finally cleared some of the miasma hanging over the Senate for over a year concerning Madison's choices

4. *Senate Executive Proceedings*, 3 vols. (Washington, D.C.: Duff Green, 1828), 2:187, 192.

for high office. Only ten days earlier, the Senate had received two nominations from Madison for vacancies on the Supreme Court and had accepted Joseph Story and Gabriel Duvall without even bothering to record the vote.[5] These three confirmations are a strong indication that the power of the Smith-Giles-Leib phalanx in the Senate was more bluster than substance and that if Madison had shown more resolve in March 1809 he probably could have called their bluff and made Gallatin his secretary of state.

Certainly Madison needed a friendly face or two in the cabinet room after Robert Smith was dismissed, for the surly ex-secretary had written a vituperative pamphlet that was meant to undermine Madison's presidency. Spewing venom right and left, Smith asserted that the president was a bundle of inconsistencies without any firm direction. But for Smith's steady hand at the tiller, the pamphlet implied, the nation would have been in far worse shape than it was. Distressed by Smith's attack, Madison recounted the firing incident to Jefferson. Perplexed by Smith's "wicked publication," Madison told his friend at Monticello that the ousted cabinet member was making wild accusations — fabrications that only the president could refute. "It is impossible . . . that the whole turpitude of his conduct can be understood without disclosures to be made by myself alone, and of course, as he knows, not to be made at all."

As Madison had predicted, Smith's ill-tempered attack backfired. The president observed the swing in public opinion and noted Smith's "infamy is daily fastening itself upon him." Although Madison kept his public silence, friends published a vindication of the president's conduct, but no defense was really required, as former Congressman James Garnett, a fellow Virginian, soon noted. Smith's ranting and raving in print, Garnett said, was "one of the rare instances of a man's giving the finishing stroke to his own character, in his eagerness to ruin his enemy."[6]

Publicly, Madison said nothing. Privately, he prepared a lengthy memorandum that underscored Smith's ineptitude, but also raised an embarrassing question: If Smith was such a nincompoop, why had Madison tolerated him for so long? Madison did not bother to vindicate his earlier judgment; instead he dwelled on the incompetence Smith had repeatedly demonstrated while a senior cabinet officer. The open break came in March 1811, Madison observed, when Smith came to the White House on some official matter and the subject drifted toward the secretary's handling of his job. "I proceeded

5. Ibid., 2:189; see also Henry J. Abraham, *Justices and Presidents: A Political History of Appointments to the Supreme Court* (New York: Oxford University Press, 1985), 88–90.
6. Madison to Jefferson, 8 July 1811, Madison Papers, Library of Congress (hereafter cited as DLC); Garrett is quoted in Perkins, *Prologue to War,* 269.

to state to him, that it had long been felt, and had at length become notorious, that the administration of the Executive Department laboured under a want of the harmony and unity which were equally essential to its energy and its success," Madison wrote. The problem was not in cabinet sessions, where the president and his secretary seemed to be in accord, but "in language and conduct out of doors, counteracting what had been understood within to be the course of the administration and the public interest."[7] For sixteen pages Madison scribbled his version of Smith's firing, noting that Smith denied all accusations of disloyalty. One jarring charge Madison made was that Smith leaked important foreign office documents to Federalists when their contents "were unknown to others, the disclosures being sometimes such as to be deemed confidential, and to be turned against the administration." On top of that, Madison said, in such important matters as the Erskine affair and the Jackson imbroglio, the letters sent with Smith's signature were actually written by the president. Smith's own letters, Madison charged, were "almost always so crude and inadequate, that I was in the most important cases generally obliged to write them anew myself."

Madison's long memorandum allowed him to purge the Smith mess from his mind. In the end, discretion overruled anger—after more thought, Madison decided to keep his case private. Had not Smith already proved that he was unfit for office? In the Philadelphia *Aurora*, which was Republican in sentiment but defensive about Smith (Editor Duane being friendly with Senator Smith), the ostensible cause of the Smith-Madison split was depicted as a difference over a policy of nonimportation and the proper means of resisting "the aggressions of G. Britain." Madison charitably did not blame Duane for distorting the truth by printing "the putative explanation of the rupture between Mr. Smith and myself," but he was worried about public reaction to his continued insistence upon the good intentions of the French. And if Madison had heard the rumor (reported in a Richmond newspaper) that his cabinet shift placed Monroe in line for the presidency in 1817, he ignored it.[8]

Madison's critics made the most of the embarrassment created by Smith's ouster, causing Madison to complain about "the ignorance and interested falsehoods which fill our newspapers."[9] Overly sensitive to any criticism from New England, Madison went out of his way to reply to a petition from

7. Memorandum in William C. Rives and Philip R. Fendall, eds., *Letters and Other Writings of James Madison*, 4 vols. (Philadelphia: J. B. Lippincott & Company, 1865), 2:495–506.

8. Madison to Jefferson, 3 May 1811, Madison Papers, DLC; Irving Brant, *James Madison*, 6 vols. (Indianapolis: Bobbs-Merrill Company, 1941–1961), 5:301.

9. Madison to Jefferson, 7 June 1811, Madison Papers, DLC.

New Haven, Connecticut, asking for repeal of the law preventing commerce with Britain on the ground that the Nonintercourse Act was unconstitutional. Madison seized on the petition as an excuse to lecture the public on what his foreign policy hoped to achieve, and at the same time the president declared that the law was well "within the necessary power and practice of regulating our commercial intercourse with foreign Countries according to circumstances." Moreover, Madison added, the law was not intended to destroy commerce (as the New England Federalists claimed) but "had for its object an entire freedom of our commerce, by a liberation of it from foreign restrictions unlawfully imposed."[10] Perhaps Madison was trying to tell New England that if war came, it would be a war forced on Americans because "an unqualified acquiescence in belligerent restrictions on our commerce . . . could [not] be reconciled with what a nation owes to itself," even if it meant that one part of the Union made more sacrifices than another.

Not all of the decisions Madison faced during the spring of 1811 were earth-shattering. One gave the president an opportunity to break a Republican tradition by vetoing a bill while making clear his ideas on what the First Amendment clause on freedom of religion meant. The incident involved a grant by Congress of a small parcel of land in the Mississippi Territory to the Salem Meeting House Baptists and a bill incorporating an Episcopal church in Alexandria (then part of the District of Columbia). Jefferson had never returned a bill to Congress with a veto message, but Madison used this occasion to send both bills back to Capitol Hill. In the Baptists' case the president merely said that the legislation ran afoul of the First Amendment; with the other instance, however, Madison said not only was the prohibition against "a religious establishment" by Congress violated but the bill went further and gave the church authority to support the poor and educate their children. The bill must be voided, Madison said, because it "would be a precedent for giving to religious societies as such a legal agency in carrying into effect [what ought to be] a public and civil duty."[11]

Madison knew he was on solid constitutional ground, but he must have been surprised by the public reaction to his veto messages. Happily, several Baptist churches in North Carolina sent the president messages approving his conduct in keeping intact the wall separating church and state. Madison replied that he had no choice because he regarded "the practical distinction between Religion and Civil Government as essential to the purity of both, and as guaranteed by the Constitution."[12] He went on to recognize that the

10. Rives and Fendall, *Writings of Madison*, 2:508–11.
11. James D. Richardson, comp., *A Compilation of the Messages and Papers of the Presidents, 1789 to 1897*, 10 vols. (Washington, D.C.: GPO, 1896–1899), 1:474–74.
12. Rives and Fendall, *Writings of Madison*, 2:508–11.

Baptists had proved their sincerity by upholding the principle "in a case favoring the interest of your brethren as in other cases." The Baptists never sent Madison a thousand-pound cheese to match their gift to Jefferson in 1802, but they acknowledged Madison's consistency from 1789 onward regarding "the free exercise of religion."

The diversions into constitutional law may have provided Madison with relief from his anxieties over the lack of hard information from Europe. The only proof coming to hand was that the cold war with Britain was heating up again; so the American navy sent the *President* to intercept any British vessels menacing New York harbor. In late May the *President* fired a broadside when attacked by the HMS *Little Belt*, wreaking havoc on the smaller British vessel while giving a boost to American pride. The pro-administration *National Intelligencer* in Washington informed readers that the American commander had fired in defense of the flag with "the approbation of the President of the United States."[13] Attention shifted to news from another vessel, the *Essex*, which was expected from Europe, bearing news of renewed trade with France or Britain's revocation of its Orders in Council. Some citizens might have even hoped for a real bonanza — French compliance and a British backoff — but that was wishful thinking. All Madison needed to vindicate his past conduct was definite news that France was living up to the letter of Cadore's message.

For American diplomats abroad, it was a spring of discontent. John Armstrong, frustrated by the maze of French diplomacy, had long since turned his office over to a secretary and headed for home. Equally confounded by London politics, William Pinkney was convinced he was up against a wall and decided to go home rather than face further frustration. Thus Pinkney had also packed his valise and booked passage on the *Essex*.

Meanwhile, unaware of the *Little Belt* incident, the newly designated British minister to the United States took his time about departing. Sir Augustus John Foster was instructed to seek a solution for the *Chesapeake-Leopard* incident (when twenty-one American sailors were killed or wounded by Royal Navy broadsides) by offering "a suitable pecuniary Provision" to "the Families of those seamen, who unfortunately fell in The Action." Before he boarded the HMS *Minerva*, bound for Chesapeake Bay, Foster was also told to protest the West Florida occupation as "the ungenerous and unprovoked Seizure of a foreign Colony" and "a most unjustifiable and Violent Invasion of The Rights both of the Monarch, and People of Spain."[14] (Many moons

13. Quoted in Brant, *Madison*, 5:320.
14. Wellesley to Foster, 10 April 1811, quoted in Bernard Mayo, ed., "Instructions to the British Ministers to the United States, 1791-1812," *American Historical Association Annual Report for 1936*, 3 vols. (Washington, D.C.: Da Capo, 1971), 3:318, 320.

later, when Foster finally looked Madison in the eye, the president and his secretary of state listened politely. It was clear Foster was only talking, not threatening, and he was courteous enough to avoid "any hostile or menacing language." Given that Madison had decided not to recognize either Napoleon's brother on the Spanish throne or the minister claiming to represent the Bourbon alternative, it was not a matter Madison or Monroe cared to discuss.)

As always, Washington was a mill of rumors. Dolley Madison complained to a relative that their summer trip to Montpelier was delayed by reports that a dispatch ship would soon reach the United States. Delays of the *Essex*, Mrs. Madison wrote, prevented the presidential party from traveling to Orange County. "Alas, it seems that it would never come, and we are precisely in the state of suspense that you left us [many weeks ago] as it regards European affairs."[15] The American envoy in London was coming home on the *Essex*, and Madison had heard that the newly accredited British minister was also expected at any moment. The president doubted if the *Essex* carried anything important, but he was hopeful that the *Minerva* bore welcome news. Trying to hold his anxiety in check, Madison wrote that he was not hopeful that the British envoy could change the present course of affairs. "On the other hand, some hope is awakened by the reports that [his mission] proceeds from the decision of the Prince Regent agst. the will of the Cabinet, and is meant to keep the path open for amicable arrangements."[16]

What Madison wanted to hear was that the prince regent in London, acting on behalf of ailing George III, was opposed to the official British position regarding the Cadore letter. Until definite proof came of France's revocation of its decrees, Britain was not budging unless the cabinet changed its position or was forced to do so. But no such luck was possible. The *Minerva* sailed up the Chesapeake Bay into Annapolis in late June, the *Essex* almost in its wake. Bulging dispatch pouches from the American ship and William Pinkney's review of events told Madison and his secretary of state what they did not want to hear: France was making Cadore's promises a dead letter by holding seized American vessels and still trying to intercept ships flying the Stars and Stripes.

In happier times, the arrival of Foster, a dashing, thirty-three-year-old bachelor bearing diplomatic credentials from the Court of St. James, would have furnished a good excuse for a plethora of drawingroom sighs. But Madison was not interested in social gatherings; he wanted some good news, so he hurried the acceptance of the British envoy's credentials as the capital prepared to celebrate the Fourth of July. In view of the events that had occurred

15. Dolley Payne Madison to Edward Coles, 15 June 1811, Cutts Papers, Massachusetts Historical Society.
16. Madison to Jefferson, 11 June 1811, Madison Papers, DLC.

on 4 July 1776 and 1783, there was good reason to see George III's representative before that historic date; so on 2 July Foster was received by the president. In short order, it was clear to Madison and Monroe that Foster had nothing new to offer.

If the president and Monroe were disappointed, the belles of Washington probably were not. Foster had served in Washington on an earlier tour of duty during Jefferson's presidency, and unlike "Copenhagen" Jackson, he was considered something of a playboy given to lavish, expensive entertainments. However, Foster's chief weakness was neither a fondness for brandy nor for pretty faces but rather the same flaw so chronic with other British ministers at Washington: He listened to the opposition party leaders too much. One after another, these career diplomats from London drank their port with smug Federalists who assured them that Madison's policies were inept and that the president lacked grass-roots support. Listening day in and day out to derogatory accounts of Madison's handling of the presidency led Foster to conclude that the chief executive was hardly the man to lead the United States into a war with anyone. When he got down to business, Foster made it clear that Britain wanted proof that France had called off its edicts, and he implied that Madison's decree impeding Anglo-American commerce justified British retaliation. Meanwhile, settlement of the old *Chesapeake* grievances concerning slain American sailors would have to await the outcome of countercharges that Britons had died in the *Little Belt* incident.

However, for the moment, the little city of Washington celebrated Independence Day and tried to forget the disappointments that had been carried into Annapolis harbor. The White House doors were opened to all citizens, who ate cake and drank gallons of punch while the president and his lady stood for hours in the receiving line and then adjourned to a celebration on the banks of the Potomac. The French minister tagged along with the Madisons, but the newly arrived British minister was discreetly absent, considering the nature of the celebration.

Foster's arrival had thrown a crimp into the Madisons' vacation plans. His stern diplomatic notes on the Florida situation had been bad enough, but the suggestion that the Cadore letter was nothing more than a bag of hot French wind had roused Madison's ire. Monroe had taken official notice of the West Florida protest, given that the British had rejected the Perdido as a demarcation line, and Monroe "himself bought West Florida in his Louisiana Purchase."[17] Soon Foster perceived that despite the ridicule heaped on

17. Henry Adams, *History of the United States of America during the Administrations of Thomas Jefferson and James Madison*, vol. 2, *History of the United States of America during the Administrations of James Madison*, Earl N. Harbert, ed. (New York: Library of America, 1986), 321 (hereafter cited as Adams, *History*).

Madison by his Federalist friends, the president and his secretary of state were neither intellectual lightweights, nor were they lacking in backbone. Monroe's reply to his West Florida note, Foster reported, had swept away their differences on that disputed territory except for the one issue that Foster could not negotiate: the Orders in Council. On 24 July Madison confided to his brother-in-law that "obscurities" still clouded the situation regarding France while the British minister "Foster shocks with one paw and scratches with the other." The dapper Foster did explain that his country would not call off the Orders in Council until it was clear beyond doubt that Napoleon had told the truth. Madison found himself locked into a diplomatic vise; but the comforting truth was "that American blood was not flowing, and there was still hope of a sudden peace in Europe."[18]

Thus, as the thermometer climbed and the humidity increased in Washington, Foster's notes and other official business kept Madison at his desk. Finally, discouraged by the diplomatic pussyfooting, Madison on 25 July helped his wife into their carriage and headed for Montpelier. He knew that a war with Britain was now likely, for rumors of the prince regent's pro-American stance had proved to be false, and despite protests from British merchants the British cabinet had made not one conciliatory gesture.

The great mystery was the French game. What was Napoleon up to, anyway? Officially the French claimed that on 28 April 1811 a decree signed by Napoleon at Saint-Cloud had carried out the promises in the Cadore letter. The French foreign office insisted that it had officially notified the American chargé in Paris of the letter's contents and had sent a second copy directly to Washington. Actually, this was more French hocus-pocus, for the evidence indicates that the decree was postdated a year after it was written (at least according to historian Henry Adams), and that Napoleon's minister had used diplomatic sleight of hand to confound and embarrass the American government.[19] If such a decree had been issued in the spring of 1811, as the French later claimed, Madison's life would have been much easier because the British would probably have revoked their Orders in Council. But by the time Madison knew of the spurious Saint-Cloud decree, the United States was at war.

Meanwhile, the Madisons relaxed on their Virginia plantation as much as the busy flow of visitors at Montpelier would allow. When Samuel Harrison Smith and his lady visited the plantation, Dolley Madison confessed that twenty-three guests were already enjoying the Madisons' hospitality.

18. Madison to Richard Cutts, 23 July 1811, Blumhaven Library, Philadelphia (1959).
19. Adams, *History*, 469–70; see also J. C. A. Stagg, *Mr. Madison's War: Politics Diplomacy, and Warfare in the Early American Republic, 1783–1830* (Princeton, N.J.: Princeton University Press, 1983), 305–7.

Dinnertime fell around four in the afternoon, followed by a separation of the ladies from the gentlemen. Dolley Madison took Mrs. Smith into her bed-chamber to escape the clouds of cigar smoke pouring from the dining area: "She said I must lay down by her on her bed, and rest myself, she loosened my riding habit, took off my bonnet, and we threw ourselves on her bed. Wine, ice, punch and delightful pine-apples were immediately brought. No restraint, no ceremony. . . . At this house I realized [how pleasant] being in Virginia, [with] Mr. Madison, plain, friendly, communicative, and uncere-monious as any Virginia Planter could be."[20] Madison told amusing anec-dotes in profusion when at Montpelier and was not the stiff, shy, little man who still wore the black smallclothes of which Federalist congressmen spoke derisively. His annual salary of twenty-five thousand dollars paid the bills at Montpelier, which kept piling up because tobacco prices stayed low and hay bills for the horses of Montpelier guests were high.

Madison fretted about tobacco prices and the Hessian flies infesting his wheat field, as planters on the eastern seaboard were inclined to do, but an even more serious problem affected farms and plantations from the Chesapeake Bay southward — soil depletion. Continuous planting of tobacco for more than a century, along with the straight-line plowing that encouraged soil erosion, was driving down land values from Maryland to Georgia and forcing farmers to look westward for cheap, fresh planting soils. Early in Madison's presidency, his onetime political associate, John Taylor of Caroline, had published a collec-tion of agricultural essays pleading for crop rotation, deeper plowing, and fer-tilizer application. Although Taylor and Madison had split politically (Taylor went over to the Tertium Quids and supported Monroe in the 1808 presiden-tial election), Madison probably had Taylor's *Arator* essays on his bookshelf at Montpelier. Taylor came back to the Senate in 1822; but long before then his extreme conservatism had placed him far to the right of Madison so that their only common ground was the soil of their plantations. Taylor made few con-verts to his conservative political ideas and was too academic for dirt farmers, as Madison must have realized. Their old friendship was as hopelessly eroded as the many acres around Taylor's Caroline County neighborhood.

Unlike their president, most American farmers showed little interest in careful land usage but were eager to acquire and exploit more lands. In 1810 farmlands in Connecticut sold for twenty to forty dollars an acre, with the proceeds often used to finance western migrations to uncleared tracts that might be purchased on credit for three dollars an acre.[21] Northern families

20. Margaret Bayard Smith, *The First Forty Years in Washington Society,* Gaillard Hunt, ed. (New York: G. P. Putnam's Sons, 1906), 81–82.

21. Curtis P. Nettels, *The Emergence of a National Economy, 1775–1815* (New York: Holt, Rhinehart & Winston, 1962), 157.

searching for cheaper farms moved into the Genesee Valley in New York or into sparsely populated northwest Pennsylvania, where new settlements added almost one hundred thousand to the state's population from 1800 to 1810. Growth in Ohio, which was granted statehood in 1803, was even more rapid during that period, climbing from 45,365 in 1800 to 230,760 in 1810. But Cleveland was still a frontier village on Lake Erie, and fewer than twenty-five thousand settlers lived in the Indiana Territory when Madison took office.[22]

In Virginia, the mountain country west of the Blue Ridge chain beckoned fewer settlers, for its lands were described as "hard-scrabble" acres, rocky and inhospitable to the row crops of Tidewater farms. But many Virginians, including some of Madison's relatives, sold out and moved to the Eden of the West, the spun-off state of Kentucky that had once been a remote county of Virginia with a population of fewer than fifteen thousand. By 1810, blue grass and limestone soils had attracted 406,511 to Kentucky, and its slave population grew in proportion. Tennessee expanded at a slower pace and its farmers stayed in the valleys east of the river that gave the state its name. Cotton was the magic crop after improved ginning brought high profits to planters, but the price fell from forty-four cents to nineteen cents early in Jefferson's administration and was back to only twenty cents when Madison took office. Demand increased, however, and in 1811 the crops of Georgia and South Carolina totaled a staggering eighty million pounds.[23] Planters in eastern Virginia and North Carolina experimented with cotton, but the fluffy bolls could not compete with the staple tobacco crops of the region. In Madison's part of the world, the bright amber-brown leaves still paid the bills and the corn crops fed the people.

As black field hands, cooks, and servants carried out the domestic business of Montpelier, messengers shuttled back and forth from the State Department and an occasional message drifted to Orange County from Monticello as Jefferson yearned for news, good or bad. Monroe often wrote to Madison from his farm in Albemarle County. In late July Madison issued a proclamation pushing the first session of the Twelfth Congress (originally scheduled for December) ahead to early November. Perhaps by then some welcome news would have arrived from Europe. If not, Madison must have reasoned, Congress would have to help him decide if the only course left was a declaration of war.

War clouds seemed distant, however, from the vista of Madison's porch at Montpelier. While Madison was on vacation, all kinds of advice on whether

---

22. Ibid., 383.
23. Lewis C. Gray, *History of Agriculture in the Southern United States to 1860*, 2 vols. (Washington, D.C.: Carnegie Institution, 1933), 2:681–83.

or not to go to war poured in from well-wishers, old friends, and strangers. Still hoping that a sizable American wool industry could be created, Madison continued to promote among other breeders the selective breeding of imported sheep; he also took horseback rides in good weather to inquire into the area's crop conditions. After he had moved up the convening of Congress, which some folks thought had ominous overtones, a letter arrived from Henry Lee, the "Lighthorse Harry" of wartime fame who was now somewhat down on his luck and hoping for better things for his four-year-old son, Robert Edward Lee. The Revolutionary War veteran complained of the "long cherished prejudices" against Britain, which he had heard with dismay, and told Madison he hoped "that a few months will prove their error not only because I should be gratified in seeing yr. measures approved . . . but from my increasing desire to see united in the bonds of amity two nations so exactly calculated to promote each others good, & between whom the torch of discord should never be lighted." Lee added that it would be tragic if "the only two nations of the many in the world who understand the meaning of liberty" should somehow "imbrue their hands in each others blood."[24]

Madison had good reason to be counted an Anglophobe, but as he rode back to Washington in October 1811, he was not ready to concede that war with Britain was inevitable. Once again, there was the anxious waiting for a dispatch ship—this time the *John Adams*—which when it finally arrived had nothing new to report. The president had settled on an appointment for the vacant American minister's post at Paris, offering that challenging job to the poet-diplomat Joel Barlow. Barlow sailed for France in late summer aboard the *Constitution;* he had been instructed to smoke out the French regarding the confusing Napoleonic decrees. Madison must have been aware of the mounting pressure of public opinion as he contemplated his next move. The president had not intended to create a crisis, but tension was mounting as news from European sources failed to let off any of the steam. Was there any hope for "a radical change of the French policy towards this Country?" Barlow was asked. The forthcoming Congress might allow American merchant ships to arm themselves, and everyone already knew that many ships flying the American flag sometimes fell in with British convoys to avoid French capture. Permitting American vessels "to arm for self-Defence," Madison told Barlow, would "scarcely fail to bring on maritime reprisals and . . . end in the full extent of war" unless the British revoked the Orders in Council.

24. Henry Lee to Madison, 19 August 1811, Madison Papers, DLC.

Altho' in our discussions with G.B. we have been justified in viewing the repeal of the French decrees as sufficiently substantiated . . . yet the manner in which the F. Govt. has managed the repeal of the Decrees, and evaded a correction of other outrages, has [caused] as much of irritation and disgust as possible. And these sentiments are not a little strengthened by the sarcastic comments on that management with which we are constantly pelted in our discussions with the B. Govt. and for which the Fr. Govt. ought to be ashamed to furnish the occasion.[25]

In the meantime, rumors printed in a Paris-based British newspaper reached Washington. According to the story, American vessels seized in contradiction to the spirit of the Cadore letter had been freed. Was the report true? Madison wondered as he took up the chore of writing his third State of the Union message.

Long simply called "the president's annual message to Congress," the State of the Union speeches (which were, in fact, read aloud by clerks ever since Jefferson had set the precedent by not appearing before Congress) were universally printed in newspapers and read carefully by citizens of every political complexion. Madison was aware of this critical communicative device as he drafted the text in October 1811, for he knew that the diplomatic impasse confronting his administration could not last forever. Eventually, the president realized, he must call either the French or the British to account. His mail was filled with assurances that the people were fed up with European diplomatic ploys, and Republican congressmen from Henry Clay down to the greenest newcomer on Capitol Hill knew that worse things than war might be their lot.

Clay was calling the tune in the House, where he had been elected Speaker at the first session. Clay knew where the action was and so had taken the unusual step of resigning from his Senate seat in order to run for the House that fall. At thirty-four he was the youngest man ever to be elected to the Speakership, and Madison's Republican philosophy of deferring to Congress for final solutions meant that Clay was the second most powerful politician in the United States. Indeed, Madison's detractors held that now Clay was the one in a position to run the country.

Clay's credentials as a staunch Republican were impeccable. A few years earlier he had fought a duel over his unreserved approval of the Jefferson-Madison embargo policy, and as House Speaker he was now in a position to appoint committee members who would support his belligerent policy

25. Draft letter, Madison to Barlow, 17 November 1811, Madison Papers, DLC.

aimed at Britain rather than France. Still, it would be unfair to say that Clay "pushed Madison into war." This new Congress had some seventy freshman members and, according to Merrill Peterson, the Twelfth Congress provided "a watershed in the history of the republic."[26] New leaders had come to the fore, including twenty-nine-year-old John C. Calhoun. These men had no memory of the Revolution; they had not helped to found the new nation, but they intended to preserve it.

President Madison was not pushed into war—he backed into it. After hinting that Britain and France had forced the United States to the limits of its patience, in his annual message Madison told the nation that the two European powers had shown "hostile inflexibility in trampling on the rights which no independent nation can relinquish."[27] The president listed the grievances accumulated under French duplicity and British arrogance and urged Congress to rearm. Although this was not a declaration of war, it came very close.

Madison then backed down a bit by sending Congress a report on the *Chesapeake* incident that seemed to end the drawn-out dispute. But while Madison was composing that note, General William Henry Harrison was directing his frontier troops in a raid on Tecumseh's village in the Indiana Territory. Reports of the Battle of Tippecanoe—full of gore and glory and hints that the Indian uprising was part of a British scheme to encourage frontier troubles—drifted into the capital. Madison officially proclaimed an American victory at Tippecanoe when he notified Congress of the action on 18 December 1811.[28] Congressman Felix Grundy of Tennessee saw the frontier action as the first shots in a war he would welcome. Yet Grundy, fiercely Republican, had misgivings that Madison must have shared. As he foresaw a declaration of war barely over the horizon, Grundy told the House of his fear that republicanism would be tested and perhaps found wanting. "We are about to ascertain by actual experiment how far our republican institutions are calculated to stand the shock of war," Grundy said, "and whether, after foreign danger has disappeared, we can again assume our peaceful attitude without endangering the liberties of the people."[29]

While Grundy worried about republicanism along the Potomac, western settlers on the Maumee had more tangible fears. Rumblings from the Old Northwest indicated that Harrison's victory had not settled all of the fron-

26. Merrill Peterson, *The Great Triumvirate: Webster, Clay, and Calhoun* (New York: Oxford University Press, 1987), 3; *Dictionary of American Biography*, 2:175.
27. Richardson, *Messages of the Presidents*, 1:476–81.
28. Ibid., 1:481–82.
29. Quoted in Adams, *History*, 390.

tier's problems, for there were reports that British fur-trading posts along Lake Erie were "focal points for hundreds of dissatisfied Indians seeking food, weapons, and support against the United States."[30]

Something had to be done, and yet Madison was not ready for the shove that would carry the United States into a war. Before Christmas 1811 Madison wrote to American envoys in Europe, warning them that another year of tension and frustration was not on his calendar. To Barlow in Paris the president suggested that Congress would allow American merchant ships to arm in self-defense. (Indeed, in his first draft of the annual message, Madison had urged Congress to take such action, but Gallatin had persuaded him to drop the bellicose recommendation.) "This can scarcely fail to bring on maritime reprisals, and to end in the full extent of war," Madison predicted, "unless a change in the British system should arrest the career of events."[31] He also told Barlow of French innuendoes that Napoleon was not going to bark if East Florida lost its Spanish moorings. Madison wanted this to be true, but he warned Barlow: "It is hoped that no unworthy attempt will be made to extract money from the occasion." With the French, all diplomacy seemed to carry a price tag!

Public meetings, mostly in the South, sent assurances to Madison that his belligerent stance toward Britain suited them to a "T" (for tough, presumably). No doubt some congressmen had spilled the beans about a meeting that the secretary of state had attended with members of the House foreign relations committee in late November. Pressed by congressmen as to administration intentions, Monroe reportedly assured them that if Britain persisted in its Orders in Council, Madison would ask for a declaration of war before the session ended in the spring of 1812. From his perspective in St. Petersburg, John Quincy Adams saw that Madison and his cabinet were walking into a snare by insisting that the Cadore letter represented genuine intentions. "It is a trap to catch us into a war with England," Adams surmised.[32] Even Jefferson had misgivings as the war clouds rolled into Washington. Madison suggested that in the event of hostilities, Congress would have to provide some leadership. "I have much doubted whether, in case of war, Congress would find it practicable to do their part of the business" as the Constitution seemed to imply, Jefferson noted. "That a

---

30. Stagg, *Mr. Madison's War*, 190.

31. Ibid., 80; Madison to Barlow, 17 November 1811, in Rives and Fendall, *Writings of Madison*, 2:519.

32. Adams to Thomas Boylston Adams, 29 April 1811, quoted in Norman Graebner, *Foundations of American Foreign Policy: A Realist Appraisal from Franklin to McKinley* (Wilmington, Del.: Scholarly Resources, 1985), 135.

body containing 100 lawyers in it, should direct the measures of war, is, I fear, impossible."[33]

Madison wanted the American public to support his policy for peace based on Britain's backing away from its provocative stance toward the United States. The only alternative was war. Thus Madison thanked the South Carolina legislature for its supportive resolutions and promised the lawmakers he had not become chief executive in order to dismantle the American empire. "Acquiescence in the practice and pretensions of the British Government is forbidden by every view that can be taken of the subject," Madison promised. "It would recolonize our commerce, by subjecting it to a foreign authority; with the sole difference that the regulations of it formerly were made by acts of Parliament, and now by orders in Council."[34]

As Madison's spine stiffened, Congress began to plan for an invasion of Canada if war with Britain came that spring. War talk had revived the old notion of invading Canada, which Americans (even those with common sense) constantly flirted with, as Gallatin's plan for 1807 had proved. In early February 1812 a Federalist congressman reported that "there is scarce a day but what we hear on the floor of the House something said about the war in which we are about to engage, i.e., when we are ready to make a rapid descent upon Canada." But this wary Yankee lawmaker saw matters in a different light. "Our yeomanry are too busy and too happy at home to embark in a wild goose chase to Canada unless they feel a greater cause of war than at present."[35] In the Republican ranks nobody seemed to think it would require a great effort to push across the Canadian border, and congressional proponents of an expanded military force to conquer Britain's northern province hinted that such an invasion would scarcely "require the utmost exertions of the nation."[36] So far as the loudest saber rattlers in the House were concerned, Canada was there for the plucking, so why raise taxes when a huge army was unnecessary?

In fact, the American army was spread so thinly across a fifteen-hundred-mile frontier that some expansion was required, war or no war. Although Madison sought authority to have ten thousand regulars in readiness when hardly five thousand men were fit for duty, Senator William Branch Giles upped the ante far beyond the president's recommendations. Giles's game,

33. Jefferson to Madison, 19 February 1812, in P. L. Ford, ed., *Works of Jefferson*, 12 vols. (New York: G. P. Putnam's Sons, 1905), 11:226.

34. Stagg, *Mr. Madison's War*, 84; Madison to South Carolina House of Representatives, 8 January 1811, in Rives and Fendall, *Writings of Madison*, 2:524.

35. George H. Haynes, ed., "The Letters of Samuel Taggart," American Antiquarian Society *Proceedings* 33 (1923): 369 (hereafter cited as "Taggart Letters").

36. Stagg, *Mr. Madison's War*, 147.

apparently, was "to ruin President Madison by the war that was threatened, and wanted to hasten the ruin before the next election," Henry Adams surmised.[37] With his crafty mind, Giles was quite capable of such deviousness, and his Senate colleagues never knew whether his motives were aboveboard or not. So out went Madison's request for ten thousand and in went Giles's change calling for twenty-five thousand, with provision made for fifty thousand volunteers.

With Congress suddenly in a fighting mood, supporters of a similar expansion plan for the navy hoped bellicose Speaker Clay would aid them in abandoning Jefferson's passive gunboat scheme by authorizing a squadron of frigates with more firepower and better maneuverability than the old gunboats. A special committee recommended that funds be found for twelve ships of the line and twenty frigates to defend American harbors and protect coastal shipping. Unfortunately, the committee noted, the timber for six ships of seventy-four guns each had been bought before John Adams left office, but the material had been wasted on gunboats. Enough timber was still around for the frigates, but a bill providing for their construction was rejected by a parsimonius House, 62 to 59.[38] With talk of war circulating in every corridor of the Capitol, the most Congress could offer was a six hundred thousand dollar appropriation to buy ship timbers over a three-year period.

Congressional niggardliness toward a naval buildup may have been due to Republican lawmakers' delusions: Most of them had a bad case of Canada on the brain, and soldiers, not sailors, would be the conquerors of that British province. From Henry Clay down to the lowliest congressman, the Republicans had convinced themselves that money spent on a navy was wasted given that a Canadian invasion would be little more than a few border skirmishes followed by an unconditional surrender. So much for conventional Washington wisdom on the eve of battle.

Canada loomed large in Madison's mind as well, for he had gotten wind of a spy story that might wake the nation up. From a rather shady source, Madison learned that the governor general of Canada, Sir George Prevost, had a secret agent in New England who was working overtime to line up possible defectors and to encourage New England to rebel against the Union. Through a French-born intermediary, Madison and his secretary of state discovered that papers were for sale that proved that the earl of Liverpool was part of a conspiracy to wrest "the eastern states" from the Union in case of war with Britain. The asking price for these letters, presumably offered by

37. Adams, *History*, 398.
38. Alfred T. Mahan, *Sea Power in Its Relation to the War of 1812*, 2 vols. (Boston: Little, Brown & Company, 1905), 1:37.

a disaffected British spy named "Captain" John Henry, was fifty thousand dollars.

The ensuing negotiations reflected no credit on either Madison or Monroe. In his eagerness to expose New England's disloyalty, Madison became a gullible pawn for the French Canadian confidence man, and Monroe willingly approved of the huge payment from a secret fund (the fifty thousand dollars, which was ultimately wasted, would have paid for a fully fitted frigate for the United States Navy). The "exposé" that Madison sent to Congress, and which was immediately printed in the *National Intelligencer* (and then in Republican papers everywhere), proved to be a dud. Nothing John Henry revealed was far beyond what a reading of the Boston newspapers could have told any intelligent observer; no names were named and no conspirators were unmasked.[39] Madison tried to make the exposé into a national alarum, but much of the noise was deadened by simultaneous reports from Europe that French warships had sunk American ships carrying flour to feed the British army fighting in Spain (another one of the anomalies permitted by the Orders in Council).

Monroe had also been ready to capitalize on the Henry exposé; thus when he heard of the latest French depredations, the secretary of state called the French minister Serurier to his office for a tongue-lashing. Monroe told the Frenchman how much damage French duplicity had dealt the administration. Making more of the Henry letters than the facts justified, Monroe told Serurier that the nation was moving toward war with Britain out of injured national pride. "It is at such a moment that your frigates come and burn our ships, destroy all our work, and put the Administration in the falsest and most terrible position in which a government can find itself placed," Monroe erupted. Monroe was not alone in his anger. A band of hotheaded congressmen heard the news of French destruction and demanded that the United States break off diplomatic relations with Napoleon. The detailed report of a French commodore's orders to burn two American vessels had sent a wave of horror through the House. "The Devil himself could not tell which government, England or France, is the most wicked," sighed Representative Nathaniel Macon.[40]

Once again, all eyes were turned toward the Atlantic as another dispatch ship from Europe was awaited. Probably at the urging of Speaker Clay, Madison asked Congress for an embargo on all shipping, a prelude to war because the purpose of the ban was twofold: to allow shippers time to bring their vessels into a safe haven and to prevent foodstuffs from going to the

39. Samuel Eliot Morison, *By Land and by Sea* (New York: Alfred Knopf, 1953), xx.

40. Adams, *History*, 429.

British armies in Spain aboard American ships. The embargo was pressed on Congress at a secret session, but the Federalists stalled for time as they sent confidential messages to shippers in port cities, warning them to load their vessels at once and thus escape any official deadline. Republicans forced the bill through; but as they debated, merchants determined to beat the clock sent flour, grain, and other provisions worth fifteen million dollars on ships bound for British-held ports. "Drays were working night and day from Tuesday night, March 31, and continued their toil till Sunday morning. . . . In this hurly-burly to palsy the arm of the Government all parties are united," *Niles' Weekly Register* reported from Baltimore, where thirty-one ships cleared the harbor in a matter of hours. At New York forty-eight ships dropped their lines in similar fashion, and departures of between thirty and forty vessels took place at both Philadelphia and Alexandria.[41] Thus "insider trading" was known in the United States during the earliest days of the Republic!

The war scare permitted speculators in American wheat and flour to dream of enormous profits before their trade was choked off, and smugglers operating in American coastal inlets from New England to Amelia Island shared this greed. The secretary of state heard that a brazen British merchant ship, the *Lady Madison*, had recently sailed to the United States and returned ladened with an illegal cargo "without entering an American port."[42] Much of the frantic activity in late March proved unnecessary, as the embargo that Congress finally enacted was not to become effective until 4 July 1812. Carrying on business as usual, American shippers operated within guidelines from the Orders in Council that permitted a Yankee ship to obtain a license for carrying provisions directly from the United States to Cádiz or Lisbon with the blessings of the Royal Navy. Profits came before patriotism when American cargoes were unloaded for the Duke of Wellington's peninsular campaign during the summer of 1812.

The American chargé d'affaires in London, Jonathan Russell, saw how the British were making a joke of American laws while the French decrees were already a joke. Russell concluded that "the great object" of Napoleon's policy was "to entangle us in a war with England."[43] What was transparent in London, however, was still murky in Washington. But then, all things take time.

Perhaps to clear the way for action against one enemy at a time, Madison threw cold water on the American invasion of East Florida lest it appear that the United States was bullying its way into the lands south of the St.

41. Quoted in Mahan, *Sea Power in the War of 1812*, 1:264.
42. Ibid.
43. Russell To Monroe, 13 July 1811, quoted in ibid., 1:268.

Mary's River. General George Mathews, who had been encouraged by the president to support any internal insurrection, found that Madison was backing off. Mathews reported that the Spanish subjects had rebelled and issued their own East Florida declaration of independence; but as he took his ragtag army in sight of St. Augustine a dispatch reached the general from the secretary of state.[44] Monroe told the Georgian that he had exceeded the president's orders and that he was fired. Mathews, convinced that he had been double-crossed by the president and the secretary of state, threatened to tell all. He was bound for Washington with promises of a juicy exposé when he suddenly became ill and died.

By early May 1812 both Madison and Monroe had more than Florida on their minds. Once again, all eyes were turned toward the Atlantic, as another dispatch ship from Europe was expected. Either the *Hornet* would be carrying news of a British retreat, or Madison would give in to pressure and there would be war. Federalists were convinced that Madison was rushing the nation into war during an election year to save his political hide. Congressman Samuel Taggart thought everything depended on Britain's repeal of the Orders in Council, which Madison would claim as "the fruit of intimidation carried by the din of our warlike preparations, an event of which the prospect is daily diminishing." The Massachusetts Federalist added: "I believe Madison's Presidential career will close with the 3d of March 1813."[45]

Reports of Madison's political demise, however, proved premature. Dolley Madison was unperturbed by rumors circulating in capital cloakrooms that DeWitt Clinton of New York was scurrying around trying to derail plans for Madison's reelection; instead of concerning themselves with such gossip, Mrs. Madison told friends that all eyes should be turned toward the ocean and the *Hornet's* imminent arrival. According to Mrs. Joel Barlow, Dolley Madison reported, the *Hornet* would bring news of French cooperation with the American administration. Seldom has a single ship's sailing drawn such national prominence. "Ever since her sailing the cant word has been, the *Hornet*, the *Hornet*," a Kentucky newspaper wailed. "What sting she will bring on her return!!"[46] Unfortunately, the ship's arrival brought no encouraging news from Europe. But Madison's enemies within the Republican ranks still failed to gain the advantage because they handled their campaign plotting so ineptly. A congressional caucus had been scheduled for 16 May, by which time DeWitt Clinton, who had made a good impression by trying to raise money for the Erie Canal project on an earlier visit to Wash-

44. Brant, *Madison*, 5:442–45.
45. Samuel Taggart to Rev. John Taylor, 20 January 1812, in "Taggart Letters," 377.
46. Lexington, Ky., *Reporter*, 10 March 1812, quoted in Perkins, *Prologue to War*, 376.

ington, was making no bones about his presidential aspiration.[47] But then Clinton "stubbed his toe" in a local squabble and was even out of the running to succeed his uncle, Vice-President George Clinton, who had died on 20 April. The caucus was not well attended—Madison's archenemies were too busy to show up—and the president was renominated in a routine manner. To replace the vice-president, John Langdon of New Hampshire was chosen as Madison's running mate. Although a northerner on the ticket was considered essential, Langdon told party leaders that he would not accept a place on the Republican ticket. Was DeWitt Clinton the alternative?

Madison's mind turned repeatedly to New England as the news of Elbridge Gerry's narrow defeat in the governor's race was interpreted as a sign of public disaffection toward both the Republican party and the administration's foreign policy. Massachusetts Republicans had outsmarted themselves, it seemed, for the famous "gerrymander" bill enacted in February 1812 apparently had rigged control of the state senate against a Federalist popular majority. Caleb Strong's upset victory placed in the Massachusetts statehouse a determined Federalist who would give no quarter to Madison. After Langdon stepped aside, Madison decided to make Gerry his running mate, but for the time he continued to regret "the incurable spirit of opposition" that "seems to have gained strength in the Eastern States."[48]

Early in April, rumors that the *Hornet* was in an American harbor had brought thrills of expectation to Washington. From Capitol Hill to Georgetown the excitement had grown until the report had proved false. Still Congress seemed in no hurry to conduct business. Legislation admitting the Orleans Territory into the Union as the state of Louisiana had been languishing for over a year. Arguments early in 1811 over the inclusion within proposed state boundaries of West Florida to the Perdido had been aired without resolution. Jingoistic pleas had led to heated exchanges, particularly from Massachusetts Congressman Josiah Quincy, who had objected to Louisiana statehood because the region was beyond the limits of the original American Union. Despite Quincy's warning that Congress was playing with a powder keg that could explode and tear the nation asunder, southern Republicans had dismissed his threat and Madison had signed legislation preparing the region for statehood. Fourteen months later had come some snipping at the border to settle Louisiana's eastern reach at the Pearl River, and in April 1812 an eighteenth star had been added to the American flag. For the first time, a state not contiguous to the existing Union of 1783 had been admitted.

---

47. Philip S. Klein, ed., "Memoirs of a Senator from Pennsylvania: Jonathan Roberts, 1771–1854," *Pennsylvania Magazine of History and Biography* 62 (1938): 227.

48. Madison to John G. Jackson, 17 May 1812, Jackson Collection, Indiana University Library.

Weeks passed before the news had reached New Orleans, but by then the nation's attention was again focused in another direction. The *Hornet* had finally dropped anchor and by the last week of May the worst was out. "France has done nothing to adjust our differences with her," Madison wrote Jefferson:

> In the mean time, the business is become more than ever puzzling. To go to war with Engd. and not with France arms the federalists with new matter, and divides the Republicans. . . . To go to war agst. both presents a thousand difficulties; above all that of shutting all the ports of the Continent of Europe agst. our Cruisers who can do little without them. . . . The only consideration of weight in favor of this triangular war as it is called, is that it might hasten thro' a peace with G. B. or F. . . . But even this advantage is not certain.[49]

Madison was weary of playing a Hamletlike role. Far in the future were Admiral Alfred Mahan's explosive views on sea power. As the leader of a neutral power without a navy worth mentioning, Madison had to press the argument that private property at sea deserved immunity in a warring world. To fight or not to fight was no longer a debatable question. Surely the pressures of another election, the promise to Clay and other congressmen that the administration would "fish or cut bait" by late spring, and the huge disappointment felt after the *Hornet* arrived all contributed to the hardening of Madison's resolve.

By the end of May, Madison was fed up, and everybody in Washington knew it except the British minister. Sir Augustus Foster's informants, mostly Federalists in Congress, led him to believe that Madison was ill-suited for duty as a wartime leader. The British minister was told by Federalist confidants that they would foil Madison by voting for a disastrous war, force him out of office when his administration collapsed, and then save the United States by suing Britain for just and honorable peace.[50] The remarkable thing is that Foster believed them. So blind was Foster to reality that he failed to realize that a letter of instructions he had received in May 1812 from Lord Castlereagh was the last nail in a much-battered coffin. Foster showed the letter to Monroe, who turned it over to Madison. The letter made it clear that the Orders in Council were firmly in place. Looking back on that fateful event, the British envoy admitted, "I did not quite expect war to take place, nor should we have [had] it, I firmly believe, but for the approaching presidential election."[51]

49. Madison to Jefferson, 25 May 1812, Madison Papers, DLC.
50. Quoted in Adams, *History*, 412-13.
51. Sir Augustus John Foster, *Jeffersonian America: Notes on the United States of America, Collected in the Years 1805-6-7 and 11-12*, Richard B. Davis, ed. (Westport, Conn.: Greenwood Press, 1980), 97.

Madison did want another term in the White House; but he had also finally admitted to himself that some things were worse than war. Convinced that the United States was still regarded by the British cabinet as a third-rate power barely beyond colonial status, Madison forgot his Republican misgivings about war and began to draft his war message to Congress. Between the lines was the admission that American foreign policy since 1803 had been a failure.

The facts showed that Britain was already at war with the United States. "A state of war against the United States" existed, the harassed president explained, and it was time to stop the bowing and scraping. Republican in name and philosophy, Madison hesitated to make an outright call for war. That decision, the president wrote, would come in answer to "a solemn question which the Constitution wisely confides to the legislative department of the Government." Between the lines it was clear, however, that "a virtuous, a free, and a powerful nation" was going to fight Britain again. "Thus the nation drifted into a state of fright and outrage leading to war, even while the actual dangers posed by Great Britain remained for most Americans too remote, abstract, or nonexistent to require an adequate defense," diplomatic historian Norman Graebner observed.[52]

Remote or not, the British threat to some influential Americans was very real. The so-called War Hawks in Congress saw the Royal Navy's impressments, the British cabinet's Orders in Council, and the Indian menace in the Northwest as all of a piece—a persistent British policy meant to limit American prosperity and expansion. Many War Hawks were in their first or second term in Congress, most were young (the leaders ranged from twenty-nine to thirty-six years old), and all were lawyers. As poker-playing, feisty men from the ebbing frontier states, they were undaunted by the risks that war involved and were eager for its potential gains, particularly if the acquisition of Canada and the Floridas came as part of the booty. "The conquest of Canada is in your power," Clay had told the Senate on 22 February 1810. "I trust I shall not be deemed presumptive when I state that I verily believe that the militia of Kentucky are alone competent to place Montreal and Upper Canada at your feet." Such arrogance fostered a confidence among the War Hawks that grew even greater after the *Hornet* came home empty-handed.

The British minister, who regarded himself as a shrewd judge of American character, looked on the War Hawks as a bunch of undisciplined dandies. Foster believed that the War Hawks regarded the war "as necessary to America as a duel is to a young [naval] officer to prevent his being bullied and elbowed in society."[53] There was, however, more than braggadocio be-

52. Graebner, *Foundations of American Foreign Policy*, 143.
53. Foster, *Jeffersonian America*, 4.

hind their saber-rattling speeches. The War Hawks were the raucous manifestation of an injured national pride, a feeling that the United States was not being treated as an equal by Britain, France, or even Spain. From their mixture of perceptions and premises the War Hawks' logic led them to believe that the British had to be taught a lesson, and if this war also involved "a double-barrelled scheme of territorial aggrandizement," so much the better.[54] How much pressure Madison felt from their importunities is anybody's guess. Surely the president must have thanked Providence for the wide Atlantic that allowed Americans to think and talk so absurdly, in magnificent isolation from war-weary Europe. And of course neither Madison nor any other Republican leader, War Hawk or not, thought there was the slightest chance that the United States might lose the war.

Nobody was ahead of the Tennessee congressman, Felix Grundy, in foreseeing the blessings to be derived from a fight with Britain. "We shall drive the British from our continent," Grundy predicted. The western War Hawk assumed that Canada would soon fall to American arms. "I am willing to receive the Canadians as adopted brethren," he said, because the annexation of Canada would have "beneficial political effects" and would preserve the "equilibrium of the government" that had worried people like Josiah Quincy: "When Louisiana shall be fully peopled, the Northern States will lose their power; they will be at the discretion of others; they can be depressed at pleasure, and then this Union might be endangered. . . . I feel therefore anxious not only to add the Floridas to the South, but the Canadas to the North to this empire."[55] Jingoism? Yes, but naive Grundy revealed on the House floor the innermost desire of the Republican majority in his audience. "Manifest Destiny" would be the rallying cry of the next generation; but as a political force it was first unleashed by the War Hawks of 1812.

Only a British about-face on the Orders in Council could have stopped the War Hawks that spring. This was still a time when wind and sail carried messages across oceans, with four to six weeks required for a normal passage between Chesapeake Bay and the southwestern tip of England. Patience and peace rarely go hand-in-hand. While Madison fretted about his war message, a force of British ironmongers and merchants pleaded with Parliament for repeal of the detested orders on the ground that their businesses had suffered and would incur ruinous losses unless the American market reopened in the summer. "The Export trade to America has been subject to very great embarrassments and distresses," they told the House of Commons in April 1812, "almost annihilating the profit attending it." During the past year, the British businessmen claimed, "there has been no Export trade to America,

54. Julius W. Pratt, *Expansionists of 1812* (New York: Macmillan, 1925), 13.
55. Quoted in Adams, *History*, 392.

and the manufacturers are reduced to a state of grievous affliction." Witnesses told members of Parliament that £500,000 in British iron exports were now rusting at Liverpool docks, but that the pre-embargo market of £800,000 a year could be restored in an instant "if the Orders in Council were repealed."[56] Their constituents were talking a language that the House of Commons understood. Thus as the Americans were buckling on their swords, the British cabinet was trying to think of a graceful way to extend the olive branch.

But why go to war with Britain, the mother country of the United States of America? To Madison, who was of the older generation, and to Clay and Calhoun, who were of the new, the answer was obvious. A war with Britain would reaffirm the commitment of 1776, for in early 1812, many American doubted whether the United States could long endure "as an independent and neutral nation."[57]

56. Quoted in Robert A. Rutland, *James Madison: The Founding Father* (New York: Macmillan, 1987), 222.
57. Gaillard Hunt, ed., *The Writings of James Madison*, 9 vols. (New York: G. P. Putnam's Sons, 1900–1910), 8:192–201.

6

★ ★ ★ ★ ★

THE DOGS OF WAR
UNLEASHED

If the United States had been prepared, things would have gone better from the start.

If the United States had been patient, the war could have been avoided.

If communications between the United States and Europe had been better, the war would not have happened.

The trouble with "ifs" is that they always come after the fact, and in the case of the War of 1812, the theories lasted so long that even Madison in his old age thought that the letter from the British foreign secretary to the minister in Washington, which the president read in May 1812, set the nation on its course for war: "In that letter it was distinctly & emphatically stated that the orders in Council to which we had declared we would not submit, would not be repealed, without a repeal of the internal measures of France. . . . With this formal notice, no choice remained but between war and degradation." That was an old man's recollection, of course, but in that 1827 letter he felt impelled to add a footnote to history. "Such was the distress of the British manufacturers, produced by our prohibitive and restrictive laws . . . that the orders in Council were soon after repealed, but not in time to prevent the effect of the declaration that they would not be repealed."[1]

Maybe. In mid-June, before the United States and Britain were formally

1. Madison to Henry Wheaton, 26–27 February 1827, in Gaillard Hunt, ed., *The Writings of James Madison*, 9 vols. (New York: G. P. Putnam's Sons, 1900–1910), 9:272–73.

at war, the House of Commons debated a motion to recall the Orders in Council. The remonstrances of the British ironmongers brought a change in attitude at Westminster, for a week later Castlereagh told the members of Parliament "from the Manufacturing Counties" of the cabinet decision to revoke the 1807 edicts, which were causing so much bad blood in Anglo-American relations. Around Manchester and Liverpool, workers and mill owners joined in a celebration of the news, and soon a stream of ships sailed out of Liverpool bound for American ports, carrying "more than 2 million yards of calico cloth as well as a supply of good English cheese for the White House."[2] Unfortunately, fate intervened, and Mrs. Madison never saw the cheese. The British cabinet decision came shortly after the assassination of the adamantly anti-American prime minister, Perceval, and perhaps that tragedy had more to do with a changed political attitude than the protest from business leaders. Perceval's negative stance had long been an obstacle to any relaxation of the tough policy imposed by the Royal Navy on neutral shipping.

These internal events in Britain could not have been foreseen in the United States. Nothing had been done hurriedly, Madison could assure critics. The pace of life and diplomacy, after all, was dependent upon unpredictable wind and sail for news from abroad. Dispatch ship after dispatch ship had returned from Europe with no genuine news of change, and thus Madison saw no reason to delay war after the *Hornet* came home empty-handed in early April 1812. Fifteen years after the fighting had started in earnest, Madison was still inclined to think the Castlereagh letter had been the last straw. In fact, however, the straws had been accumulating for so long, and the patience of Congress was so exhausted, that the unfortunate letter to Sir Augustus Foster was almost irrelevant.

Americans, as their congressmen discerned, were sick and tired of being treated like colonials. Everywhere except in New England, citizens apparently thought they had reached the point where a test of arms was necessary to establish American independence without any ifs, ands, or buts. Curiously, New England men had been the ones impressed by the Royal Navy, and New England ships were the ones towed into British ports as prizes of war. Yet the public men of these northeastern states found excuses to justify British depredations. Ultimately, it was the way the rest of the country perceived these insults that seemed to matter.

For his part, Madison wanted to believe that the United States had been forced into the war by British arrogance and cupidity. The House took his message, sent it to its foreign relations committee, and took its time about

2. Bradford Perkins, *Prologue to War: England and the United Sates, 1805*–1812 (Berkeley: University of California Press, 1968), 337–38.

declaring war. In the committee report, Calhoun sounded the battle cry with his statement of the war aims of the United States. The current generation of Americans, the report vowed, would show "the World, that we have not only inherited that liberty which our Fathers gave us, but also the will and power to maintain it."[3]

The earlier vote on the embargo had been a tip-off of the troubles ahead, for not only had the New England Republicans lost the state election of 1812, but Senators Giles and Smith had opposed this last step before out-right war. That measure carried the Senate, 20 to 13, but the vote was close enough to worry Madison. The president told Jefferson that some senators wanted an embargo as a way of preventing war, whereas others hoped merely to postpone a war and to allow time for Americans to bring their ships home. Madison saw the embargo as a signal to the world that war was at hand. In its original form, the embargo was limited to sixty days. "Its ex-tension to 90," Madison wrote Jefferson, "proceeded from the united votes of those who wished to make it a negociating instead of a war measure, of those who wished to put off the day of war as long as possible."[4]

The mood of a restless Congress, before Madison sent his war message, had favored adjournment. Sensing what was in the wind, John Randolph de-cided once again to lecture the Madison administration on the real condition of the country. "I know that we are on the brink of some dreadful scourge," Randolph said. Words of doom rolled from Randolph's tongue: "Go to war without money, without men, without a navy! Go to war when we have not the courage, while your lips utter war, to lay war taxes! When your whole courage is exhibited in passing Resolutions!"[5] So far as we know, humor was not part of Randolph's personality, but he may have been amused by the Re-publicans' confusion. Party unity had all but disappeared during Jefferson's last year in office; now the idea of a long-overdue war, rather than party loyalty, made the War Hawks eager to vote. As the Clays, Johnsons, and Grundys rallied around the war banner, the staunchest Republican in Madi-son's cabinet, Gallatin, was given to second thoughts toward an immediate declaration of war against Britain. Gallatin's natural conservatism made him doubt the wisdom of a struggle with that world colossus. And "probably four

3. Quoted in Merrill Peterson, *The Great Triumvirate: Webster, Clay, and Calhoun* (New York: Oxford University Press, 1987), 4.

4. Madison to Jefferson, 24 April 1812, Madison Papers, Library of Congress (hereafter cited as DLC).

5. Quoted in Henry Adams, *History of the United States of America dur-ing the Administrations of Thomas Jefferson and James Madison*, vol. 2, *History of the United States of America during the Administrations of James Madison*, Earl N. Harbert, ed. (New York: Library of America, 1986), 440 (hereafter cited as Adams, *History*).

fifths of the American people," historian Henry Adams noted, "held the same opinion."[6]

As a matter of fact, the public was ignorant of the fight inside Congress. Both the House and Senate met in executive sessions, their doors closed to all visitors, including newspaper reporters. House Federalists tried to "go public" with a resolution calling for open doors, but when their proposal lost by a thirty-vote margin they retreated into surly silence. While Federalists in the Senate maneuvered for Madison's embarrassment, if not his defeat on the crucial question, the leading newspaper in Washington simply told readers that an important matter was before Congress and then added to the speculation by printing copies of recent diplomatic correspondence from London.

Still working behind closed doors, the House on 4 June passed the bill declaring war on Britain, 79 to 49, and sent it to the Senate. Washington society was abuzz with excitement, but officially a grand pantomime was being enacted on the capital stage. On 6 June the *National Intelligencer* gave the public a cryptic paragraph that concluded, "Report says that some measure of a decisive character has passed the House, and has been sent to the Senate for concurrence." Federalist Abijah Bigelow leaked nothing to the newspapers but told his wife, "Madness, rage and folly are the order of the day."[7] He added: "The taxes will not be laid this session, war or no war, because it might endanger Madison's reelection."

The public might have been in the dark, but the British minister knew as much about the debates as the president. When Senator Andrew Gregg of Pennsylvania proposed allowing American ships to arm and issue letters of marque and reprisal, the measure was seen as an alternative to all-out war, but it failed by only a tie vote. Senator Leib in a desperate move called the question up again, adding a proviso that the armed ships might fire at French as well as British vessels if Napoleon's withdrawal of his decrees proved to be more French mendacity.[8] Not until 18 June did the Senate finally pass the House war bill, 19 to 13. Senators Leib, Giles, and Smith made the difference — otherwise, an embarrassing tie vote was in prospect! The official word was still not out, but Sir Augustus Foster learned how close the vote had been and he was willing to go along with the mystery. Madison immediately signed the war measure. That same evening Foster went to the White House, nonchalantly moving about until he wandered over "to Mrs. Madi-

6. Quoted in ibid., 449.
7. *National Intelligencer,* 6 June 1812; "Letters of Abijah Bigelow, Member of Congress, to His Wife, 1810–1815," American Antiquarian Society *Proceedings* 40 (1930): 339.
8. Perkins, *Prologue to War,* 414.

son's drawing room where I found them all shaking hands with one another, but the President was white as a sheet."[9]

Newspapers in 1812 were not sold on Washington streets and did not carry headlines related to vital topics of the day; thus not until 20 June could the *National Intelligencer* note, "The veil is at length removed from the Secret Proceedings of Congress." The United States was at war with Britain! In an adjoining column appeared Madison's presidential proclamation to prove it. The next day, wrote Richard Rush in his diary, Madison bestirred himself: "He visited in person — a thing never known before — all the offices of the departments of war and the navy, stimulating everything in a manner worthy of a little commander-in-chief, with his little round hat and huge cockade."[10] The United States was at war, yet the casualness of the constitutional declarative process, the public stillness, and the sudden revelation of the state of war all seem in retrospect to be actions taken in slow-motion cinematography.

Yet the events of 1812 were clearer to spectators. "The long forbearance of our government," a North Carolina congressman told constituents, "which has been imputed to a want of energy in our councils . . . will now be attributed to its true cause, a love of justice, and a sincere desire to cultivate peace. A trial is now to be made [of] how far a free government is capable of its own preservation. On the issue of this interesting experiment rests the fate of the only free republic on earth." Virginia Representative Hugh Nelson told voters that the war had been forced on the United States by two powers — Britain and France — both aiming "at universal domination." A clash with Britain could not be avoided without sacrificing "national honor, character, and independence."[11]

But Federalist Samuel Taggart thought the secrecy in Congress allowed a bad bill to sweep through without the opposition that would have formed naturally had the proceedings been made public. "A majority in Congress has been mad enough to vote a declaration of war," the New England congressman observed, but had the matter "been debated openly and fairly, the discussion probably would have been a long one and so many petitions would have come in from all quarters [of the nation], that they would not have dared to proceed."[12] When the bill became law, Taggart simply looked to the

9. Sir Augustus John Foster, *Jeffersonian America: Notes on the United States of America, Collected in the Years 1805-6-7 and 11-12*, Richard B. Davis, ed. (Westport, Conn.: Greenwood Press, 1980), 100.

10. *National Intelligencer*, 20 June 1812; Richard Rush to his father, 20 June 1812 (quoted in Adams, *History*, 229).

11. Noble E. Cunningham, Jr., ed., *Circular Letters of Congressmen to Their Constituents*, 3 vols. (Chapel Hill: University of North Carolina Press, 1978), 2:793-95.

12. Taggart to Rev. John Taylor, 5 June 1812, in George H. Haynes, ed., "The

heavens with resignation, declaring that his colleagues who had voted for war "were deprived of all that share of common sense which God had originally given in the manner in which it is like[ly] to be conducted."

Sour-faced Taggart was right. Congress was better at declaring a war than at running one. The war thus launched was to end after thirty months of frustration, humiliation, and a series of military miscues that only a strong nation could survive. Eighty years later another New England man, Henry Adams, believed that Madison had picked the wrong time and the wrong enemy. Reviewing the events of early 1812, Adams said that the reasons given for fighting Britain "were weaker than they had been in June, 1808, or in January, 1809. . . . In 1807 England would have welcomed a war with the United States; in 1812 she wanted peace."[13] All of these judgments came seven decades after Madison signed the war bill into law. Hindsight has never prevented a war; nor has it won a peace.

By the time news of the repealed Orders in Council reached the United States, it was too late to call off the war. British businessmen had achieved what American diplomacy could not — forced the British cabinet into submission. The door was not slammed with finality, however; for Madison sent instructions to London via a diplomatic courier, offering "the termination of the war by an armistice." The president's conditions were that Britain must agree to stop impressment, to release American seamen already captured, to pay the indemnity for seized American vessels converted to Royal Navy ships, and to give up its "paper blockades" of European ports authorized by the Orders in Council. Assured on these matters, Madison might have suspended hostilities until a treaty could have settled the outstanding grievances. On 24 August the American envoy in London sent the terms to the British cabinet, and five days later the answer came back a firm "no." The cabinet refused to consider suspension of impressment, "a right upon which the naval strength of the empire mainly depends."[14] (Curiously, Madison was simultaneously rejecting a British offer tendered in upstate New York.) The war in Europe — and crushing Napoleon — dominated the British ministers' perspective. If the American upstarts insisted on a war, so be it.

Letters of Samuel Taggart," American Antiquarian Society *Proceedings* 33 (1923): 402 (hereafter cited as "Taggart Letters").

13. Adams, *History*, 449.

14. Lord Castlereagh to Jonathan Russell, 29 August 1812, in *American State Papers: Documents, Legislative and Executive*, 38 vols. [Foreign Relations] (Washington, D.C.: Gales & Seaton, 1832–1861), 3:589–90.

The temptation to treat the War of 1812 as a "bad dream" episode of the Madison presidency is strong. American historians have made it fashionable to detest all wars in one generation and then to assure one another that some wars had to be fought. They have had it both ways with the War of 1812. Another negative factor was Madison's personality. The chief executive was the kind of man who jumped when a gun went off, and to him war was not blood and gore but an abstract power struggle conducted with Grotius's *De jure belli et pacis* for a rule book.

Never for a moment did Madison forget that the Atlantic moat would keep the war to a modest size, sans large troop movements on a Napoleonic scale. Not for Madison was the vision of a war with heavy casualties, raping, looting, and an army of widows after peace returned. It is perhaps worth remembering that on the day Napoleon's army crushed the Austrians at Wagram, at a cost of eighty thousand casualties, Madison was vacationing at Montpelier and may have been swatting flies on his back porch. In Madison's mind the war with Britain would be fought on American terms with more diplomacy than marching, with more talking than shooting, and ultimately—and this was the whole point—with the British backing down. Madison wanted no British territory, no reparations, no humble surrender. His war aims were limited. All he desired was an admission by British leaders that the United States was not a second-cousin dependent but an honest-to-God sovereign power in the world family of nations.

As the first president in American history to conduct a war, Madison had to feel his way into the constitutional provision that made him the commander in chief. Madison knew that the whole point was to keep the reins of government in civilian hands, and he had no problem asserting his role as the ultimate decision maker. Beyond that, however, Madison fell into a trap that would ensnare other chief executives before the century ended. Madison, Polk, Lincoln, and McKinley listened to armchair generals who speculated that the war that had just begun would be of brief duration. Only once were they right. In the first instance, with Madison at the helm as commander in chief, they were dead wrong.

Congressional wisdom was part of the problem. Ruled by passion rather than reason, the War Hawks looked on the war as a combined picnic and international shooting match. During the debates over declaring war, Representative John C. Calhoun spoke for his generation when he said that the war would start with a cakewalk into Canada. "I believe that in four weeks from the time a declaration of war is heard on our frontier, the whole of Upper Canada and a part of Lower Canada will be in our power," the South Carolinian assured the House.[15] Similar boasts on Capitol Hill may have in-

15. Quoted in T. Harry Williams, *The History of American Wars from 1745 to 1918* (Baton Rouge: Louisiana State University Press, 1981), 98. For the military

fluenced Madison's cabinet, but given that the army and the navy would be fighting the war, Madison turned to his senior army officers and beheld an aged, inexperienced, and somewhat bewildered band of has-beens and would-bes.

Nobody expected the nation's first wartime president to mount a white charger and take to the field. Besides the constitutional fact there was the matter of Madison's physique, for he was far better fitted for an armchair than a saddle. His temperament was no more warlike than his frame. Thus Madison, in conducting a war of nearly twenty months' duration, had to look to his generals and naval officers for guidance. The biggest decisions would be his, but for tactics and strategy Madison had to rely upon his senior commanders.

What the public did not know—and Madison also appears not to have been aware of it—was the extreme partisanship that permeated the United States Army from top to bottom. Captain Winfield Scott, a Virginian by birth and a Republican by choice, would recall that in 1812 the older officers drank too much and the younger ones were loyal Republicans without military merit: "Party spirit of that day knew no bounds, and, of course, was blind to policy. Federalists were almost entirely excluded from selection [military service], though great numbers were eager for the field, and in New England and some other States, there were but very few educated Republicans. Hence the selections from those communities consisted mostly of coarse and ignorant men."[16] If Scott's memory is close to accurate, the patronage-minded Republicans in the army and navy passed over bright applicants for commissions and instead chose "swaggerers, dependants, decayed gentlemen, and others 'fit for nothing else,'" party hacks who "always turned out" to be the castoffs of society, "utterly unfit for any military purpose whatever."

Scott's description probably best fitted the general with the most seniority: Henry Dearborn. Major General Dearborn, sixty-one years old in 1812, had served in the Revolution but had spent the intervening decades waist deep in politics. Dearborn knew how to win elections but not battles, and he had no conception of overall grand strategy. Neither did his colleague, sixty-three-year-old Major General Thomas Pinckney, another Revolutionary War veteran with impeccable political credentials. Of the nine brigadier generals, James Wilkinson, whose reputation was still under a cloud, was senior in rank. These officers commanded an army of fewer than seven thou-

phase of the War of 1812, I have (in most cases) replied on this survey, particularly Chapters 5 and 6; on Harry L. Coles, *The War of 1812* (Chicago: University of Chicago Press, 1965); and on John K. Mahon, *The War of 1812* (Gainesville: University Presses of FLorida, 1972).
16. Winfield Scott, *Memoirs*, 2 vols. (New York: Sheldon & Company, 1864), 1:35.

sand regulars, more than half of whom were little more than raw recruits. A cadre of noncommissioned officers, so vital for the expansion required by war, was needed to train the volunteer army authorized by Congress; but no thought had been given to organizing a veteran corps that could prepare recruits for the rigors of battle.

Although a decade had passed since the instruction of army cadets in military engineering began at West Point, fewer than one hundred officers had been trained at the military academy by 1812. This paucity of trained young officers, Winfield Scott recalled, allowed a surplus of "imbeciles and ignoramuses" to serve as junior officers. The pity, Scott said, was that West Point had not turned out more officers, "for a booby sent thither, say at the age of 16, 17, or even 19 — and there were many such in every new batch — is, in his term of four years, duly manipulated, and, in most cases, polished, pointed, and sent to his regiment with a head upon his shoulders; whereas, if a booby be at once made a commissioned officer, the odds are great that he will live and die a booby."[17] Shielded from such candor, Madison signed all the commissions placed on his desk. Surely the president knew that the chief test of qualifications usually ended with the knowledge that the commission seeker was either a Republican or Federalist. William Eustis and his clerks had no intention of strewing favors among men who were critical of the Republican party or its titular head.

Rigid Republican doctrine, apart from party loyalty, also harmed the war effort. Republican views concerning the use of the state militia proved to be a genuine albatross. In 1798 Republicans had argued that the Constitution limited the use of the militia (today's National Guard) to executing federal laws within its borders, suppressing insurrections, and repelling invasions. Could the president call on the militia to invade Canada or the Floridas? No, said doctrinaire Republicans and Federalists alike, and no bill passed by Congress in the months before Madison's war message gave the president any power to order state-supported units for service beyond American borders. Thus the clear message was that only regular troops and volunteers could be sent across the Canadian border.

To make matters worse, Congress set its own time limit on the process by passing legislation that included one-year enlistments, and Madison went along with the short term. In the name of expediency, Madison said, an adequate force could "be obtained in a short time, and be sufficient to reduce Canada from Montreal upward." The success of American arms would buy time for a while, then a "durable force . . . would be able to extend as well as secure our conquests."[18]

17. Ibid., 35–36.

18. Madison to Gallatin, 8 May 1812, Gallatin Papers, New York Historical Society.

Madison was as beguiled as the War Hawks and the paunchy generals into believing that the British forces in Canada would be pushovers. In fact, the 6,000 regular British troops stationed in Canada when the war started were the equal of the attenuated American army, and the redcoats were reinforced by 2,100 Canadian auxiliaries and perhaps 3,000 Indian allies ready to pick up the war hatchet. The president did not know the extent of the British forces, of course, for the War Department had no intelligence information beyond vague rumors drifting across the Canadian border. Not only were the generals also ignorant of these facts, but even though they had listened for years to talk about an invasion of Canada, they had never concocted a strategic plan or mobilization orders.

Everybody agreed, however, that the conquest of Canada was to be the first order of business. How could an inexperienced civilian and aged veterans of a war fought thirty years ago plan a war of conquest? The ultimate decision, reached about the time Congress adjourned on 6 July, was made by Madison in consultation with Eustis and Dearborn. Listening to his military experts, Madison approved their recommendation that three American armies carry out the task. One column would move from Lake Champlain toward Montreal, another would strike along the Niagara River, and a third, western force would march from Fort Detroit across Upper Canada (the region south of the Ottawa River). Resistance would be swept away in a drive across Upper Canada, Montreal would fall, Quebec would surrender, and the Canadian invasion would end in an American triumph, thus forcing the British to make concessions.

Madison appears to have thought that a single "rapier thrust" at Montreal would have been enough, for with Montreal in American hands the Great Lakes stations would have been cut off and Upper Canada left helpless. Rumblings of dissent in New England jeopardized this scheme and Madison abandoned it, for troops from the northern border states had to cooperate in such a plan to make it effective. The real enthusiasm for the war was in the South and West, hence the three-pronged strategy made more sense. Much depended on coordination between the three invading American armies, but Dearborn shirked from overall command, and Eustis had no stomach for great responsibilities either. In some vague way, General William Hull in the West, Dearborn in the East, and a joint-command force in the middle would converge on Montreal and bring Canada to its knees.

With inland Montreal and Quebec as the main targets, there seemed to be no need to involve the secretary of the navy in any strategic planning. Initially, Secretary of the Navy Paul Hamilton told the president that the best thing to do was to acknowledge British superiority and order the American vessels into drydock. Madison and his other cabinet members rejected this plan and instead Hamilton was urged to issue orders for American ships to avoid confrontation with the Royal Navy, dart in and out of safe harbors to harass British merchantmen, and afford at least token coastal defenses when possible. In fact, there was little more the American navy could accomplish. To match the eighty-odd Royal Navy ships working out of the American stations at Halifax and in the West Indies the Americans had fewer than a dozen seaworthy vessels, hundreds of useless gunboats inherited from the Jefferson administration, and a civilian-led Navy Department. There were no admirals and no fleet to command. The two navies were on equal footing in only one respect—they both depended on winds for movement. And as Captain Alfred Mahan noted, "The supply, if fickle at times, was practically inexhaustible."[19]

The War Hawks' fixation with the conquest of Canada by land had led to a deliberate policy of avoiding a naval buildup. "The partisans of England here have endeavored much to goad us into the folly of choosing the ocean instead of the land, for the theatre of war," Jefferson told General Thaddeus Kosciusko in June 1812. "That would be to meet their strength with our weakness, instead of their weakness with our strength. I hope we shall confine ourselves to the conquest of their possessions, and defence of our harbors, leaving the war on the ocean to our privateers." When it came to wartime commerce, Jefferson was for leaving that up to private American enterprise. Legalized privateers, he predicted, would "swarm in every seat, and do more injury to British commerce than the regular fleets of all Europe."[20] In all the wild talk about conquering Canada, not enough attention had been paid to the Great Lakes, where the British ensign flew on the masts of a small but respectable collection of armed vessels. Ship for ship, the Americans were outnumbered there, eleven to two.

Bad as the situation was, however, the American navy did have a few assets in its younger officers. Thirty-nine-year-old Commodore John Rodgers favored making the most of the small American force by sending out squadrons to raid British shipping. With only three frigates available—the *Constitution*, the *United States*, and the *President*—the strategy might have worked. But after Rodgers chased a British convoy across the Atlantic, only to lose it, the idea of sending out squadrons was abandoned for a makeshift, single-ship strategy. Through the remainder of the war, the well-armed American frigates proved superior to the enemy in armament and gunnery, but after some initial successes they were restricted by the shifting of British vessels to American waters until the odds were too lopsided.

19. Mahon, *War of 1812*, 38–39; Alfred T. Mahan, *Sea Power in Its Relation to the War of 1812*, 2 vols. (Boston: Little, Brown & Company, 1905), 1:284.

20. Jefferson to Kosciusko, 28 June 1812, in P. L. Ford, ed., *Works of Jefferson*, 12 vols. (New York: G. P. Putnam's Sons, 1905), 11:259.

As the Royal Navy had become the acknowledged master of the high seas after the Battle of Trafalgar, Americans looked inland for that quick opportunity which would deal the enemy a knockout blow. Perhaps the hysteria that led Madison and the country into a Canadian invasion with patchwork planning and poorer execution was the result of a long-standing policy fomented by the president himself. Historian J. C. A. Stagg saw the Canadian debacle as the outcome of Madison's failed policies of economic coercion in Anglo-American relations going back to 1783: "Madison's decision to wage war for Canada was not basically inconsistent with the diplomacy of peaceful commercial restriction he had advocated prior to 1812."[21] In this context, the long-frustrated Madison hoped that the capture of Canada would deprive the British of vital raw materials and force John Bull to the negotiating table. The flaw in this argument is its assumption that Madison had a strong hand on the tiller when he began steering the nation into war in the summer of 1812. Madison's ignorance of military strategy, his total dependence on generals who had not heard a shot fired in anger for over a generation, and his willingness to go along with public opinion rather than to shape it all suggest that Madison had no firm policy that made war inevitable. Instead, Madison fell into a trap shaped by British inflexibility, pressures from public opinion, and his own gullibility.

The president also listened to a great deal of advice, most of it bad. Jefferson, who should have known better, told Madison that a successful prosecution of the war depended on only two factors: "1. To stop Indian barbarities. The conquest of Canada will do this. 2. To furnish markets to our products." To reinforce his argument, Jefferson told Madison that a host of volunteers had already rallied to the colors in Virgina and that "they all declare a preference of a march to Canada." Jefferson surmised to another friend that "the acquisition of Canada this year, as far as the neighborhood of Quebec, will be a mere matter of marching."[22] Madison was only human so he must have given credence to such irresponsible talk. Who could doubt that an invasion of Canada was Providence's answer to American prayers?

Thus Madison, unlike President Polk, had no grasp of the military situation as the war clouds rolled up the Potomac. Instead, the president relied on his cabinet for guidance of a war he had earnestly tried to avoid. Madison took the advice of Secretary of War Eustis and General Dearborn and approved their plan for the conquest of British North America. The early

21. J. C. A. Stagg, *Mr. Madison's War: Politics, Diplomacy, and Warfare in the Early American Republic, 1783–1830* (Princeton, N.J.: Princeton University Press, 1983), 6–7.

22. Jefferson to Madison, 29 June 1812, and Jefferson to William Duane, 4 August 1812, in Ford, *Works of Jefferson*, 11:262, 265.

strategy of a three-pronged thrust into Canada was based on the uninformed belief that British resistance might be little more than token. No timetable existed, which meant that the three efforts would be launched in helter-skelter fashion. Not the best way to start a war.

General William Hull, commandant of a large garrison at Fort Detroit, had some idea of what the overall plan was, for he had been in Washington early in the spring of 1812. Hull was en route to Detroit with nearly two thousand militiamen and regular troops when he learned on 1 July that war had been declared. Hull then received orders from Washington to march into Canada, seize Fort Malden, and head east. Hull feared that the enemy was formidable, but in fact only a few hundred British regulars were then on duty at Fort Malden. Nevertheless, after crossing into Upper Canada, Hull procrastinated until reinforcements reached the still outnumbered British. While Madison confidently assumed that a large American force in the Michigan Territory was poised to sweep across Upper Canada, Hull allowed a smaller British-Canadian force to trap him. Hull never gave his troops the order to fire, and he panicked when a British shell exploded in the officers' mess hall. To climax a series of decisions, the Revolutionary hero was humiliated into surrendering his forces and control of the entire region between Detroit and Fort Dearborn (Chicago). Hull's decision on 16 August to send a white flag was a low point in the war, but to call the consequence "the greatest loss of territory that ever before or since befell the United States," as Henry Adams did, is a great overstatement.[23] The land was sparsely settled, and if the British now had a free hand in the Old Northwest it was only temporary.

Hull's surrender still rankled Madison a decade after he left the White House. Disappointment is too mild a word to use in expressing Madison's reaction to the old man's humiliation. "He had acquired during the Revolutionary War the reputation of a brave & valuable officer," Madison recalled. "He was of course an experienced one" and had long dealt with the Indians and the terrain around Detroit. (Hull had also served as superintendent of Indian affairs in the region.)

> With such qualifications and advantages which seemed to give him a claim above all others to the station assigned to him, he sunk before obstacles at which not an officer near him would have paused, and threw away an entire army, in the moment of entering a career which would have made the war as prosperous in its early stages . . . as it was rendered by that disaster, oppressive to our resources, and flattering to the hopes of the Enemy. By the surrender of Gen. Hull, the people of Canada, not indisposed

23. Adams, *History,* 528.

to favour us, were turned against us; the Indians were thrown in to the service of the Enemy . . . and a general damp spread over the face of our Affairs.[24]

Madison's scenario of a Hull victory portrayed a different ending. "A triumphant army would have seized on Upper Canada," Madison asserted, and Lake Erie would have become an American pond. "The Indians would have been neutral or submissive to our will," enlistments would have soared in the enthusiasm generated by triumph, and, perhaps most important, "the intrigues of the disaffected would have been smothered in their embrio [sic] State." In 1812, however, none of this happened. In time poor Hull was released by his captors and came home to face a court-martial that found him guilty of cowardice and negligence. He was sentenced in 1814 to face a firing squad, but Madison had no wish to humiliate the old man further, and he pardoned Hull. Meanwhile General Henry Dearborn had also managed to botch up his part of a planned second invasion of Canada, aimed at the capture of Montreal.

Amid political infighting, Dearborn had divided the command of forces assembled to cross into Canadian territory opposite Fort Niagara, assigning forces to a joint command (involving Generals Stephen Van Rensselaer and Alexander Smyth) where nobody was in charge. Van Rensselaer was a New Yorker, Smyth a Virginian. Dearborn apparently was trying to please everybody and at the same time protect his own reputation because the base of operations was in New York State and he was an outsider. In truth, however, New Yorkers seemed indifferent to the war on their doorstep, judging from the lag in enlistments. "What is to be done with respect to the expedition agst. Montreal?" Madison complained. "The enlistments for the regular army fall short of the most moderate calculation. . . . The volunteer act is extremely unproductive. And even the Militia detachments are either obstructed by the disaffected Governors, or, chilled by the federal spirit diffused throughout the region most convenient to the Theatre."[25]

Politics in time of war astounded the president. How could Federalist governors drag their feet when the success of the quick-campaign strategy depended on supplementary troops from the state militias? Madison also saw the flaw in a divided command, but did not move fast enough to remedy it. A host of "guardhouse lawyers" insisting that the militia did not have to fight outside the continental United States now appeared in the militia encampments, making the use of militia a questionable endeavor. The situa-

24. Madison to Henry Wharton, 26 February 1827, Madison Papers, DLC.

25. Madison to Gallatin, 8 August 1812, Gallatin Papers, New York Historical Society.

tion worsened when New York militia troops, claiming that they were a defense force not obligated to fight on foreign soil, held back. General Van Rensselaer, goaded by political considerations, asked Smyth to wheel his forces in line and join in an assault on the Canadian defenses. Smyth refused.

To his credit, Van Rensselaer thought a soldier's duty was to fight; so he finally ordered an attack on the Niagara peninsula. Most of the New York militia stayed in camp, forcing volunteers and regulars to bear the brunt of an American attack on Queenstown Heights. The initial American thrust succeeded, but the tide turned when reinforcements were lacking, even though the British lost General Isaac Brock in the fierce combat. Caught in a deadly cross fire, nearly thirteen hundred Americans began retreating to a beachhead. Late in the day about nine hundred Americans, cut off from supplies and denied additional firepower, surrendered. Winfield Scott was among the prisoners, and he had some choice words to describe the New York militia. "These vermin, who infest all republics, boastful enough at home, [but] no sooner found themselves in sight of the enemy than they discovered that the militia of the United States could not be constitutionally marched into a foreign country."[26] Fed up with militia punctilios and the strutting General Smyth, Van Rensselaer resigned.

Some of the gloom created by embarrassing reports from the battle fronts on land was scattered on 30 August 1812 by the triumphant return to Boston harbor of another Hull — Captain Isaac Hull — aboard the *Constitution*. A local Republican, Dr. Nathaniel Ames, smarting under the Boston town meeting call for a state convention to resist the war effort, recorded the unexpected victory in his diary:

> *Constitution* returned from glorious cruise. . . . Isaac Hull, Captain, arrived at Boston from short cruise, having taken sundry British prizes and took and sunk the *Guerriere*, Captain Dacres, after short conflict in which she was cut and mangled most effectually by our guns — just chastisement for the bragging Dacres that he wished to engage not one but two Yankee frigates of his own force, both at once, but found more than his match in one of inferior force! His was 28, ours 44 guns!

Ames's joy was short-lived, however, for two days later he and all New England learned of William Hull's capitulation.[27] "Having 2,500 men," Ames recorded, "he surrendered to the British general Brock with only 1,800 men, Indians and all, without firing a gun."

26. Scott, *Memoirs*, 1:63.
27. Charles Warren, ed., *Jacobin and Junto: In Early American Politics as Viewed in the Diary of Nathaniel Ames, 1758–1822* (Cambridge, Mass.: Harvard University Press, 1931), 256.

The *Constitution's* feat was for the president like a cool drink of water at a desert outpost. There was so much bad news, and so little to brag about! Madison was baffled by the disappointing news from the New York front, which came while the Washington know-it-alls were still reeling from the Detroit fiasco. Like kingpins, the American generals were being toppled by supposedly inferior forces. In the latest sad episode another trusted general had been humiliated, another had resigned, and still another sulked in his tent. Dearborn, placing his own reputation above all other considerations, disclaimed responsibility for the New York disaster. And even though Smyth was now in charge, he ultimately made a bad situation worse. A southerner and dyed-in-the-wool Republican who knew little of the New York–Ontario borderlands and less about its parade-ground politics, Smyth's insulting remarks about the New York militia's lack of courage alienated the troops he needed for an effective command.

Madison needed no geography lessons to tell him how the Detroit and Queenstown losses had harmed the American cause. Hard on those disasters came reports from the key fur-trading post at Fort Mackinac, in the straits that joined Lakes Huron, Erie, and Superior. A tiny American force had been overwhelmed by the British. Here was another signal to the northwestern Indian tribes that the redcoated warriors were in command of the disputed territory. This setback, coupled with Hull's fiasco, made Madison more attentive to the visiting Indian delegations than was usually the case. Chieftains from the Sauk, Fox, Osage, and other tribes living along the Missouri River joined lesser chiefs from the Sioux tribes on the upper plains to formally call upon the Great White Father. The Indian visitors pitched their tents at Greenleaf's Point near Washington and wondered at the Potomac River traffic moving by their makeshift village.

When the colorfully clad chieftains called at the White House, Madison took pains to explain the war with Britain. The quarrel now engulfed "the 18 fires," pitting these eighteen united states against their old enemy, "the British King." George III had sent out agents from Canada, Madison told the grave-faced Indians, to foment strife by carrying

> bloody belts . . . to drop among the red people, who would otherwise remain at peace. . . . The British, who are weak, are doing all they can by their bad birds, to decoy the red people into a war on their side. I warn all the red people to avoid the ruin this must bring on them. . . . Your father does not ask you to join his warriors. Sit still on your seats: and be witnesses that they [the Americans] are able to beat their enemies and protect their red friends. This is the fatherly advice I give you.[28]

28. Merrill D. Peterson, eds., *James Madison: A Biography in His Own Words*, 2 vols. (New York: Newsweek Books, 1974), 2:328.

In a sense, Madison was smoking the peace pipe with the wrong crowd. The tribes across the Mississippi were too remote to become involved in this white man's war, but the southern Indians, the Creeks in particular, needed to be impressed by American prowess. In time, a Creek faction known as the Red Sticks broke with their older chiefs, who were inclined to side with the Americans. When the Red Sticks rose up as allies of the British to challenge the Americans, Madison learned that he actually did have a reliable general who could handle a crisis: Andrew Jackson. Clearly Jackson was not from the same character mold as William Hull.

Remote from the scenes of battle, Madison listened for any encouraging news. Instead, the papers flowing over his desk during the late summer and autumn of 1812 told of disgrace, dissension, and failure on the Canadian front. By Thanksgiving 1812 there was not much to be thankful for at the White House table. The three-pronged attack on Canada had turned into a nightmare, for after some hemming and hawing General Smyth called off the invasion aimed at Montreal and left the Canadian frontier guarded by only a token force. To save face, Smyth fought a duel to fend off charges of personal cowardice; shots rang out, but nobody was hurt. As winter approached, dreams of a quick, easy, and triumphant march into the British provinces vanished.[29] Mocking editorials in the Federalist newspapers printed in the shadow of Faneuil Hall made it clear that some Americans were not sorry.

Newspaper barbs against the Madison administration aside, the hostility of New England governors toward federal calls for militia showed Madison that one section of the country was still out of step. Perhaps if the Canadian invasion had proceeded smoothly, the resistance from Federalists might have crumbled before the force of public opinion. But letters home from disgruntled militiamen who complained of bad food, no shoes, and inept commanders seemed to reinforce local politicians' charges that the conflict was a Republican war but a Federalist fight. There was for the time no southern theater of action, so the burden of war remained at the Canadian-American border. As the effects of the abortive 1812 campaign sank in, New England continued to drag its feet, its leaders almost exulting in the Madison administration's embarrassment.

The apathy and constant hostility of New England baffled Madison, who was a Union man to the core. Four years earlier, the New England smugglers' defiance of the embargo had also mystified him. To Madison, e pluribus unum was more than a motto—it was the guidon of his political career. In amazement the president learned that the Massachusetts House of Representatives had passed a resolution urging citizens to resist the war effort, and

29. Stagg, *Mr. Madison's War*, 246–51.

the governor set aside a day of fasting and prayer to ask Divine Providence to protect the people from "entangling and fatal alliances with foreign powers," leaving little doubt that France was the nation to be avoided. A Boston town meeting in August 1812 condemned the war and Governor Strong denied Madison's request for militia to aid in the march toward Canada. The governors of Connecticut and Vermont were similarly unresponsive or openly hostile, and Nicholas Gilman of New Hampshire was only coolly cooperative.

Despite the legal hairsplitting of the New England governors that kept their state militia units at home, there is another side to the story worth telling, and one that President Madison must have known. As historian Harry Coles reminds us, "The number of recruits furnished the regular army [by volunteers from] Massachusetts was second only to New York."[30] Eager Yankee farm boys and store clerks who joined the Massachusetts Ninth and several other New England volunteer regiments fought with valor at Lundy's Lane, Fort Erie, and other pitched battles on the Canadian border.

Madison was disheartened by these events even before he knew of the tragedy at Fort Detroit. Perhaps in his frustration he overreacted when the British made one last effort to halt the war. Convinced that the repeal of the Orders in Council made continuing the war farcical, the British dispatched orders to Canada to seek a truce that might produce, after negotiations, a permanent cessation of hostilities. General George Prevost sent an officer under a flag of truce to meet Dearborn near Albany on 8 August. Ill and unsure of himself, Dearborn issued orders for a truce and sent an express rider to carry the news to Washington for Madison's decision.

Although Madison's own inquiries for potential peace were already en route to Britain, he was in a bad mood when the message from Dearborn arrived. Smarting from the defiance encountered in New England and mystified by the failure of the British to mention the impressment issue, Madison shot back a quick reply: no deal. On the day Dearborn had held his parley with the British truce team, Madison had urged Dearborn to move on to Montreal. "The expedition agst. Montreal should be forwarded by all the means in your power," Madison had pleaded. But Madison was discouraged, and he told Jefferson a week later that "the seditious opposition in Mass. & Cont. with the intrigues elsewhere insidiously co-operating with it, have so clogged the wheels of war, that I fear the campaign will not accomplish the object of it."[31]

In London, rumors of a disaffected New England brought a prompt re-

---

30. Coles, *War of 1812*, 241.

31. Adams, *History*, 574; Mahon, *War of 1812*, 51; Madison to Dearborn, 9 August 1812, in Hunt, *Writings of Madison*, 8:206; Madison to Jefferson, 17 August 1812, Madison Papers, DLC.

sponse. British policy encouraged a loosening of the bonds of loyalty by exempting the region from the Royal Navy's coastal blockade. After the truce negotiations collapsed, the king's fleet threw down an iron net from Narragansett Bay south along the coast to Georgia, but gave American ships free access to the sea lanes from Newport northward. There was more than a hint of insult in the whole business as in Boston's parlors East Indian tea was poured into English bone china cups, both the tea and the cups having been recently shipped from Liverpool. Defiant High Federalists delighted in this trade with the enemy, for they regarded Madison as a detestable creature who deserved no allegiance. Was he not the puppet of that madman Napoleon? Chagrined by these developments, the old patriot and former president living at Quincy, Massachusetts, was almost as amazed as Madison. John Adams urged a turnaround of attitude so "that this disaffected Part of the Nation may be gradually reconciled to a cordial Participation in this righteous and indispensable War."[32] Adams's plaintive call had few echoes in New England.

Federalists who charged that the war was only an election-year trick to reelect Madison suffered more disappointment when the votes were counted. The fall election returns finally put the quietus on DeWitt Clinton's presidential aspiration, but the Federalists' "peace party" rolled up immense leads in areas of New England that had once been nominally Republican. No one saw through young Clinton's obstinacy and ambition more clearly than historian Henry Adams, who, after studying the New Yorker's political moves, concluded:

> No canvass for the Presidency was ever less creditable than that of DeWitt Clinton in 1812. Seeking war votes for the reason that he favored more vigorous prosecution of the war; asking support from peace Republicans because Madison had plunged the country into war without preparation; bargaining for Federalist votes as the price of bringing about a peace; or coquetting with all parties in the atmosphere of bribery in bank charters — Clinton strove to make up a majority which had no element of union but himself and money.[33]

Clinton courted support from Federalists, disgruntled Republicans, "peace party" merchants hurt by the war, and the remnants of his late uncle's cadre in New York politics.

32. Adams to Benjamin Waterhouse, 23 March 1812, in Worthington C. Ford, ed., *Statesman and Friend: Correspondence of John Adams with Benjamin Waterhouse* (Boston: Little, Brown & Company, 1927), 95 (hereafter cited as *Adams-Waterhouse Correspondence*).

33. Adams, *History*, 581.

Madison, following custom, acted as though reelection were the furthest thing from his mind — he made no speeches, wrote no campaign letters, and shook no hands in search of votes. Congressman Samuel L. Mitchill, a New York Republican loyal to Madison, decried "the arts of strategem and intrigue . . . put in motion to supplant M[adison]." Mitchill told his wife that "emissaries and agents have been dispatched to most parts of the union to cry down the administration and beg or buy votes" for Clinton. Until the election results were known, Mitchill observed, "the Presidential drawing room was thin and solemn," but as the returns drifted in, anti-Madison men in Congress became "less exulting and impudent . . . and I suppose the Levees [at the White House] will be thronged with an additional press of company."[34] Although Madison was unaware of John Adams's support of his candidacy, he would surely have been delighted to know that at least one Federalist in New England approved of him. "If I had a vote I should give it to Mr. Madison at the next Election," Adams wrote a friend, "because I know of no man who would do better."[35]

Most Federalists were not so charitable. A rumor in early November that Ohio had defected from the Republican ranks sent a thrill of hope through the dissenters in Congress. "The result of the late elections in New Hampshire and Massachusetts have struck them, like an unexpected clap of thunder, or an Earthquake," Federalist Bigelow exulted. "The report from Ohio, that Clinton will have the votes of that State is another damper, and they begin to entertain serious doubts of Madison's election."[36] This was a Federalist exercise in self-delusion, however, for the West and South (including the recently admitted state of Louisiana) were solidly in Madison's camp. Despite the bad news from upper New York and the Canadian frontier, Madison had cause to celebrate as the electoral tally became clearer in the weeks before Christmas 1812. Clinton had won all of New England except Vermont, had swept New York and New Jersey, and had taken 5 of Maryland's 11 electoral votes to amass a total of 89. Madison carried all the states below the Potomac and west of the Appalachian mountains, a total of 128 votes. The first wartime election set the tone for all others: The incumbent president was reelected handsomely.

The 1812 elections provided additional bonuses for Madison. His acer-

34. Samuel L. Mitchill to his wife, 24 November 1812, Mitchill Papers, Museum of the City of New York.

35. Adams to Benjamin Waterhouse, 11 March 1812, *Adams-Waterhouse Correspondence*, 77.

36. "Letters of Abijah Bigelow, Member of Congress, to His Wife 1810–1815," American Antiquarian Society *Proceedings* 40 (1930): 343 (hereafter cited as "Bigelow Papers").

bic enemy in the House, John Randolph of Roanoke, was *defeated* because he opposed the war; newcomer Daniel Webster of New Hampshire was *elected* because he opposed it. The House remained decidedly Republican, 114 votes to 68; the Senate was more Republican than it had been in Madison's first term, with 22 Republicans facing 14 Federalists or independents. As problems of supply and finance loomed, Madison and Gallatin must have scanned the list of new congressmen with more than ordinary interest. They needed votes to carry on the war, and the bigger the majority the better.

The dearth of good news from battle fronts was temporarily relieved before the year was out by Commodore Stephen Decatur's capture of the HMS *Macedonia*. Bonfires and illuminations welcomed the news of an American victory, and guns that were fired at the Washington Navy Yard to celebrate the news probably rattled White House dishes. A few days before Christmas, the Madisons attended a ball in the capital where the captured flag from the British ship was on display. "Queen Dolly was at the ball," a disgruntled Federalist noted. "Young Hamilton, son of the secretary of the Navy . . . brought the [captured] colours . . . and laid them at the feet of Mrs. Madison."[37]

Socially, Washington somehow avoided the turmoil of war, but in the president's official family there was plenty of cause for worry. The Royal Navy had blockaded the coast to New Orleans, but in an effort to wean New England from "Mr. Madison's war," the British still left its ports open. Madison was also facing opposition in the capital. Daniel Webster, newly elected to Congress as a "peace party" candidate, went to the White House on a social call but was not overwhelmed by the presidential presence. "I did not like his looks," Webster said of the president, "any better than I like his Administration."[38] Even within his own party, Madison found the going perilous. During the winter recess, Speaker Clay had told Attorney General Rodney his frank opinion that Madison was "wholly unfit for the storms of War." Clay admired the president as a person but now believed that "Nature has cast him in too benevolent a mould. Admirably adapted to the tranquil scenes of peace — blending all the mild & amiable virtues, he is not fit for the rough and rude blasts which the conflicts of Nations generate." Clay thought Madison's peaceful demeanor must give way to reforms within the cabinet. "And here again he is so hesitating, so tardy, so far behind the National sentiment, in his proceedings towards his War Ministers, that he will lose whatever credit he might otherwise acquire by the introduction of suitable characters in their places."[39] Clay was never a patient man.

37. Taggart to Rev. John Taylor, 21 December 1812, "Taggart Letters," 416.
38. Quoted in Peterson, *The Great Triumvirate*, 39.
39. Letter of 29 December 1812, in James F. Hopkins et al., eds., *The Papers of Henry Clay*, 9 vols. (Lexington, Ky.: University Press of Kentucky, 1959–), 1:750.

The reverses of the army in the north called for a scapegoat or two, of course, and Secretary of War Eustis resigned to clear the way for a more experienced cabinet officer. Monroe temporarily wore two hats, as secretary of both state and war, and Madison flirted with the idea of making him commander of the western army. But when Monroe's taking to the field was discouraged by western congressmen, Monroe stayed put and the War Department was turned over to John Armstrong. Remembered in history as one of the disgruntled amy officers at Newburgh who had tried in 1783 to threaten Congress by heavy-handed action, Armstrong had married well and was thought to be presidential timber in some circles along the Hudson River. His brother-in-law was Robert R. Livingston, whom he had succeeded in 1804 as American minister at Paris. Armstrong had stayed at that thankless post for six years. Madison knew that Armstrong harbored political ambitions (he had served briefly in the Senate), had a powerful connection with the Livingston family, and was bound to be considered Monroe's rival. Madison weighed all the pros and cons and then decided that Armstrong's military background would help him to restore order to the shattered War Department.

Meanwhile, Secretary of the Navy Hamilton had long outlived any usefulness obtained through his southern connections. At the ball celebrating the surrender of the *Macedonia* in December 1812, Hamilton had appeared in such a drunken state that Madison could no longer tolerate his behavior. The president allowed Hamilton to resign, publicly gave him credit for his "uniform exertions and unimpeachable integrity," and started the search for a replacement. The choice soon fell on William Jones, a Philadelphia mariner-merchant who had once served in Congress and was thus easily confirmed.[40] Armstrong had enemies, but not enough to block his confirmation by the Senate, 18 to 15. With most of the dead wood in the cabinet replaced, Madison turned to the state of the army and sought to raise the pay of enlisted men from five dollars to eight dollars per month. With some reluctance, Congress finally voted for the pay raise, but not until Josiah Quincy made a long speech denouncing the president as Napoleon's vassal. Some things never seemed to change.

A running account of the various land and sea battles taking place in the next year and half offer no proof that Madison was an effective commander in chief. The tiny American navy of three frigates and thirteen smaller ships was no match for the British, but by late 1814 nearly five hundred privateers were authorized to harass the enemy's merchant fleet. Several sensational American naval battles doubtless helped Madison at the polls and certainly injected needed support into the nation's morale. These early

40. Irving Brant, *James Madison*, 6 vols. (Indianapolis: Bobbs-Merrill Company, 1941–1961), 6:126–286.

American victories forced Francis James Jackson to observe in late December 1812, "As to the Conduct of the naval war against the Americans, it would disgrace the sixth form of Eton or Westminster."[41] John Adams, who considered the navy his own creation, boasted that the American successes would startle Europeans, and "they will ferment in the Minds of this People till they generate a national self respect, a Spirit of Independence and national Pride which has never before been felt in America."[42]

Despite the lack of enthusiasm in Congress for a navy, the war planners in Washington regarded control of Lakes Ontario and Erie, with their water routes to the West, as vital. After the dismal reports from the several fronts sank in, Madison lectured Dearborn on the need to fortify the Great Lakes region. "The command of the Lakes, by a superior force on the Water, ought to have been a fundamental point in the national policy from the moment the peace [treaty of 1783] took place," Madison wrote his general. "Whatever may be the future situation of Canada, it ought to be maintained, without regard to expence. . . . Without the ascendancy over those waters we can never have it over the savages, nor be able to secure such posts as Makinaw." The unceasing defeats and surrenders were weakening Madison's commitment to Republican frugality.

Although outnumbered initially, the American lake flotilla drew first blood when Captain Isaac Chauncey was moved from the New York Navy Yard to Sackett's Harbor with orders to build a squadron and dominate Lake Ontario. Chauncey set about building eight ships and sent to Lake Erie an enterprising young officer, Lieutenant Jesse D. Elliott. Elliott still had no ships when in October 1812 two British armed brigs were sighted off Fort Erie. One of the vessels was the *Detroit*, which had been the American ship *Adams* until it had been surrendered by Hull. The other ship was the HMS *Caledonia*, a key force in the fall of Fort Mackinac.[43]

Lacking a suitable ship, Elliott made a daring decision by sending two long boats on a surprise mission. Some one hundred forty American sailors and a few troops borrowed from the army boarded and captured the two British vessels in a fight lasting only ten minutes. The *Caledonia* was beached at the temporary American navy yard, but the *Detroit* ran aground and had to be burned. That same month the American eighteen-gun frigate *Wasp* cap-

41. Francis James Jackson to George Jackson, 22 December 1812, in Lady Jackson, ed., *The Bath Archives: The Diaries and Letters of Sir George Jackson*, 2 vols. (London: R. Bentley & Sons, 1873), 1:448.

42. Adams to Waterhouse, 23 March 1813, *Adams—Waterhouse Correspondence*, 95.

43. Madison to Dearborn, 7 October 1812, in Hunt, *Writings of Madison*, 8:217–18; Mahan, *Sea Power in the War of 1812*, 1:354.

tured the British *Frolic* in a fight off the Delaware capes; although a larger British ship then swamped the *Wasp*, the victory was significant because it proved that American marksmanship was superior to that of the Royal Navy.

Americans needed something to be proud of, for the inauspicious, not to say embarrassing, 1812 overland campaigns against Canada had revealed the incompetence of American staff officers; the senior generals were a particularly sorry lot. Secretary of War Armstrong began the new year by ordering the most inept generals to sleepy commands at military district headquarters. But the leavings inspired no confidence in demoralized battalions that waited out the winter clad in shoddy uniforms. Moving a finger down the list of field commanders, not one name stood out in terms of bravery, battlefield experience, or notable success. As Jefferson said in dismay, "So wretched a succession of generals never before destroyed the fairest expectations of a nation."[44]

News from the lakes and oceans was a constant stream of good and bad. Close to seventy American merchant ships had been captured by the British early in the war, but the Yankee sailors knew how to reply in kind. The 473-ton *America*, a merchantman refitted and heavily armed, sailed out of Salem harbor in the fall of 1812 bound for European waters as a privateer. Carrying a vast amount of sail, the *America* outran the British ships it encountered while cruising south of the English Channel toward the Canary Islands. In several four-month cruises the *America* took forty-one prizes, "twenty-seven of which reached port and realized $1,100,000" in profits.[45]

Not to be outdone, the British Admiralty stepped up its blockade of American ports but granted special licenses to New England–based ships that sometimes flew flags of convenience that bore no resemblance to the Stars and Stripes. This ruse allowed British goods to reach northern ports and permitted the Americans to operate under the protection of the Royal Navy. Madison was aware of the situation and finally sent Congress an angry special message calling for an end to the two-faced British policy through a complete embargo of all American ports. The transparent aim of Britain's half-hearted blockade, Madison said, was "to seduce and separate" one part of the Union from the other. "The insulting attempt on the virtue, the honor, the patriotism, and the fidelity of our brethren of the Eastern States, will not fail to call forth their indignation and resentment," Madison noted as he asked for tighter laws.[46] Congress balked, however, and Madison was un-

44. Jefferson to Benjamin Rush, 6 March 1813, quoted in Marshall Smelser, *The Democratic Republic, 1801–1815* (New York: Harper & Row, 1968), 251.

45. Mahan, *Sea Power in the War of 1812*, 1:399.

46. Message to Congress, 24 February 1813, quoted in Peterson, *Madison*, 2:330–31.

able to put his embargo in place until the war had dragged on for almost eighteen months.

In the Northwest, the American Forts Mackinac and Dearborn had fallen or been hastily abandoned. The United States could do nothing until the Great Lakes were again under American control, and with Canada still infested by redcoats there was no prospect of an early peace with the restless Indian tribes that seemed to prefer British trading goods, such as wool blankets, rifles, and rum, to American ones. In the South, General Wilkinson, whom Madison could have sacked after the court-martial of 1811/12, had been restored to full command. He led an occupation force into West Florida early in 1813, and on 15 April the Spanish commandant at Mobile surrendered his eighty-man garrison to the Americans. Wilkinson was then promoted to major general and ordered to join the American forces assembling at Lake Ontario for another drive into Canada. Slowly Wilkinson headed for the Canadian border headquarters. Madison hoped that the man he had given a second chance might deserve it.

Meanwhile, the situation in East Florida was no nearer a solution, and there were reports of Indian unrest, fomented by British agents, in the region. Despite an attack on American marines occupying the smuggler's haven at Amelia Island, the Senate rejected a bill passed by the House that would have empowered the president to send troops into Spanish Florida. Thwarted in that area, Madison asked the governor of Tennessee to send 1,500 militiamen to New Orleans in case the British attacked. General Andrew Jackson, picked to command the Tennessee volunteers, had been itching for a chance to shoot down unruly Creeks and Seminoles, but one of Armstrong's early moves after he had taken office was to cancel the Tennesseans' expedition. Jackson had been miffed, but obeyed his orders. As the disappointed Tennessee troops trudged home, a force of 750 Kentuckians was surprised near the Raisin River not far from Lake Erie and routed; in the ensuing chaos the Indian allies of the British were said to have tomahawked some wounded prisoners and burned others alive. Frontier warfare had returned to its bloody, brutal pattern.

Not only were the battlefields in disarray but the nation's finances were also no source of consolation to the president or his secretary of the Treasury. Before war came, Gallatin had estimated that at least ten million dollars would be needed to carry on the initial stages of the fighting, but his estimates of income from tariffs were far too generous. Congress, of course, was reluctant to impose old taxes, even for a war. Rather than passing a tax program on the eve of war, Congress had even considered reopening trade with Britain in a blatant admission that customs duties were needed. This strange legislation was defeated by Speaker Henry Clay's casting vote. With war now a stark reality, Gallatin was authorized to borrow eleven million dollars, a sum that the *National Intelligencer* and other Republican newspapers insisted would show the patriotic colors of the financial community. Instead of a tremendous subscription, only six million dollars came into the Treasury coffers, and the New England bankers, who might have easily taken the entire war loan, took less than one million dollars in bonds. Although the South and West were enthusiastic about the war, they were almost broke; thus the financiers of New York and Philadelphia kept the government from extreme embarrassment.

In this uncertain war, tidings from Captain William Bainbridge's command, the *Constitution*, gave American morale a temporary lift. The *Constitution* had so completely destroyed the forty-nine-gun HMS *Java* off the coast of Brazil that there was no prize money for the crew to share. Exuberant congressmen, ordinarily so tightfisted when considering naval appropriations, voted fifty thousand dollars to salve the crew's disappointment.[47] But then came the gloom, following reports of Napoleon's retreat from Moscow in the winter of 1812/13 and the shocking news that American minister Joel Barlow had died in Poland while chasing the French emperor. Furthermore, a British fleet had moved into Chesapeake Bay and was said to be menacing the coast outside Norfolk; rumors from this vulnerable port told of a request for federal defense aid that had been denied by the White House. "Such a ferment is raised that it is thought that if the Presidential election was to take place now," a New England congressman jibed, "Madison would not obtain a single vote in Virginia."[48]

The election was history, however, and on 4 March 1813 Madison rode up to Capitol Hill, stood before Chief Justice John Marshall, took the oath of office, and kissed the Bible as he withdrew his right hand. In his inaugural address Madison invoked "the smiles of Heaven" to assure the nation that the war was headed toward "a successful termination." Madison repeatedly spoke of "the justice of the war," as if to reassure citizens that they were not fighting Britain out of caprice but because of their enemy's outrageous violations of American independence. Thus the nation had no choice but to prosecute "an unavoidable war" and hope that it was still possible to marshal the nation's strength "to render the war short and its success sure."[49]

The somber mood produced by the news of military reverses and the president's remarks was offset by the outpouring of public interest in the ceremony. "The crowd was so great that by eleven o'clock the stairs of the Capitol were filled with a press of persons thriving to enter the Representa-

47. Brant, *Madison*, 6:143–47.
48. Taggart to Rev. John Taylor, 11 February 1813, "Taggart Letters," 427.
49. James D. Richardson, comp., *A Compilation of the Messages and Papers of the Presidents, 1789–1897*, 10 vols. (Washington, D.C.: GPO, 1896–1899), 1:509–11.

tives Chamber," a friendly witness reported. Congressman Mitchill told his wife, "I got in, after a hard Scuffle. . . . Having once entered, all was free and easy. . . . You never saw at this place a greater throng."[50] As in 1809, Davis's Hotel was decorated with bunting for the inaugural ball, and a radiant First Lady made her presence felt; on the following night the Madisons (perhaps the president was showing a "stiff upper lip" in the face of news of adversity) went to a festive dinner party at the Russian minister's house where the company was "brilliant & pleasant."[51]

The importance of Madison's social call became apparent a few days later when the *National Intelligencer* revealed that the Russian minister, André Daschkoff, had handed the president an offer from Tsar Alexander I to serve as peacemaker. Earlier, unofficial reports that the Russian emperor was anxious to mediate a peace between the United States and Britain had reached Washington. Madison apparently delayed official notice of the Russian offer until Congress had adjourned and the inauguration was out of the way. Then Madison accepted the tsar's "humane and enlightened" offer, noting that Russia was "the only power in Europe which can command respect from both France and England."[52] The president said he would appoint a special commission to treat with the tsar's emissary, and at once placed the American minister at St. Petersburg, John Quincy Adams, on the delegation. Who could be trusted from the cabinet to take another place at the peace table?

Some of the pleasure of the inaugural festivities was dampened by further news of Barlow's tragic death in Poland. At one of the functions, Madison took Monroe from the subdued merriment to discuss Barlow's replacement. Before the evening ended, Monroe was instructed to tell the French minister that Senator William Crawford, a loyal Madison supporter who was president pro tem of the Senate, would take the Paris post. Maybe Crawford would be able to catch up with Napoleon.

In the midst of war, life in the White House moved smoothly along under the watchful eyes of the first lady. Dolley Madison had the first bathtub installed in the executive mansion; but her major expense had been a carriage built by the best coachmaker in Philadelphia. Benjamin Henry Latrobe, the official federal architect, oversaw its construction and advised Mrs. Madison that "the fashion requires them to be painted which can be done here very elegantly."[53] She insisted that brass-fitted mountings be placed on the

50. Samuel L. Mitchill to his wife, 4 March 1813 (2d letter), Mitchill Papers, Museum of the City of New York.

51. Dolley Madison to Phoebe Morris, 6 March 1813, photostat, Papers of James Madison, University of Virginia.

52. Brant, *Madison*, 6:156–57.

53. Latrobe to Mrs. Madison, 22 March 1809, in William T. Hutchinson et al.,

harnesses for the two teams that would pull the new carriage. The musically inclined first lady also asked Latrobe to find her a guitar while he was in Philadelphia.

Madison was usually quite careful in spending his presidential salary; but on one occasion he displayed a surprising speculative spirit by joining William Thornton in investing in a champion stud. His wife loved high-fashion clothes and her tendency to take a dip of snuff now and then made that habit more acceptable in Washington. The snuff in Mrs. Madison's dainty china boxes was of the best grind and quality. The president himself enjoyed an after-dinner cigar, and perhaps he too dipped occasionally, but he never *chewed*. The many spittoons visitors noted at the White House were not there for Mr. Madison's use. Thus with trivial matters left to Mrs. Madison's care, the president concentrated on the business of state, particularly whether Russia's offer to mediate had the potential to bring about a peaceful settlement. Then there was the matter of the peace delegation.

Monroe had Madison's confidence, but the real rock of the cabinet was Gallatin. The British blockade was strangling government revenues, and the indispensable Gallatin asked Congress to release five million dollars impounded as duties on illegal imports from Britain before news of the war's outbreak reached that island. Gallatin allowed sale of the goods at a huge profit, but he desperately needed this accidental windfall. Congress slammed the door on Gallatin's request, however, voting 64 to 61 in the House to return all forfeitures on goods owned by Americans and shipped from Britain before 15 September 1812.[54] Although Congress took note of the precarious state of the Treasury by authorizing a war loan of sixteen million dollars in January 1813, Gallatin soon learned that the New England bankers were still not interested in buying government bonds, even if the interest rates were unusually high. Yet the customs house at Boston was one of the nation's busiest, for with the British navy allowing commerce to come and go freely, ships with British crews but flying the flags of Spain or Portugal arrived loaded with sugar and fruit and then left loaded with American grain to feed Wellington's army. By law, British goods could not be imported, but sly Yankee seamen figured out ways to evade customs cutters on the prowl for smugglers. In the last year of the war, blockaded Virginians paid $4,000 on their imports, but the collections in Massachusetts came to $1.6 million.[55]

Although the Boston merchants laid the foundations for Beacon Hill

eds., *The Papers of James Madison*, 16 vols. [Presidential Series] (Chicago and Charlottesville: University of Chicago Press and University Press of Virginia, 1962–), 1:73 (hereafter cited as *Madison Papers*).

54. Adams, *History*, 600–603.
55. Ibid., 1072–73.

mansions, their consciences would not allow them to help the federal government raise money to carry on the war. Gallatin struggled to find bankers who would pay hard cash for the $16 million war loan, but he was able to sell only $75,000 at Boston and less than $500,000 in New England as a whole. This trifling sum sent a loud message to Gallatin and Madison, but fortunately the New York bankers took $5.72 million, and Philadelphia's financial circles bought $6.8 million.[56] If the American war effort had depended on Boston for its money, hostilities might have ended by the summer of 1813. Scarcely a month after Madison's second oath of office, Gallatin had his $16 million, but the interest rate was regarded as outrageously high — 7.48 percent.

Federalists had used the artillery of their press to denounce the war loans as a devious means of prosecuting a wicked war. As in the Mexican and Vietnam wars, the opposition likened support for Madison's policies to a covenant with the Devil. Hardly an issue of the Boston *Columbian Centinel* reached readers without an essay blasting the administration for prosecuting an "unnecessary war." Better that a citizen should purchase a pistol and blow out his brains, the New York *Evening Post* warned, than that he should buy the government's war bonds.[57] But the heat was off Gallatin once the book on loans closed. He told Monroe that a place on the American peace delegation to Europe was his desire "if the president thought him worthy." Thus Madison knew he had his loyal man on the delegation and made the interim appointment with his fingers crossed. Perhaps the Invincibles would welcome a way to get Gallatin out of the country! Madison decided to also appoint former Senator James Bayard of Delaware, a respected Federalist, to the delegation as a bipartisan link with Congress.

Congress had adjourned with much business unsettled. At least the silence on Capitol Hill had its compensations. Before the adjournment an intemperate attack on the administration by Josiah Quincy had shown unusual ferocity. A Boston Brahman with a pathological hatred of both Jefferson and Madison, Quincy had called the administration a "despotism" and said the Republican leaders in the House were "fawning reptiles, who crowded at the feet of the president, and left their filthy slime upon the carpet of the palace."[58] Henry Clay had left the speaker's podium to meet anger with anger and spent three days defending Madison and the war effort. Widely reprinted, Clay's defense of the president and "Mr. Madison's war" won plaudits in the South and West but was passed over in silence by most northern newspapers.

56. Ibid., 648–49.
57. Brant, *Madison*, 6:157–58.
58. Quoted in Peterson, *The Great Triumvirate*, 40.

Madison decided to keep Congress busy as the problems of finance, military supply, and generalship multiplied. He called for an unusual early meeting of the Thirteenth Congress on 24 May 1813. (The session would ordinarily not have begun until December.) Madison took this unorthodox step to raise sorely needed revenue for the Treasury and to implement the tsar's offer, provided the British agreed to mediate at a neutral site. The possibility of a negotiated peace appealed to Madison's political instincts, although he must have seen weaknesses in the American position at the bargaining table.

To keep the Senate coterie off guard, Madison waited until his appointees to the St. Petersburg conference—Bayard and Gallatin—were on the high seas. Bayard had lost his Federalist rancor and had come around to Madison's way of thinking about the war; Gallatin, exhausted by his work on the war loan, had told Madison another cabinet member could control the Treasury during his absence. An unexpected bonus for Madison was the decision to send attachés with the commissioners, including his stepson, John Payne Todd. Dolley Madison's son had postponed his matriculation at Princeton and was spending his days in Washington, courting pretty belles and acquiring a reputation as a man-about-town. Mrs. Madison agreed that six months in Europe, where Payne could practice his French linguistic skills, would be a valuable experience for the twenty-one-year-old dilettante. No doubt Madison sighed with relief when Payne dashed out to be fitted for a lieutenant's gaudy uniform. Madison, having made these appointments in haste, bade the two envoys and their young aides godspeed. He had already chosen the resident minister in Russia, John Quincy Adams, as the third member of the American mission. By 9 May, Bayard, Gallatin, and their entourage were on their way to the Baltic.

Thus Madison's second administration began with a gamble. The opportunity had been created, in part, by the Russian tsar's desire to play a crucial role in European affairs. Tsar Alexander had first broached the offer in September 1812, but the British were not too pleased by this Russian meddling, and definitive news of the emperor's effort only reached Washington in March 1813. After discussing with his cabinet the Russian offer and the reasons for presuming British acceptance, Madison presented Congress with a fait accompli, although if Washington rumor mills worked as well then as they do now, the mission must have been an open secret by the time Congress assembled. What is important, however, is that the mission, secret or not, was Madison's uncharacteristic way of seeking an end to the war. The president explained to Congress that the Russian offer "was immediately accepted" and that "three of our eminent citizens [were] accordingly commissioned . . . to conclude a treaty of peace" with Britain.[59] Madison said that

59. Richardson, *Messages of the Presidents*, 1:511–15.

a wait-and-see attitude toward the scheme was proper, but he presumed the British were inclined to cooperate with Tsar Alexander toward achieving peace, which would bring them to the negotiating table.

Turning to other matters, Madison noted that the sixteen-million-dollar war loan had been tagged with an extremely high interest rate, and he asked Congress to levy taxes that would render the nation's finances "more extended and less precarious." Madison ignored the fact that his most able cabinet minister was on his way to St. Petersburg and that Gallatin had made enormous concessions to find the money in New York and Philadelphia to round out that loan. Although some Republicans thought the high interest rate scandalous, as Henry Adams noted, the "terms were not excessive when it was considered that New England in effect refused to subscribe" and that the deal was made firm at the "moment the Treasury was empty, and could not meet the drafts of the other departments."[60]

A British safe-conduct pass helped the American envoys bound for St. Petersburg to glide out of Chesapeake Bay. From the decks of the *Neptune*, they passed the charred remains of the village of Havre de Grace on the Maryland shoreline. A British raiding party had moved at will in the area above Annapolis in the spring of 1813, causing rumors to reach Washington of a full-scale British invasion. The president was warned by Jonathan Dayton, a former congressman discredited in the Burr plot, that a conspiracy was afoot to kidnap the president and whisk him to a Royal Navy ship lying at anchor on the Potomac.[61] Nothing came of the flurry of wild stories except that the cry of "wolf" may have caused Americans to discount similar reports the next summer.

Not until the war in Vietnam would one segment of the American population try so persistently to embarrass the national administration as did the New England forces seeking to discredit Madison in the summer of 1813. The very label that New England gave this fight — "Mr. Madison's war" — was used in derision in order to distance the northern end of the Union from any commitment to wholeheartedly join in the struggle. In June 1813 Representative Webster introduced resolutions aimed at the heart of the president's credibility. When did the president learn of the French decree in Saint-Cloud, which he had used to justify declaring war on Britain? What were "the reasons [for] that decree being concealed from this government and its minister for so long a time after its date?"[62] Madison had already answered these questions when asked by the Senate earlier, but now Federalists wanted to place

60. Adams, *History*, 650–51.
61. Dayton to Madison, 29 March, 9 April, and 19 April 1913, Madison Papers, DLC.
62. *National Intelligencer*, 11 June 1813.

in the spotlight the mendacity of the French (the decree was backdated a year) and the gullibility of the president.

As the Federalists warmed to their work, Madison became ill and was reportedly suffering from "a remittent fever," or, as the president himself called it, influenza. For over a month, Madison's health was precarious. Servants tiptoed around the White House, and Mrs. Madison canceled her weekly receptions. The weather in Washington grew more humid and hot, and Congressman Bigelow lamented, "The President has been sick of a fever, Eppes Chairman of the Committee of Ways and Means is sick [and] to tell you the truth I am almost homesick. . . . I think I pay pretty dear for my six dollars a day."[63]

Instead of wrestling with the impending financial crisis, the House was tied up by the Federalists, who wanted the president to confess that the French had tricked the United States into declaring war. As the president lay fighting for his life, the Federalist attack reached gutter levels, forcing the *National Intelligencer* to comment, "Search the records of the British Parliament . . . search annals of the councils of any free people [and none will reveal] a single precedent in which such a freedom, bordering upon rudeness, has been exhibited to the Chief Magistrate of a nation."[64]

To prevent endless debate on a hopeless topic, Clay allowed the resolutions to pass and then sent Webster to the White House to deliver them to the ailing president. "I went Tuesday to the Palace to present the Resolutions," Webster told a friend. "The Presidt was in his bed, sick of a fever. His night cap on his head — his wife attending him &c &c. I think he will find *no relief* from my prescription."[65] Madison recovered as a wave of anxiety swept through Washington in June 1813 after reports of a British fleet in Chesapeake Bay reached the capital. The city's defenses were less than adequate, but after a hurried reconnaissance toward the south by Monroe, the cabinet and key members of Congress pronounced all was in readiness if the British tried to invade Washington. Meanwhile, the Senate took up Madison's nominations for the Russian peace mission and looked hard and long at Gallatin's name. Who would handle his Treasury duties in his absence? Madison answered that Secretary of the Navy Jones was competent to perform the duties of both positions, but then a Senate committee began narrowing its focus and a resolution was adopted denying the right to allow one cabinet officer to fill two posts.

63. "Bigelow Letters," 365.
64. *National Intelligencer*, 24 June 1813.
65. Webster to Charles March, 24 June 1813, in Charles M. Wiltse et al., eds., *The Papers of Daniel Webster: Correspondence*, 10 vols. (Hanover, N.H.: University Press of New England, 1974–), 1:152.

Madison's dander was now aroused. He came off his sickbed to say to a Senate delegation that his mind was unchanged. This seemed an act of defiance to Senators Leib, Giles, and Samuel Smith, and they spearheaded a drive to reject Gallatin's nomination. They succeeded by one vote, 17 to 18, and then rubbed salt in the wound by in effect rejecting the president's nominee for a ministry at Stockholm. Madison believed he had been the victim of a double-crossing senator or two, for he told Gallatin the close vote "proved that the final purposes of certain individuals on whom the turning of the scale depended, had been miscounted." The Senate Invincibles resolved that no American minister was needed in Sweden; so a vote on Madison's appointee was useless. The Senate action also infuriated Monroe, who told Jefferson the anti-Madison clique in the Senate was conspiring to make Giles the next president. With Madison feeling poorly and Vice-President Gerry also on the sick list, the president pro tem of the Senate was next in line for the White House and, Monroe said, the Leib-Giles-Smith coterie were happily awaiting news that both Madison and Gerry were beyond recovery.[66]

Madison was tougher than the disaffected Republican senators imagined. Nursed by Dolley Madison and treated by an army physician (who advised Madison to have a daily horseback ride before breakfast once he recovered), the president shook off his fever and was eager to escape the Washington heat by late July. By then the American peace commissioners were in Russia and beyond the lash of vindictive senators. However, Britain had decided it was not interested in a Russian-sponsored peace parley. As Madison yearned for the vista from his porch at Montpelier, the American commissioners took the diplomatic developments in slow doses. (For example, Gallatin did not learn until October 1813 that the Senate had rejected his appointment.) In the meantime, the chore of answering Webster's snide resolutions fell to Monroe, who wrote a lengthy paper that was more a paean than a reply, but the Federalists continued to think that they had Madison on the run. "I am fully of opinion," Webster observed, "that the Administration now looks forward to its own certain downfal[l], unless it can have a peace. But if it does make Peace, it will have all the West &c in arms agst it. Poor Madison does not know what to do."[67]

Madison was not as dispirited as his foes believed. A special message was sent to Congress asking for an embargo to thwart the British designs for acquiring American commodities and shipping them in "neutral vessels or to British vessels in neutral disguises."[68] Madison apparently wanted to choke off trading with the enemy in Bermuda and areas where the Union Jack flew.

66. Monroe to Jefferson, 28 June 1813, quoted in Adams, *History,* 662.
67. Webster to Charles March, 28 June 1813, in Wiltse, *Papers of Webster,* 1:153.
68. Richardson, *Messages of the Presidents,* 1:516–17.

Congress balked, and Abijah Bigelow told his wife, "The President and his advisers . . . hate the federalists of the eastern States quite as bad as they do the British." The president, Bigelow added, "they say is quite testy and cross. He does not like it that his friend Gallatin has got to come back with a flea in his ear."[69] To make matters worse, the hastily appointed Russian peace mission seemed to have been on a wild-goose chase; it was now common gossip in Washington that the British had rejected the tsar's olive branch.

Exhausted by his illness and distressed by the news from military camps, Madison felt relieved when Congress hurriedly passed a taxation program and the special session adjourned. Arrangements were made to send daily messengers to Montpelier, and by 10 August the Madisons were on the road leading to the plantation. Heavy rains made the carriage wheels churn through mud up to the axles, but at last the pillars of Montpelier were in sight. Jefferson was setting out for his summer retreat at Poplar Forest, but he promised a reunion at Monticello before the Madisons returned to Washington. The mud around Washington gave way to the dust in Orange County, and Jefferson seemed more concerned about the drought (only one rain since 14 April made him think of the dreaded year 1755 "when we lost so many people by famine") than the war.[70] Though it was hot and dry, Madison was home. All he needed for a tonic was some favorable news, and every messenger spotted from the Montpelier portico brought the president renewed hope.

69. "Bigelow Letters," 368-69.
70. Jefferson to Madison, 15 August 1813, Madison Papers, Rives Collection, DLC.

7

★ ★ ★ ★ ★

THE FUSE OF WAR
SPUTTERS

Fortunately for the American cause, Yankee sailors were better led in the War of 1812 than were their counterparts in the United States Army. Although the Royal Navy dominated the high seas — spectacular victories such as that of the *Constitution* over the *Guerrière* were isolated instances of American ocean prowess — in the Great Lakes region American shipbuilding and leadership produced victory. On the high seas the Royal Navy had over five hundred ships of the line against which the Yankees tried to make headway with a force of a dozen vessels, only three of them outfitted for a full-dress battle. Thus the Americans had to pick and choose their battle sites to preserve any chance of survival.

General William Henry Harrison, chosen by Madison to command the western forces, called for a halt in the land war and urged a fleet buildup to harass or halt British usage of the Great Lakes for supply routes. To protect the British supplies, a six-ship squadron moved onto Lake Erie on 9 September 1813. Commander Oliver Hazard Perry moved his nine-vessel force into position against the British ships with orders to engage the enemy at close range, and on his flagship he hoisted to the mast a pennant inscribed "Don't Give Up the Ship." After the American flagship *Lawrence* suffered unbelievable casualties (85 of 103 on board were killed or wounded), Perry moved from the disabled vessel to the *Niagara*, and from its quarterdeck he directed American gunners until the British squadron was crippled. To General Harrison the young commander sent the message that became a tonic for American morale: "We have met the enemy and they are ours." At last Americans had cause to celebrate. "Perry's victory swept the British off Lake

Erie for the balance of the war."[1] Curiously, the farther one went inland, away from the seaboard, the more enthusiastic Americans seemed to be over these victories. The "landlubbers" stayed loyal to their Republican leanings, whereas the seamen in New England were often employed in endeavors that had the strange appearance of trading with the enemy.

As Madison was unwinding on his Montpelier vacation, the American forces under General Harrison followed up on Perry's triumph. The British had abandoned Detroit and retreated from their Lake Erie positions, hoping to find a safe haven on Lake Ontario. Harrison's army caught up with them near Thamesville, Ontario, on 5 October 1813. A combined force of British army and Canadian militia units, supplemented by an Indian force under Chief Tecumseh, was easily overwhelmed at the Battle of the Thames. As newspapers relished the end to a long string of military defeats with full reports of "the Late Accounts from Lake Ontario," Madison received the news of these latest victories and called it "the gratifying confirmation" of earlier rumors.[2]

Sixty years earlier, Benjamin Franklin had made a prediction that time had proved true: "I do not believe we shall ever have a firm peace with the Indians, till we have well drubbed them." After Tippecanoe, the eastern Indians from above the Ohio River had one good fight left in them; but after the retreat from Detroit and the British defeat at Thamesville, the issue of Indian rebellion was all but settled. Beyond their loss in numbers, the Indians were demoralized when Tecumseh, "the genius of Indian resistance in the West," as T. Harry Williams notes, was killed by an American bullet. Within a few years, the West extending as far as the Mississippi was to become an American parade ground. The scalping knives rusted and the war hoop was heard no more.

Reports of Tecumseh's death (his body was never found) were important because, as Madison sensed, news of a British setback would affect Britain's allies in the southeast—the Creek Indians. As secretary of state, Madison had seen how vast the nation was even before the Louisiana Purchase. Now the United States was so immense it took weeks or months to send reports to and from Washington. Sometimes, however, it seemed that rumors flashed far ahead of the express riders. Indeed, Madison expected the southern tribes to be impressed by Harrison's victory—"this happy turn in our affairs."[3]

1. T. Harry Williams, *The History of American Wars from 1745 to 1918* (Baton Rouge: Louisiana State University Press, 1981), 121–22; John K. Mahon, *The War of 1812* (Gainesville: University Presses of Florida, 1972), 170–75.

2. Madison to Monroe, 18 October 1813, Monroe Papers, Library of Congress (hereafter cited as DLC).

3. Franklin is quoted in Daniel J. Boorstin, *The Americans: The Colonial Experience* (New York: Random House, 1958); Madison is quoted in Irving Brant, *James Madison*, 6 vols. (Indianapolis: Bobbs-Merrill Company, 1941–1961), 6:219.

In a war where competent commanders were at a premium, Madison might have been distressed by the manner in which Harrison and Perry, the two leaders most responsible for those much-needed American victories, dropped from sight. Harrison, angered by Armstrong's treatment, thought he was being slighted and resigned. Perry was made a captain but languished under the command of a dilatory senior officer. He pleaded for sea duty but found none and was soon placed on shore duty. Thus Harrison and Perry, both tested fighting men, were for all practical purposes out of the war.

Harrison's victory had resulted from careful planning and coordination, something the American generals on the eastern front seemed unable to do. Early in the spring of 1813 the new secretary of war had submitted a scheme calling for the occupation of upper Canada from Lake Erie to the St. Lawrence. Armstrong's offensive was aimed at Montreal. He pressed his strategic plan until Madison and the other cabinet members deferred to his judgment.

Armstrong had probably treated Harrison shabbily because he saw the frontier general as a threat to his own political ambitions, but he saw none in Dearborn. Dearborn, ailing and unsure of himself, was a threat to no one, least of all the British-Canadian forces he was supposed to destroy. Thus with the president's approval, Armstrong instructed General Dearborn to cross Lake Ontario and capture Kingston while the secretary himself established a headquarters at Sackett's Harbor to keep track of the planned invasion.

Dearborn and his naval subordinate, Captain Isaac Chauncey, started their expedition in April 1813, but then they heard that Kingston was stoutly defended so they altered their orders. Instead of Kingston they attacked by land and by water the village of York (now Toronto), the tiny capital of Upper Canada. After a short, intense battle in which they burned some public buildings, the Americans triumphed. In the melee, however, they lost able Brigadier Zebulon Pike, who was killed in a powder-magazine explosion. Dearborn returned to Niagara and from a safe distance watched as American troops forced the British out of Fort George, which had also not been stoutly defended. Thereafter, Dearborn's men marched a great deal but never fast enough to reach the right place before a battle. A force of two thousand Americans was encamped at Stony Creek when two of their brigadiers were captured after the sentries fell asleep. A skirmish took place, with both sides retreating in confusion. His confidence shaken, Dearborn picked a fight with Armstrong and was summarily ordered to concentrate his forces. Have it your way, Dearborn said, and he ordered the scattered American units to regroup at the border fortifications at Forts George and Niagara, where they remained for the rest of the summer. For all of Dearborn's bluster and his army's marching and countermarching, the 1813 summer campaign ended with the paltry snare of "one fort barely on Canadian soil." Armstrong blamed Dearborn for the lack of progress, and the cabinet considered a demand for his resignation. Armstrong continued to bad-mouth Dearborn until Madison signed an order for his retirement "until your health be reestablished."[4]

A slow learner, Armstrong then picked as Dearborn's replacement the nefarious James Wilkinson; thus Armstrong traded one old, incompetent general for another. Wilkinson, however, was nimble when it came to reputations. Armstrong thought his plan to attack Kingston or bypass that strategic point and storm Montreal would still work. If Montreal was to be the main objective, Armstrong promised reinforcements from four thousand troops commanded by Major General Wade Hampton, at Plattsburg. Unfortunately, Wilkinson and Hampton despised each other, and a successful linkage of their two armies was made impossible when Wilkinson frittered away valuable time (he too decided to avoid Kingston) before he finally told his staff officers to call off the campaign and go into winter quarters. The younger men succeeded in persuading him to let them attack, using flatboats to carry men and matériel down the St. Lawrence. On 13 November 1813, near a spot known as Chrysler's Farm, they pulled into an embankment and sent out skirmishers to drive away small British units that were taking potshots at the boats. A smaller British-Canadian force assembled, drove the Yankees back, and before the fighting ended the Americans had retreated pell-mell back to Wilkinson's command post. Meanwhile Hampton, after a border foray, had pulled back his troops and set up his winter encampment.

As the campaigns of 1813 faded into the mists of frustrations, the British retained control of Fort Mackinac and retook Fort George; they then smashed Fort Niagara and put Buffalo to the torch. Wilkinson was recalled and another court of inquiry was formed to look into his conduct. But by this time the scoundrel was immune to military disaster, public opinion, or presidential outrage. He demanded that another court-martial be formed and conducted by generals. Predictably the court-martial gave Wilkinson another clean bill.

Madison realized that the war was being fought on two fronts — the real battles and the internecine ones in Boston, Philadelphia, Baltimore, and Washington. Soon after he left for his vacation, Madison read a warning from Virginia Republican William Wirt. Confessing that he saw new signs of party division, Wirt told Madison that he was "alarmed at this newly

4. Mahon, *War of 1812*, 142–43; Williams, *History of American Wars*, 124; Henry Adams, *History of the United States of America during the Administrations of Thomas Jefferson and James Madison*, vol. 2, *History of the United States of America during the Administrations of James Madison* (New York: Library of America, 1986), 739 (hereafter cited as Adams, *History*).

threatened breach of the republican corps."⁵ What was the source of this threat? Not the old Federalists, who were always naysayers. Instead, the rumblings came from dyed-in-the-wool Republicans. "The complaint is the impotency of the war in Canada," Wirt observed.

> It has been answered that the government could not be expected to make soldiers like Cadmus — that they must await enlistments . . . but the complainers reply that the governt. might send militia. We [loyal Republicans] answer that several of the States have refused on constitutional grounds to permit their militia to pass the limits of the U.S. and that the [governors] . . . regard them under the constitution, as a domestic defence merely.

Wirt went on to say "that no state to the south or west of New York" refused to furnish militia for a Canadian invasion. "The willing states were not only able by their militia to over-whelm Canada, but to reduce the treacherous members of the Union themselves to their duty." In short, the South and West could teach a patriotic lesson to disloyal New England, if the president used his executive powers forcefully.

Nobody needed to remind Madison of the problems created by New England's lukewarm support of the war. "I have not been unaware of the disappointment and discontent gaining ground with respect to the war on Canada," Madison replied from Montpelier. "I have not been less aware that success alone would put an end to them. This is the test by which public opinion decides more or less in all cases, and most of all, perhaps, in that of military events."⁶ But Madison was not looking for excuses, and he added that it was too early to blame the field commanders, Congress, or himself. The executive branch had chosen to commence the war when it did, Madison admitted, to take Britain off guard by assembling "such a force as might be obtained in a short time, and be sufficient to reduce Canada, from Montreal upwards before the enemy would be prepared to resist." This plan had miscarried, Madison admitted, and thus had forced Congress into a round a lawmaking to authorize more troops; but the increase in troops had caused acute supply problems, necessitating thorough reform of the commissary system.

So the cat was finally out of the bag, and a dead cat it was. For Madison admitted that when he had agonized over which major power to fight early in 1812, he had been persuaded by self-styled military experts that

5. William Wirt to Madison, 20 August 1813, Madison Papers, Rives Collection, DLC.
6. Madison to Wirt, 30 September 1813, in Gaillard Hunt, ed., *The Writings of James Madison*, 9 vols. (New York: G. P. Putnam's Sons, 1900–1910), 8:262–65.

Canada was there for the taking in a surprise attack. Believing these advisers, Madison had envisioned using Canada as a bargaining chip at a peace parley with the British. Harsh facts and cold steel demolished that chimera, Madison now acknowledged.

Finally, with republican frankness, Madison said that the United States was ill-prepared militarily because of the nature of its government. Confusion and error in the officer ranks were "an inconvenience of the most serious kind, but inseparable, as it always must be, from a Country among whose blessings it is to have long intervals of peace, and to be without those large standing armies which even in peace are fitted for war." Knowing that his letter would cross many hands back in Richmond, Madison reminded Wirt that a Republican government was a low-cost but high-risk government. Sometimes it seemed that the national motto was "Liberty, Equality, and Parsimony." In short, mistakes had been made, but they were being corrected. Meanwhile, Republicans need not apologize for following their principles!

This was vintage Madisonian doctrine. Before the president returned to Washington it was clear that the Lake Erie and Thames River victories had not been repeated in the muddled commands of Generals Wilkinson and Hampton. These inept officers sulked in their winter-quarters tents until Wilkinson accused Hampton of "beastly drunkenness" and demanded his arrest and a demeaning court-martial.[7] Madison might have excused a heavy drinker if the general had been sober enough to fight; but the boozing, backbiting, and accusations, linked with the cowardice and indecision, must have made the commander in chief wonder if there was a competent general in command anywhere.

As the Thirteenth Congress assembled for its first regular session, Madison heard from his secretary of war of arguments over seniority, squabbles that made sense only to bumbling old men jealous of their rank and oblivious to their ludicrous posturings. Armstrong was rid of Dearborn, but the replacements were no better. With Madison's approval the quarrelsome duo of Wilkinson and Hampton was relieved, replaced by Jacob Brown and George Izard. In War Department corridors, the newly promoted young generals were likened to a fresh breeze; but only Brown proved to be a mover and a shaker willing to risk a hard campaign. Izard, only thirty-seven and trained for war in European academies, never reached his potential.

Meanwhile, reports from the South indicated that General Andrew Jackson's campaign against the militant Creeks — the Red Sticks — had stalled. The Creek warriors destroyed Fort Mims above Mobile, massacring over

7. Quoted in J. C. A. Stagg, *Mr. Madison's War: Politics, Diplomacy, and Warfare in the Early American Republic, 1783–1830* (Princeton, N.J.: Princeton University Press, 1983), 346.

half the five hundred fifty captives trapped inside the barricades. Jackson retaliated on 13 November 1813 by destroying the Creek encampment at Talladega, but morale among his band of farm-boy volunteers was volatile. Homesick militiamen were threatened with death by firing squad, and the American base at Fort Strother struggled along with a complement of fewer than one hundred thirty-five men. As the frosts gave way to snow in the North and freezing weather in the upper South in December 1813 the fighting ceased, but the outlook for 1814 against foes in any direction seemed less than auspicious.

Financing the war was another problem. Over thirty-four million dollars had been borrowed to pay for everything from horseshoe nails to frigates, and another war loan of nearly ten million had to be offered to bankers early in 1814. Public land sales, once thought to be a treasure trove for the Republic, were never up to Treasury Department estimates of around six hundred thousand dollars annually. Settlers moved to the Old Southwest during the war years, hoping for easy credit terms on one-hundred-sixty-acre quarter sections of newly surveyed lands in cotton-raising climates. Wartime dislocations and the lack of a stable market caused droves of public land buyers to petition Congress for debt relief in January 1814 as they blamed the war for their plight:

> The National Interest, the National Character called for war. War just and righteous as it was, has stripped them of the means of fulfilling their engagements. They will not say that the Declaration of War was the Act of the Creditor, and has deprived the Debtor, against his will of the means of Discharging his Debts. No! Though your memorialists had no voice in Declaring war they approved of the measure; and are [proud to be] regarded as parties in it. But if their Lands, their Houses and their Homes, be swept from them in consequence of the War, they will be more than equal sharers in its disasters.

The Mississippians asked Congress to postpone demands for their installments "till peace shall Smile upon them again."[8] Congressmen found reasons for leniency, but they did not abolish the credit system until 1820.

Only one man in Washington seemed concerned about financing the war — William Jones, Gallatin's stand-in at the Treasury. Gallatin had not yet returned from Europe to resume his old post, and Jones begged Madison for relief. "Here I am a perfect galley slave . . . obliged to row *double banked,"* the secretary holding two jobs lamented.[9] Jones drafted a military budget for

8. Memorial of the Legislative Council and House of Representatives of the Mississippi Territory, 11 January 1814, in Jack M. Sosin, ed., *The Opening of the West* (New York: Harper & Row, 1969), 101–3.

9. Quoted in Brant, *Madison*, 6:234–35.

1814 that called for another thirty million dollars for the war effort. Where would most of it come from? Taxes? Not from this Congress, Jones realized, as he fretted about the cost of fighting this wretched war for another year. Secretary of War Armstrong had no crystal ball either, but as he peered into the future he worried over the same numbers game every military leader faces. Recruiting was "at a standstill," a Republican congressman said. Thousands of short-term (twelve to eighteen months) enlistments would end in 1814, and the effort to sign up volunteers had been a total failure in New England; it had been more successful in the West and South but was still discouraging. Worse still, Governor Martin Chittenden of Vermont ordered his state militia to come home and stay there. Not the first military man to believe that with superior numbers the aims of the war might be achieved during the ensuing year, Armstrong decided to urge the commander in chief to raise the regular army to fifty-five thousand by calling up the militia by stages or classes. Monroe, as secretary of state, regarded Armstrong with suspicion (Monroe thought Armstrong also coveted the 1816 presidential nomination) and warned Madison that Armstrong was attempting to run roughshod over the Constitution and was personally corrupt to boot. "My advice," Monroe wrote Madison, "is to remove him at once."[10]

The president was probably confused by the contrary opinions of the two experienced military men in his cabinet, although neither had ever held a genuine command. Because Madison himself had never shouldered a Brown Bess musket, he was too inclined to believe men who had. Thus in his annual message to Congress in early December 1813, after noting the victories of Perry and Harrison and praising Jackson, Madison paid lip service to the militia "as the great bulwark of defense and security for free states." Then he suggested to Congress a revision of militia laws to make possible the embodiment of the state units into the regular army. Madison also urged Congress to consider a way to pay states for the "first assembling as well as the subsequent movement of detachments called into the national service."[11] Clearly, the president wanted to make it easy for the states to acquiesce when calls for more troops were issued, but he never hinted that any army as large as fifty-five thousand was his goal.

As Congress began sorting out the requests for men and money, the week following Christmas Day 1813 found the newspapers filled with stories about the New York frontier clashes that led to the burning of Buffalo. Morale faltered as reports of light battle casualties were discredited. The Canan-

10. Quoted in ibid., 6:239; Stagg, *Mr. Madison's War*, 366–67.

11. James D. Richardson, comp., *A Compilation of the Messages and Papers of the Presidents, 1789–1897*, 10 vols. (Washington, D.C.: GPO, 1896–1899), 1:523.

daigua, New York, newspaper, the *Ontario Repository*, said on 7 December 1813 that the 339 reported dead or wounded in an earlier skirmish had been greatly underestimated: *"We believe the American loss to be more than double what is* [officially] *stated.* . . . As the time of the three months drafted militia have expired, their return to their families is daily expected. The *patriotism* of the *volunteers* has probably become a little cooler, and they may also be looked for soon."

Along the New York border, hysteria seemed to reign, and Governor Daniel Tompkins implored Madison to dispatch 2,500 troops to the area or else all resistance to the British forces would collapse. Madison tried to reassure Tompkins that the sky was not falling—yet. "A regular force of the amount you suggest, would be the best provision for that station," Madison answered, "could it be spared from the armies below and the objects elsewhere kept in view."[12] Politely Madison told the governor to keep his shirt on and wait until a defense plan for the whole region could be implemented. Had Madison read the Boston newspapers while he was corresponding with Tompkins, he would have seen suggestions, made in all seriousness, that Massachusetts might negotiate a separate peace with Britain. Were the Yankee Federalists mad?

Not by their own estimation, for Massachusetts High Federalists such as Timothy Pickering and Josiah Quincy believed that the Republic was being destroyed by southerners who had captured the White House and had selfishly and wickedly placed sectional interests before the national good. Very well, they seemed to say, if you want to see sectional interests exploited, we will give you a lesson in sectionalism. Encouraged by Massachusetts business interests and with their purses wide open, New England producers sent an illegal flow of foodstuffs across the Canadian border to help feed the king's troops; the British paid in cash for the beef and flour consumed in their regimental messes. In fact, by late 1813 the hard money supply below the Potomac had dried up, whereas New England enjoyed a surplus of specie as it thrived on a vigorous, illegal cash-and-carry importing business. Determined to make Mr. Madison repent for starting his war against their wishes and interests, the Massachusetts legislature gladly paid the bills to maintain a well-armed and drilled seventy thousand–man state militia. The governors of Massachusetts, citing the Constitution as their source of authority, saw to it that not a single man from this force ever faced the British during the entire war. Behind all these maneuvers the New England Federalists played a waiting game. "They believed," historian T. Harry Williams wrote, "that

12. Daniel Tompkins to Madison, 3 January 1814, Madison Papers, DLC; Madison to Tompkins, 25 June 1814, Madison Papers, DLC.

eventually the national government would be unable to raise men and money and would have to come to the states for support, and the states could then demand peace."[13]

The war effort reached its darkest hour in the winter of 1813/14 when Madison was finally forced to admit that the British cabinet had rejected the tsar's mediation offer. He also learned that "Light-Horse Harry" Lee's informal peace mission to the Barbadoes had foundered as the impressment issue. In his State of the Union message, Madison reported his disappointment that "the British cabinet, either mistaking our desire of peace for a dread of British power or misled by other fallacious calculations," had rejected the Russian mediation plan.[14] The president did not tell of the diplomatic backing-and-filling going on in Europe, but only warned Congress that "there is no evidence . . . that a change of disposition in the British councils has taken place or is to be expected." The wandering American envoys were left unmentioned, even though as Madison spoke the slow-grinding mills of diplomacy were beginning to crank in London.

There were countervailing forces to dispute the sanctimonious New England stance. Charles Ingersoll, a graduate of Madison's alma mater who was a Philadelphia jack-of-all-trades, had won a seat in the House of Representatives in the fall of 1812 and had then clamored for war with Britain. The setbacks of 1813 had not dampened Ingersoll's desire to twist the lion's tail. In fact, Ingersoll told a friend in December 1813, "This holy war has advanced us a century *per saltem* in power and character."[15]

Holy war? There were no metaphors suggesting a crusade in Madison's December 1813 message to Congress, wherein more was left unsaid than explained. Smuggling by American citizens had not been mentioned, nor had the president alluded to the notorious trade carried on with the enemy through sailing ships flying spurious "third country" flags. But a few days after he reported to the nation, Madison sent Congress a secret message repeating an earlier call for an embargo. Present laws tended "to favor the enemy, and thereby prolong the war," the president said. Bad enough that British troops were being fed with American wheat, Madison observed, but perhaps worse was the "British fabrics and products [that] find their way into our ports, under the name and from the ports of other countries; and often in British vessels, disguised as neutrals, by false colors and papers." To stop this trading

---

13. Williams, *History of American Wars*, 105.

14. Leonard D. White, *The Jeffersonians: A Study in Administrative History, 1801–1829* (New York: Macmillan, 1951), 184–85; Message to Congress, 6 January 1814, House of Representative Records, National Archives.

15. Quoted in Steven Watts, *The Republic Reborn: War and the Making of Liberal America, 1790–1820* (Baltimore: Johns Hopkins University Press, 1987), 99.

with the enemy, Madison asked Congress to enact at once an embargo on exports.[16] The president also wanted a nonimportation act to cover non-British textiles and rum, with tighter regulations to make legitimate the registry of ships coming into American ports. Because the British blockade prevented all commerce except in New England, the embargo was clearly aimed at the region giving the Madison administration so much grief.[17] With uncharacteristic speed, Congress in a matter of days gave Madison his embargo act.

New England reacted angrily. As the govenors of the northern states had refused to cooperate with the War Department by declaring that they would not release the state militia for a foreign invasion, the lawmakers in Boston now claimed that an overbearing federal legion was interfering in the daily lives of the Bay State's citizens. "It was the embargo of December 1813 — which prohibited the coasting trade and which the administration enforced with a rigor disastrous to the flourishing smuggling enterprises of New England's borders and to the people of Nantucket—which put an end to Federalist patience," historian James Banner discerned.[18] In late December the town meeting at South Hadley, Massachusetts, instructed its state legislators to consider ways to avert a crisis. When the Massachusetts General Court convened in January 1814, the Federalist opposition was on a course of total opposition to "Mr. Madison's war."

Meanwhile, forces operating independently of Madison's domestic quarrels were taking shape. A British ship carrying a diplomatic pouch dropped anchor at Annapolis on 30 December 1813, with a letter aboard addressed to the secretary of state. The British foreign secretary was offering to negotiate directly with the American commissioners sans Russian mediation, in either London or the Swedish port of Gothenburg. Madison leaped at the chance to save the aborted peace mission. Before the week was out, he sent Lord Castlereagh's letter to Congress along with his reply accepting the proposal. This may have been a trial balloon on the president's part, for when he saw that the reaction in Washington was favorable Madison sent the Senate a surprise list of peace commission appointees; for a political stroke the president had included the name of one of the most popular leaders in Congress — House Speaker Henry Clay. When the Senate took only a few days for the confirmation process, Madison grew bolder and sent Gallatin's name as an additional envoy. (Gallatin had managed to stay in Europe, hoping for such a break.) But the president sugarcoated the pill for the Leib-Giles-Smith

16. Hunt, *Writings of Madison*, 8:275–76.
17. Adams, *History*, 873.
18. James M. Banner, *To the Hartford Convention: The Federalists and the Origins of Party Politics in Massachusetts, 1789–1815* (New York: Alfred Knopf, 1970), 313.

faction by also naming a cabinet replacement for Gallatin. The unpopular Pennsylvanian was to be followed in the Treasury post by George W. Campbell, a likable Tennessean who had served in the Senate. On 9 February 1814 the Senate approved this job swap by an unrecorded vote.[19]

If Madison drank an extra glass of Madeira that night, he deserved to celebrate. For one of the few times since he became president, Madison had made a bargain and achieved his goal in the Senate. Undoubtedly Madison hoped that the Clay appointment would prove to New England his serious commitment to end the war. Although Madison's coup in placing Gallatin on the commission was of first importance, Clay's addition gave the delegation a western representative who would be useful in the ratifying process — if that day ever arrived.

The decision to grab the opportunity Castlereagh offered for peace forced Madison to check the plans drafted by Secretary of War Armstrong for a vigorous campaign on the Canadian border during the spring of 1814. Armstrong, responding to frightened New Yorkers, was ready to use Indian allies to harass British settlements on the Niagara peninsula and form a pincers movement to eject the British from Fort Niagara.[20] But Madison was opposed to using Indians on the frontier and preferred a defensive posture until the diplomatic signals from London were clearer.

Armstrong, never enamoured of the Russian peace offer and convinced that the British would never surrender their self-proclaimed "right of impressment," began a closet backbiting campaign of his own. He tried to interest Federalists in a political alliance that would derail Monroe's presidential ambitions, and he threatened to resign if the proposed Niagara campaign was canceled by Madison. For his trump card, Armstrong suggested to a New York congressman that Congress adopt a resolution favoring the annexation of Canada by the United States.[21] Madison's addition of Clay to the peace commission and Monroe's instructions to the envoy, including the possible cession of Canada to the United States, took the sting out of Armstrong's little intrigue, but how long the president could tolerate a grumbler in his cabinet became a matter of concern.

Increasingly Madison saw the peace conference, now scheduled for Gothenburg, as his ace in the hole. If the nation's financial situation was precarious, Congress had no choice but to approve more loans as long as the peace mission held out hope for an early settlement of the lengthy list of British wrongs. American rights, including the end of impressment, might be vin-

19. *Senate Executive Proceedings*, 3 vols. (Washington, D.C.: Duff Green, 1828), 2:470–71.

20. Stagg, *Mr. Madison's War*, 370–71.

21. Ibid., 373.

dicated without pressing the claim to Canadian soil. After all, the French had been retreating across Europe since October 1813. While Napoleon's armies triumphed, the United States could expect to find the British military commitments to the American war half-hearted. The crushing defeat of Napoleon's army by the allies at Leipzig forced the French to fall back beyond the Rhine. Surely Madison must have wondered what might happen if the British decided to throw more troops into the American campaign. Where would they send an armada? New Orleans, with its rich storehouses of cotton and other commodities, was not ruled out as a potential target. And what if British troops landed in East Florida on a punitive expedition headed for Georgia?

Madison was unaware of the diplomatic maneuvers taking place in Europe, but he benefited from the master stroke of placing Gallatin in de facto charge of the American mission. Fed up with the inaction at St. Petersburg, the American commissioners had departed for Amsterdam late in January 1814 to await developments; there a discreet message from across the Channel told Gallatin that more direct negotiations were a possibility. Although French armies were everywhere on the run, Gallatin was granted safe passage to visit London at a time when American fortunes seemed at low ebb. "The world has seen President Madison plunge into a war from the basest motives," crowed the London *Times* early in 1813, "and conduct it with the most entire want of ability."[22] Since then, American arms had been tarnished by the fiasco at Chrysler's Farm and the burning of Buffalo, so that except for the Great Lakes victories, there was little room for an American foothold in any diplomatic contest. Gallatin's ability to negotiate, a skill honed by his financial dealings with hardheaded businessmen like John Jacob Astor and Stephen Girard, was the chief American asset when the British cabinet took up the nuisance war across the Atlantic. With Napoleon's armies on the verge of collapse in March 1814, the British were more concerned about the shape of postwar Europe than the echoes of war from imperial outposts.

Congress gave Madison his embargo in short order, but balked when the president sought companion laws to give teeth to his restrictive policy. Madison urged the passage of bills that (among other things) forbade the ransoming of ships captured by the enemy and that would have closed American ports to any importation of British woolens, textiles, or "ardent spirits." These measures died in committee as Congress wrestled with the old problem of money, brought forward in a new form by Gallatin's replacement. Pro-

22. Quoted in Adams, *History*, 866.

viding money for the army, which was far below authorized strength with fewer than thirty-four thousand men in uniform, was an unending task. Congress abandoned the idea of a draft and approved a bill that offered recruits a cash bonus ($124) and a half section (320 acres) of public land for enlisting. Secretary of the Treasury Campbell's revised estimate indicated that $40 million would be needed for the war effort in 1814. Of course, the New England banks were teeming with money, but there was no hope that they would help the Treasury survive another crisis.

Jefferson heard the Macedonian cry for more money and thought that it could be found by "the continual creation of new [state] banks . . . for already there is so much of their trash afloat that the great holders of it shew vast anxiety to get rid of it."[23] In a somber mood, Jefferson told Madison the emission of paper money "will ensure your loan for this year; but what will you do for the next?" Jefferson thought it likely that the nation's financial structure "must blow up before the year is out and thus a tax of 3[00] or 400 millions will be levied on our citizens who had found it a work of so much time and labour to pay off a debt of 80 millions."

How Madison reacted to his predecessor's gloomy prediction is not known, but there was revived talk in Congress of chartering the Bank of the United States, and after much haggling a new loan of twenty-four million dollars was authorized. The best that Madison's friends could obtain as a stopgap for the expected fifteen-million-dollar deficit was further legislation permitting the issuance of five million dollars in Treasury notes, and if these borrowed funds fell short, the president was permitted to approve the printing of another five million dollars.

In the midst of the budget battle, Madison's stock in the Senate suddenly rose as the result of a misstep by Postmaster General Gideon Granger. Granger ignored warnings from Republican friends that the appointment of Senator Michael Leib to the vacant postmaster's office in Philadelphia would irritate Madison. For reasons of pride if nothing else, Granger defied the naysayers and appointed Leib to the lucrative post; whereupon Madison in a matter of hours ordered Granger fired. On 2 March 1814 the *National Intelligencer* took pains to assure readers that Granger was never told that the Leib appointment had White House approval.[24] Granger's standing in the Republican party was ruined, and the incident rebounded in Madison's favor for the troublesome Leib was now out because he had resigned to take a new job. Moreover, reports from Virginia made it likely that Leib's partner in attacking the Madison administration — Senator Giles — had no chance of reelection.

23. Jefferson to Madison, 16 February 1814, Madison Papers, DLC.
24. *National Intelligencer,* 1 March 1814.

The embargo Madison sought and obtained had denied customs revenue for the Treasury but had not perceptibly affected British commerce. Enterprising Yankees continued to smuggle British-labeled goods across Lake Ontario in alarming quantities. On the high seas, Britain was now the master, and with Napoleon in full retreat Madison decided not to make an issue of the embargo (which the New England delegations in Congress derided) any longer. On 31 March 1814 he sent a special message to Congress recommending the end of the embargo and the resumption of exports and imports "in vessels of the United States and in vessels owned and navigated by the subjects of powers at peace with them." Only goods produced in Britain would remain on the president's list of interdicted products.

Southern and western Republicans, who had defended the Jefferson-Madison embargo from 1807 onward, were confounded by the sudden abandonment of a basic party policy. After much debate the necessary bills passed both houses and Madison signed the law on 14 April. "From that day the restrictive system," historian Henry Adams gloated, "which had been the cardinal point of Jefferson's and Madison's statesmanship, seemed to vanish from the public mind and the party politics of the country."[25]

More to the point, Madison saw the end of the embargo as a pacifying measure. Pressure from New England and the difficulty of enforcement may have caused Madison to reverse himself. As a *National Intelligencer* essayist wrote, "Removal of the cause of the disaffection of the East [New England] will reunite the East with the South. . . . I hope to see the bear of the East and the wolf of the South lie down with the lamb of the Centre, and that as a House divided against itself cannot stand, by this measure the union will be again restored [and] all will rally round the standard of our common country."[26] Madison himself could not have said it more optimistically; this phrasing would hang in a deep recess of the nation's memory.

Thus by surrendering on the embargo issue Madison hoped to dampen the fires of disunion burning at Hartford, Boston, and Marblehead. He also realized that with Napoleon's collapse the British had no need to make themselves the policemen of the world's sea lanes. Peace in Europe seemed the likely prospect, and with peace would come the resumption of normal commerce. In short, Madison was facing the facts. If abandoning the embargo would bring needed dollars into the national cash box and deprive New England merchants of their chief cause of complaint, why insist on an outmoded policy? Critics of Madison's presidency have taken pains to note the inconsistencies of his attitude toward the Bank of the United States, of his use of the embargo, and of his policy toward Spanish Florida. The White

25. *Niles' Weekly Register,* 23 April 1814; Adams, *History,* 881.
26. *National Intelligencer,* 14 April 1814.

147

House occupant can never escape criticism, either in office or in the cemetery, but most presidents have bent to the winds of expediency. James Madison certainly did.

As Congress hurried to finish its business, Madison's mail sacks were filled with the usual requests for patronage, resolutions from state legislatures supporting his war plans, and plaintive pleas for relief from businessmen who had risked their fortunes on cargoes now seized and bonded in warehouses. The president tried to ignore requests for his intervention on behalf of office seekers, but he had to find replacements for cabinet officers who were weary of Washington life or the demands of public service. William Pinkney, who had replaced Caesar Rodney as attorney general, was miffed when Congress debated a bill requiring the mandatory residence of the attorney general in the capital (most men who held the post had continued their law practices at home). Pinkney, who lived in Baltimore, angrily resigned as the House of Representatives considered the bill's merits. Richard Rush, a Pennsylvania lawyer with excellent credentials, was persuaded to take the post. Return J. Meigs, a man as capable as his name was remarkable, was appointed to the vacancy left by the fallen Granger's departure. To be sure, the cabinet missed Gallatin, but with the noisy critics in the Senate almost silenced, Madison had reason to believe that his official family was as much improved as his rapport with the Senate.

Some of Madison's interludes had little to do with mulish senators or congressmen. As president-elect, Madison had joined other dignitaries early in 1809 to watch Robert Fulton demonstrate a wicked-looking "harpoon gun" at the Kalorama estate outside Washington. Now Fulton, giddy with the success of his steamboats on the Hudson, invited Madison to support his proposal for construction of defensive "Steam floating batteries." When Congress approved the construction of his invention Fulton wanted the president's advice. "Should there not be money in the treasury for the purpose I can make the loan in New York on the guarantee of the government and any interest over 7 per cent[?] . . . One word from you will give Vigor to the operations."[27] Whether Madison gave the word is not certain, but Congress did authorize funds and eventually the *Steam Frigate* was launched.[28]

Proof that domestic affairs were swinging Madison's way was furnished by the final solution to the "ancient" Yazoo land scandal. Born of a corrupt deal in the Georgia legislature twenty years earlier, the Yazoo affair involved land titles that had presumably been bought by innocent third parties. While in Jefferson's cabinet Madison had served as a commissioner in an attempt

27. Fulton to Madison, 23 March 1814, Madison Papers, DLC.
28. Cynthia O. Philip, *Robert Fulton: A Biography* (New York: Franklin Watts, 1985), 325.

to bring justice into the midst of that fraud and had drawn Randolph's wrath for his efforts. Now the settlement was muddied by the 1810 *Fletcher v. Peck* decision in the Supreme Court. Denounced in the South as a judicial usurpation, the Marshall Court decision held that the fraudulent titles were part of a contract that could not be broken, hence the present titleholders (mostly northerners) were entitled to their lands. As a commissioner in 1805 Madison had hoped to settle the matter and go on to more urgent problems, but the compromise brought out the worst in John Randolph. As long as Randolph was in the House, the Yazoo case was his whipping boy, but when he lost his seat in the 1812 election a glimmer of hope for a settlement appeared. Four years after the Supreme Court announced its decision, legislation needed to implement a $5 million cash settlement was dropped into the Senate hopper. Thirty days after the Senate acted favorably, a companion measure passed the House. The New England investors (who eventually pocketed $4,282,151) were happy, and Madison was finally relieved of the Yazoo "tar baby" that had first left its smear on his reputation in 1791.[29]

Congress went home in late April 1814, and the Madisons seized the opportunity for an early trip to Montpelier. They reached Orange County as the dogwoods were bursting into bloom. Vexing problems, such as the twenty-three American partisans held in a British jail on charges of treason, seemed remote from the Montpelier porch. Meanwhile, newspapers in Washington repeated rumors of an armistice after a New York journal told of a March meeting in Sweden at which British and American diplomats conferred, "and it is expected a peace will result." Madison must have seen the article, for the *National Intelligencer* scotched "The Rumor of the Day" by declaring, "It is not true, as was very currently reported yesterday, that an armistice has been concluded by our government with the enemy."[30]

Madison probably wondered where such stories originated. And, as he rode out to check the Montpelier wheat crop, his mind might have wandered to the motives of his secretary of war, John Armstrong. A man of strong opinions with good connections in New York political circles, Armstrong saw that his chances for the presidency in the 1816 election hinged on personal military success. He was willing, therefore, to do whatever was necessary, even appear on the battlefield, to vault him ahead of Monroe, who the southern Republicans assumed would be the caucus choice. Although his nomination as secretary of war had squeaked by the Senate, Armstrong acted as though he had the full confidence of the nation. His reforms in the chain

---

29. William T. Hutchinson et al., eds., *The Papers of James Madison*, 16 vols. (Chicago and Charlottesville: University of Chicago Press and University Press of Virginia, 1962–), 14:21–22n.

30. *Niles' Weekly Register*, 28 July 1814; *National Intelligencer*, 25–26 April 1814.

of military command had removed some of the dead wood inherited from Eustis; but the swashbuckling William Henry Harrison had also been removed, perhaps because Armstrong saw him as a presidential rival. At any rate, Armstrong had made no apologies for offending the hero of Tippecanoe after he had questioned Harrison's administrative integrity, causing him to resign "in a huff."[31] There were two sides to the story, of course. Harrison had a frontiersman's careless disdain for strict accountability—he was a soldier, not a bookkeeper. Harrison's letter explaining his resignation reached Washington while the president was enjoying the Blue Ridge scenery.

"A very seasonable spring has given a fine countenance to the country," Madison wrote a cabinet member; but he feared "an exception is about to take place in our Wheat fields which abound with the Hessian fly." Lovely as it was at Montpelier, there was always a hint of impending disaster. One reason for the president's anxiety was the lack of news from the peace negotiators in Europe. The Allies had occupied Paris in March 1814 and had sent Napoleon into exile; but no word from the American envoys had reached Washington. "Neither have we any accts. from England," Madison added in a letter to Jefferson; however, he thought that the British cabinet "can not do less than send negociators to meet ours; but whether in a spirit of ours is the important question."[32]

At that point Madison received a dispatch from his secretary of war in Washington. Without checking with Madison, Armstrong had sent Andrew Jackson notice that he would be elevated to the major general's vacancy created by Harrison's angry resignation. Unaware of Armstrong's precipitate offer to Jackson, Madison told the secretary of war that he thought the way was clear to promoting Jackson (whose forces had won an important victory in March 1814 over the Creeks at Horseshoe Bend); but, Madison added, "I suspend a final decision however until I see you [in Washington]."[33]

When Madison returned to the White House in the spring of 1814, he learned of Armstrong's quasi-appointment of Jackson. He was not pleased but decided to let Jackson's elevation stand. Meanwhile, another instance of Armstrong's high-handed methods came to the president's attention when he heard from his former secretary, Isaac Coles. Coles, who had resigned from Madison's official family in 1809 after publicly whipping a congressman who criticized his boss, had taken a commission in an infantry regiment. Early in June 1814 Coles, angered because he had been passed over for promo-

31. Stagg, *Mr. Madison's War*, 399–400.
32. Madison to George W. Campbell, 7 May 1814, in Hunt, *Writings of Madison*, 7:276–77; Madison to Jefferson, 10 May 1814, Madison Papers, DLC.
33. Madison to Armstrong, 24 May 1814, Madison Papers, DLC.

tion, claimed that Armstrong had favored Coles in public but "at the same time . . . gave *private assurances* to Col: Preston's friends that he should be promoted over Col: Coles."[34] What was Armstrong trying to do, playing up to a crowd at one moment and double-dealing with Madison's kinsman in the next? Patience seemed warranted, Madison decided, and he let the matter rest for the moment.

In late June Madison called a cabinet meeting to consider the British peace treaty terms. A ship from Europe had broken the diplomatic silence, and the American negotiators needed direction. Since 1763 the British had pushed for an Indian buffer zone between the United States and Canada, and they included this demand in the peace terms. Creating such a state from the ceded Northwest territory defied common sense, argued the Americans, and, furthermore, it had been among the grievances that had led to the Revolution. That British demand was preposterous! At any rate, "shall a treaty of peace, silent on the subject of Impressment be authorized?" Madison asked his cabinet. A cabinet majority said no, and the negotiators were instructed "to insert or to annex some declaration or protest, agst. any inference from the silence of the Treaty on the subject of impressment, that the British claim was admitted or that of the U.S. abandoned."[35]

Madison and his cabinet were in truth wasting their time and energy, for the American negotiators had to move on their own or seem weak-kneed to the British. Thus while the Madison administration talked tough, the American diplomats parried with their British counterparts. The only progress made by the late spring of 1814 was a joint agreement to move the treaty discussions from Sweden to Ghent in Belgium. Although the Flemish city was "a British military camp," it was a far more comfortable rendezvous than Gothenburg; also, because it was closer to London, the Queen's envoys would be able to communicate more easily with their home office.[36] Not until 6 July 1814 were all the American commissioners ready to look across the table at their British counterparts, and they slowly backed down from their insistence that some part of Canada be turned into American soil. With a restless British army only a few miles away, the Americans wondered what devilment the War Office in London might attempt in order to weaken their bargaining position.

Armstrong and Madison wondered, too. Vice-President Gerry, who was resting in New England, had asked Madison to keep him informed for he knew little about the plans for the 1814 summer campaign. Madison replied

34. Isaac Coles to Madison, 4 June 1814, Coles Papers, Chicago Historical Society.
35. Cabinet memorandum, 23–24 June 1814, Madison Papers, DLC.
36. Fred L. Engelman, *The Peace of Christmas Eve* (New York: Harcourt, Brace & World, 1962), 95, 116.

that the country had little choice, so long as the negotiations proceeded, but to be vigilant. "It is a reasonble expectation that with the facility afforded by the peace in Europe, an adjustment with us may take place," Madison wrote. But if the British became belligerent "out of a misconceived state of things here, we can see nothing before us but another combat, *pro aris et focis.*"[37] That is, Americans would protect their "altars and firesides" should the British have an offensive up their sleeves.

Armstrong was aware that Madison was paying more attention to his conduct of the land warfare, too. As the outlines of a campaign to invade Ontario emerged, Madison in the spring of 1814 asked for the cabinet's opinion on a two-pronged, land and water, attack on the peninsula "& proceeding towards York." All except Monroe thought the plan a good one, and Monroe "did not positively oppose but thought the measure hazardous."[38] The president also asked Armstrong for a report on troop strength and naval preparedness for key positions on the lake. Then Madison sent the secretary notes on the disposition of troops and gave advice on how to placate governors who were reluctant to order their state militiamen to battle zones.[39]

Trouble developed when two of Armstrong's choices for high command, Generals Izard and Brown, fell to quarreling. Brown, eager to fight the British rather than Izard, led his army to recapture Fort Erie and defeated a superior force at the Battle of Chippewa on 5 July. After failing to join with Commodore Chauncey at Fort George, Brown was attacked by the British on 25 July at Lundy's Lane. Both armies took a beating, with each losing about eight hundred men, and although both sides claimed victory, it was actually a draw. At month's end, the battered American army was back where it had started. Brown and Commodore Chauncey started blaming each other for the failed campaign, and in the shouting match that ensued, neither man gained much credit.

Armstrong took Brown's side and said Chauncey needed disciplining, a chore normally reserved for Secretary of the Navy Jones. Jones, who had threatened to resign in April and was staying on only because of pressure from Madison, was reluctant to censure Chauncey. Late in July, Jones relieved Chauncey and gave Stephen Decatur the Lake Ontario command. Armstrong pleaded with Madison for a direct-order, joint army-navy assault to win control of the vital lake, but Madison inferred that most of the problem was centered in Izard's reluctance to cooperate with Brown.

Confusion lay ahead, for Izard became testier as Armstrong issued orders that undercut the strategic defense of Lake Champlain. In August 1814 Izard moved his four thousand men from Plattsburg to Sackett's Harbor. Ul-

37. Madison to Gerry, 9 July 1814, Madison Papers, DLC.
38. Cabinet memorandum, 7 June 1814, in Hunt, *Writings of Madison*, 7:279–80.
39. Memorandum to the secretary of war, 6 July 1814, Madison Papers, DLC.

timately, a British siege of Fort Erie was lifted, but nothing more was accomplished along the Canadian-American border during the summer of 1814. By September a strong British force of nearly twelve thousand veterans was poised above Plattsburg for a land and water campaign that had been planned in London to strengthen Britain's hand at the Ghent bargaining table. American illusions of a quick conquest of Canada were now gall-and-wormwood, for the military situation on land was essentially the same in September 1814 as it had been in July 1812.

Meanwhile, diplomatic dispatches from Belgium and France added to Madison's dismal reading. The so-called great powers — including Louis XVIII — were truckling to Britain, and the once-friendly Russian tsar had snubbed the American minister in Paris. Madison decided that he had to share his burden with Congress and issued a proclamation on 8 August calling for a special session to consider "great and weighty matters" in mid-September.[40] Madison had read a news packet from London that mentioned more British treaty demands, including the exclusion of American ships from the Newfoundland fisheries. What was their game?

Everybody on the American side was unhappy, but none more so than Armstrong, who thought that Monroe had hopelessly snarled all his plans by conniving with Jones and Izard. Then on 13 August Madison sent Armstrong a "massive reprimand . . . over the way he had been running his department." Delicately but unmistakably Madison told Armstrong that he had overstepped his authority when he consolidated regiments "without the knowledge or sanction of the President" and applied "certain rules & regulations" without executive sanction. Indeed, Madison said, he did not learn of the new orders until he read of them "in the newspapers." Madison listed other grievances and then spelled out his orders for Armstrong's future conduct: All general or permanent orders, orders for courts-martial, commissions or dismissions, acceptance or refusals of resignations from field-grade and general officers, all instructions relating to the militia or Indian treaties, and any changes in military district boundaries required prior presidential approval.[41]

Armstrong took his dressing-down in manly fashion. Then Madison looked at the inspector general's report concerning unfit officers and decided to ask Armstrong for his own evaluation of those whose records qualified them to remain in the army. It was not a pleasant chore. Armstrong's torment was not finished, however, for within two weeks both the president and his secretary of war would know humiliation unlike any that Americans in high offices have felt before or since.

40. Richardson, *Messages of the Presidents*, 1:544.
41. Marshall Smelser, *The Democratic Republic, 1801–1815* (New York: Harper & Row, 1968), 257–60; Stagg, *Mr. Madison's War*, 399–407; Brant, *Madison*, 6:282–83.

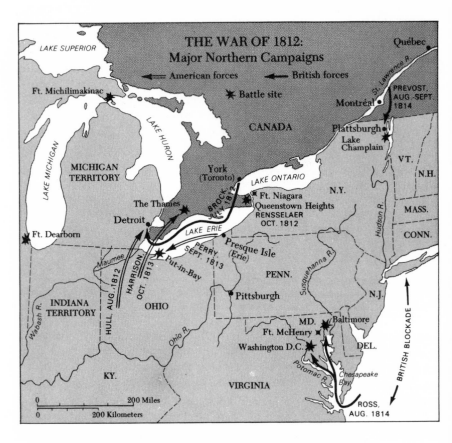

Source: George B. Tindall and David E. Shi, *America: A Narrative History* (New York: W. W. Norton & Company, 1989), p. 223. Reprinted with permission.

8

★ ★ ★ ★ ★

A CAPITAL'S
NOT FOR BURNING

Early in July 1814, while there was still hope that the Canadian campaign would force the British to keep all their troops in northern defensive positions, the president spoke to John Armstrong about "a systematic provision against invading armaments" so that "this City [Washington] and Baltimore" would be defended.[1] The president asked his secretary of war to report on general coastal defenses, using the information and estimates discussed at their 1 July cabinet meeting, when it was assumed that 3,140 regular troops and 10,000 militiamen could be mustered to defend the nation's capital. Even though the negotiators were still huddled in Ghent and land forces were under orders to take the offensive in upstate New York, Madison had every reason to be concerned about defending the major American ports. British landing parties had been foraging along the coast since the war began, but there were recent, disturbing reports that a full-fledged redcoat invasion was possible. Starting in the spring of 1814 newspapers periodically reported rumors of "a large British force coming to America." One such rumor appeared in the *National Intelligencer* on 30 March. It told of a Royal Navy armada that was laden with 4,000 British marines and headed for the United States, carrying "Congreve rockets, shrapnel shells," and other accoutrements of modern warfare.[2]

Usually these reports were wrong as to numbers and timing, but in this

---

1. James Madison to Armstrong, 2 July 1814, in Gaillard Hunt, ed., *The Writings of James Madison*, 9 vols. (New York: G. P. Putnam's Sons, 1900-1910), 7:281-82n.
2. *National Intelligencer*, 30 March 1814.

case there was fire behind the smoke. The French army was broken. Napoleon had abdicated early in April 1814 and was headed for Elba. With the return of peace in Europe, the British had a large land force that would need to be disbanded or sent where the fighting continued. The United States was the natural target of much speculation as the British cabinet pondered the effects of peace after over twenty years of battling against the American quasi-ally, France.

Even before Madison knew of Napoleon's collapse he had authorized armistice talks with the British in Canada at a conference called to discuss exchanging prisoners of war.[3] Nothing came of the meeting, however, because the president made the cessation of hostilities dependent on a naval as well as a land force ceasefire. As long as the Royal Navy harassed American coastal cities, Madison figured that a punitive invasion of Ontario was simply tit for tat. Madison was also aware of the American weakness at the bargaining table, which became evident when news reached Washington on 9 June that Napoleon had abdicated, a hard fact that brought smiles to Federalist faces as their predictions of a bad war and a worse peace seemed nearly realized. In Massachusetts the state lawmakers decided to rub it in and, by a joint resolution, called on the Madison administration to end the war. In such circumstances, Madison's cabinet discussed the instructions for the American negotiators and debated whether to drop the subject of impressment. Someone suggested that the negotiators be told to say that the issue of "impressment along with that of commerce [could be left] to a separate negotiation."[4]

What the Americans needed was an escape hatch that would allow the war to end with only a slight whimper. Gallatin, ever the realist, warned the secretary of state that the British government was ready to punish its former colonies by revoking some rights in the 1783 peace treaty and even — incredible as it sounded — forcing the United States to return Louisiana to the Spanish empire.[5] This news shocked the cabinet, shocked Madison, and led to the 27 June vote to drop impressment as an adamant American bargaining point.

With Napoleon gone and France in disarray, public opinion in Britain was now directed at the upstart United States of America. Newspaper editor-

3. J. C. A. Stagg, *Mr. Madison's War: Politics, Diplomacy, and Warfare in the Early American Republic, 1783–1830* (Princeton, N.J.: Princeton University Press, 1983), 385.

4. Cabinet memorandum, 23–24 June 1814, Madison Papers, Library of Congress (hereafter cited as DLC).

5. Gallatin to Monroe, 6 June 1814, quoted in Stagg, *Mr. Madison's War,* 395.

ials called for retaliation for its having "stabbed us in the back," and Gallatin had digested many such demands when he wrote Monroe in June 1814:

> This is a very general sentiment of the nation; and that such are the opinions of the ministry was strongly impressed on the mind of ——— by a late conversation he had with Lord Castlereagh. Admiral Warren also told Levett Harris, with whom he was intimate at St. Petersburg, that he was sorry to say instructions given to his successor on the American station were very different from those under which he had acted, and that he feared very serious injury would be done to America.[6]

Warren should have known, for his relief was furnished by Vice-Admiral Sir Alexander Cochrane on 1 April 1814, and this new commander of the Atlantic and Gulf stations was eager to teach Americans a lesson. "I have it much at heart," he told Lord Bathurst, "to give them a drubbing before peace is made." Cochrane expected to enlist American slaves under His Majesty's banner once the British invasion of the Chesapeake region became a reality, and he predicted that the freed blacks wearing red coats would "be as good Cossacks as any in the Russian army, and more terrifying to Americans than any troops that can be brought forward."[7] Cochrane assured General Prevost, the British commander of the thrust at Lake Champlain, that he would order British forces to cause havoc on American towns and cities from the St. Croix River to the St. Mary's on the Florida border. In short, the Royal Navy was extending its blockade north to include New England. All Americans were to be treated as enemies, and many were going to suffer the agonies of war.

Action by the Royal Navy early in April 1814 had been an indication that the world's mightiest military machine was ready to step up its trans-Atlantic war. The immunity New England had enjoyed vanished 7 April when the Royal Navy descended the Connecticut River to Pettipaug and burned more than twenty seaworthy Yankee ships. In June the king's sailors destroyed a smaller fleet of American merchantmen at Wareham, Massachusetts, and smaller numbers of Yankee ships were involved in brief actions elsewhere on the defenseless New England coast. Then in July the British ousted the small American force on Moose Island, in Passamaquoddy Bay, and made good their threats to move onto the American mainland by heading toward the Maine District of Massachusetts. While President Madison and his cabinet worried about the rumors of British sails sighted in Chesapeake Bay, the enemy occupied Machiasport on the Penobscot River and menaced Castine.

6. Gallatin to Monroe, 13 June 1814, quoted in Alfred T. Mahan, *Sea Power in Its Relation to the War of 1812*, 2 vols. (Boston: Little, Brown & Company, 1905), 2:332.
7. Ibid., 2:331.

Monroe read the diplomatic dispatches from Europe and decided it was time to bestir the administration. Reciting the warnings from Gallatin in London and Crawford in Paris, Monroe was blunt. "We may therefore expect the worst and ought to be prepared for it," he told the president. Madison took the hint and on 9 August he issued a call for a special session of Congress to begin 19 September. Then, joined by his cabinet, Madison boarded a navy barge on the Potomac and went downstream to Fort Washington, the sole defensive bastion below the capital. With some fanfare the president and his cabinet members inspected the batteries of heavy artillery recently mounted on limbers so they could be fired down on the British if they tried to navigate past the natural defenses at Kettle Bottom Shoals.

Meanwhile, Brigadier General William Winder (one of the Americans captured at Stony Point and then later exchanged) had been chosen by Madison as commander of the capital's defenses. In a flurry of activity, Winder issued calls for militia regiments from Maryland, Virginia, and Pennsylvania, gradually increasing his demands until he would have commanded fifteen thousand men if all the orders had been followed. Winder wanted to bring the militiamen who responded to a rendezvous point between Baltimore and Washington. A fatal flaw in the chain of command appeared when Secretary of War Armstrong disagreed with Winder's strategy. Keep the militiamen on the ready but do not bring them into camp, Armstrong advised, until "the spur of the occasion" demanded action. Winder was alarmed. "What possible chance will there be of collecting a force, after the arrival of the enemy, to interpose between them and either of those places?" Winder asked. Winder's request to bring six thousand men from Maryland into camp was granted, but Armstrong labeled a rumor that the British would strike from the Chesapeake as patent nonsense.

Congressman Philip Stuart, a militia general already in the field, knew better. After driving a small British force away from the Maryland shore, Stuart sent an urgent plea to Armstrong for more ammunition and larger guns. His request was ignored; so Stuart decided it was useless to ask Armstrong for help and sent his plea to the president instead. Madison overrode Armstrong and ordered powder and shot sent to Stuart and then told General Winder to dispatch three hundred fifty regular troops to help Stuart's militia at Upper Marlboro, at the headwaters of the Patuxent River.

Madison still expected his secretary of war to ensure that the capital was safe from British attack, but Armstrong (perhaps unwilling to place his military reputation at risk) treated the defense of Washington as a local matter. American intelligence was pitifully inadequate; so no one realized that the British strategy was to have General Prevost sweep down from the north with the main attack while a diversionary force would threaten Washington with a feint that might provide opportunities to harm the Americans on their front doorstep. However, Prevost ended up taking his men and plodding toward Plattsburg and obscurity. The expedition planned by Cochrane, in contrast, took its mission seriously. Major General Robert Ross, a veteran of the Napoleonic wars, was placed in command of the land forces carried by Cochrane's fleet. Rear Admiral George Cockburn knew the terrain and was sent along as an adviser. Ross's plan was to strike quickly at designated targets and then withdraw. Any plunder that fell into British hands was, of course, to be considered prizes of war and shared by the victors according to established British custom.

On the American side, false alarms raised by every unidentified sailing ship were offset by a tendency to dismiss all rumors as groundless. When a British squadron sailed into the mouth of Chesapeake Bay in mid-July, the American commander at Norfolk passed the information along but gave no credit to reports that transports bearing twelve thousand soldiers would soon follow. The number of redcoats rendezvousing in Bermuda, General Moses Porter reported, was closer to five or six thousand and they would be split into three forces headed for different theaters of action. Confidently Armstrong insisted that the reports of a huge force bearing down on Baltimore or Washington were "palpably a fable." Madison heard similar reports from another source who said that the British troop strength on the Potomac was about three thousand. "This must be a great exaggeration," the president informed Monroe early on 22 August.[8] By nightfall the president knew differently.

The most humiliating episode in American history was about to unfold. Whether the disastrous sequence of events could be blamed, as Captain Alfred T. Mahan insisted, on the bullheaded policies of "the men who for a dozen years had sapped the military operations of the nation" is beyond proof. Certainly Presidents Jefferson and Madison had long paid homage to the Republican dogma that the militia should be the reliable, frugal defense of the nation. One must remember, however, that in a war in which most troop movements had been painfully slow and months had been wasted in marching and countermarching in the northern front, the debacle at Washington occurred in only a few days. No one was prepared for the rapid military onslaught that would be called a blitzkrieg in the twentieth century.

On the day that Madison had dismissed reports of a large British contingent sailing up the Chesapeake Bay, thirty-four hundred British regulars supplemented by seven hundred Royal Marines, having landed two days earlier, reached Upper Marlboro and were marching past the remains of a hastily abandoned American gunboat flotilla. Commodore Barney had or-

8. James Madison to Monroe, 22 August 1814, in Hunt, *Writings of Madison*, 7:291–92, 293n.

dered his gunboats burned and had retreated with about four hundred sailors to a crossroads at Oldfields, six miles east of the capital. In a matter of hours, Ross's redcoats were closing in on General Winder's motley brigade of six thousand regulars and hastily assembled militiamen encamped nearby.

Madison, learning of the bold British move, rode to Winder's camp with several cabinet members (including Armstrong) in his mounted entourage to inspect the defense lines. The president and his advisers spent the night at Winder's headquarters, and the morning of 23 August Monroe joined them as Madison rode through the camp, making himself visible as more troops straggled into the cantonment. Winder did not seem worried when he predicted that the British force was probably headed for Annapolis, where he expected that General Ross would establish a base for an attack on either Baltimore or Washington. Reassured, the president sent a note to his wife, reporting that "the troops . . . are in high spirits and make a good appearance. . . . The reports as to the enemy have varied every hour. The last and probably truest information is that they are not very strong . . . and of course that they are not in a condition to strike at Washington." Madison hinted to the first lady, however, that the British "may have a greater force or expect one, than had been represented or that their temerity may be greater than their strength."[9]

The situation changed hour by hour. Two British deserters who came into camp apparently talked to the president and told an aide that the British force was larger than the Americans assumed. The perceptive young officer then predicted that the British might move on the American position soon, but Armstrong discounted the possibility of an immediate attack. Madison started to worry and wrote Dolley Madison a second message, warning her to be ready to flee. Frightened residents in the capital were ahead of the president in expecting trouble, and by nightfall the roads west of the city were choked with wagons laden with furniture and other valuables that would fit into buckboards and buggies. Early on the afternoon of 23 August the president, accompanied by Secretary of the Navy Jones and Armstrong, returned to Washington. The British army was only an hour's march behind them.

More confusion ensued, as there were rumors that the British were swinging south to attack Fort Washington from the rear in a coordinated movement with Royal Navy ships that had skirted the Potomac shoals. (In fact, Fort Washington was abandoned with unseemly haste by the American defenders.) Madison was back in the White House, but in the babel of rumors nobody knew where the British were headed. To be safe, Mrs. Madison

9. James Madison to Dolley P. Madison, [23] August 1814, in Hunt, *Writings of Madison*, 7:293–94.

began packing official papers into trunks and became resigned to the loss of their chinaware and furniture if the British were bent on invading the capital. Around midnight on 23 August Madison received a note from Monroe at Winder's headquarters. "The enemy are in full march for Washington," Monroe warned. "You had better remove the records."[10] The exhausted president sent Monroe's message to Armstrong's nearby lodgings, with orders to awaken the secretary of war if necessary. Then the Madisons tried to get some sleep.

The next day, 24 August, was a nightmare come true. An urgent message from Winder took Madison away from the breakfast table. A surprised Winder reported that the British were bound for Bladensburg. The president had the note relayed to Armstrong and then hurried to Winder's headquarters, where he found the general giving orders to blow up a bridge leading into Washington. Winder commissioned nearly five hundred men to do a job that six could handle and then rode toward Bladensburg. Armstrong arrived, but Madison was the one who decided Winder's judgment was faulty and he ordered Commodore Joshua Barney's sailors to hurry north with five naval guns to join the general's army forming along the Bladensburg Road. As the critical hour approached, Armstrong seemed more a spectator than the president's chief military adviser.

What was going on? Treasury Secretary Campbell, dismayed by what he saw, thought somebody ought to speak up. Campbell told Madison that "he was grieved to see the great reserve of the Secretary of War . . . who was taking no part on so critical an occasion." Armstrong's excuse was "that as the means of defending the District had been committed to Genl Winder, it might not be delicate to intrude his opinions without the approbation of the President."[11] Armstrong, fearing criticism, was hiding behind Madison's earlier reprimand of him so that the blame would fall on poor Winder.

The president would not allow Armstrong off so easily, however. Upon hearing Campbell's comments, Madison wheeled his horse around and told Armstrong that he was surprised to see the secretary so unperturbed. Madison said that his memorandum of 13 August ought not be misconstrued and that in the crisis they faced, Madison expected a man of Armstrong's experience to hurry to Bladensburg and "be of any service to Genl. Winder he could." Later, when Madison rode to the American defense lines near Bladensburg and found Winder accompanied by Monroe and Armstrong, the president asked "the latter whether he had spoken with Genl. Winder" about troop dispositions and defenses. "He said he had not."[12] Whether he

10. Quoted in Irving Brant, *James Madison*, 6 vols. (Indianapolis: Bobbs-Merrill Company, 1941–1961), 6:297.
11. Memorandum, 24 August 1814, in Hunt, *Writings of Madison*, 7:293–94.
12. Quoted in Brant, *Madison*, 6:300.

realized it or not, Armstrong's goose was cooked. The president at that very moment had trouble handling his horse and then the shooting started; so Madison prudently suggested that they all fall back to observe the battle. The fighting was over in three hours. Annapolis had never been part of General Ross's plan. Early on 24 August an order from Admiral Cochrane reached Ross. His troops were to return to the Maryland shore. But after arguing with Cockburn, Ross decided to continue the attack. He moved his troops before daybreak, following the original orders to capture Washington, disrupt the civil government, destroy public buildings, and cause general havoc in the nation's capital. Winder's story was not the usual too little too late, but rather a sad tale of bad guesses, faulty orders, and poor judgment. With nearly six thousand militiamen and Barney's sailors, the Americans outnumbered the British, but many of the untried milita riflemen were more eager to flee than to fight. Two thousand men were ordered to retreat before they had time to cock their guns and get off a single shot.

Monroe, mounted and frustrated, charged onto the field and tried to give some orders that made sense, but confusion invaded the American force faster than the British bayonets. A rumor rippled through the ranks that the president himself was coming down to see how Americans reacted to cold British steel, but nothing stiffened the Yankee spines. After some desultory fire, most of the militiamen ran pell-mell for the safety of nearby woods. Barney's sailors held firm and their guns ripped holes in the British lines. Unaccountably General Winder ordered his troops to fall back, leaving the road to Washington undefended. A veteran British officer who saw the spectacle said he had never seen troops "behave worse" than the frightened Americans.

Among the few American casualties was Commodore Barney, who, in trying to rally the retreating forces, was wounded and captured. Only ten or twelve Americans had been killed, and perhaps fifty wounded had been left on the field; the British, in contrast, had sixty-four killed and one hundred eighty-five wounded. Only a handful of Americans who were not wounded were captured. "The rapid flight of the enemy," General Ross reported, "and his knowledge of the country, precluded the possibility of many prisoners being taken."[13] The vaunted militiamen had hightailed for home. Except for the moaning of the wounded and the distant rattle of the scattered, retreating army, all was quiet on the Bladensburg Road. It was only four o'clock; with plenty of daylight left, the British began to move down the pike toward Washington. Thus the victors, almost unopposed, made a leisurely march into the capital of the United States. A sniper killed Ross's horse, after which a token force of three hundred armed Americans scattered.

13. John K. Mahon, *The War of 1812* (Gainesville: University Presses of Florida, 1972), 300; Mahan, *Sea Power in the War of 1812*, 2:351.

Ross was anxious to return to Cochrane's fleet; so he rapidly gave orders as his troops went on a spree of burning and looting. As pillaging armies go, the British showed restraint, but some Americans did not. The *National Intelligencer*, recapping the battle, recognized the British decorum and added, "No houses were half as much *plundered* by the enemy as by the knavish wretches about the town who profited by the general distress." As cinders and soot swirled around, Admiral Cockburn went to the offices of the *National Intelligencer*, the only newspaper that had been singled out for British fury. He ordered the British marines to wreck the presses and throw away the type, with an injunction to "destroy all C's so they can't abuse my name."[14]

If witnesses can be believed, the British relished the chance to set bonfires and teach the Americans a lesson in humiliation. A member of Congress wrote his wife that Admiral Cockburn assured a group of ladies that the British hoped to capture the president before they evacuated the capital. "You may thank old Madison for this," Cockburn said, "It is he who has got you into this scrape." Cockburn, perhaps in jest, added, "We want to catch him and carry him to England for a curiosity."[15] The British overall were quite restrained when it came to looting. One officer claimed that he traded his dirty shirt for a clean one left behind at the White House. Certainly Madison lost his shirt and more, but nobody expected the president to stay behind and risk capture. An explosion at the navy yard, touched off by Americans who wanted to destroy anything useful to the enemy, confused citizens, who figured that the destruction was increasing and that the British were about to run amok.

Bedlam did not follow, however. Private property was for the most part bypassed for the torching of public buildings — the Capitol, the White House, and offices used by the executive departments. The targets appeared to be so carefully selected that rumors of a British sympathizer guiding the torchbearers began to circulate. The French minister, residing in the Octagon House a few blocks from the executive mansion, reported this vivid scene to his French superior:

I never saw a scene at once more terrible and more magnificent. . . . A profound darkness reigned in the part of the city that I occupy, and we were left to conjectures and to the lying reports of negroes as to what was passing in the quarter illuminated by these frightful flames. At eleven o'clock a colonel, preceded by torches, was seen to take the direction of the White House, which is situated quite near mine. . . . [A letter was sent to the Brit-

14. Mahon, *War of 1812*, 301; *National Intelligencer*, 31 August 1814.
15. George Dangerfield, *The Awakening of American Nationalism, 1815–1828* (New York: Harper & Row, 1964), 5n.

ish officer, asking that the French minister's residence be spared and] my messenger found General Ross in the White House, where he was collecting in the drawing room all the furniture to be found, and was preparing to set fire to it. The general made answer that the King's Hotel should be respected as much as though his Majesty were there in person.[16]

Before the darkness ended, a heavy squall arose, and rain drenched the fires. After the storm subsided, Ross gave orders to prepare for a forced march back to the ships anchored at Benedict, Maryland, where the whole episode had begun four days earlier.

What had happened to the president? Wisely, Madison had not waited to watch the final rout of the American militia. "When it became manifest that the battle was lost," Madison noted, "I fell down into the road leading to the city and returned to it," jostled by fleeing militiamen and civilians.[17] For the first time in his life, James Madison heard the sound of combat. Before he headed for the White House, Madison told his cabinet members that if the British captured the city he would meet them at Frederick, Maryland, for "Executive consultations." Early that evening, Madison reached the abandoned White House and then slipped across the Potomac into Virginia, hoping to find his wife (who had already left the White House) before nightfall.

Dolley Madison had waited for the president to return until it became a matter of endangering her friends. After three o'clock she ordered a wagon pulled up to the front door and "had it filled with the plate and most valuable articles belonging to the house," including Gilbert Stuart's magnificent painting of Washington, which was taken off the dining-room wall, removed from its frame, and rolled up like a scroll. Mrs. Madison gave the portrait to "two gentlemen of New York for safekeeping" and made her escape into Virginia.[18] An earlier plan to meet near Great Falls was altered, and the president's wife hustled her servants and precious cargo of china and silverware to Salona, a friend's house located above the Little Falls bridge. Their plans miscarried, however, and Mrs. Madison ended up spending an anxious night in a Falls Church tavern while the president waited for her at Salona. The next day they met at an inn near Great Falls, where Dolley Madison remained while the president rode over to Maryland in pursuit of the remnants of the American forces marching toward Baltimore. The first lady was in no hurry to re-

16. Henry Adams, *History of the United States of America during the Administrations of Thomas Jefferson and James Madison*, vol. 2, *History of the United States of America during the Administrations of James Madison*, Earl N. Harbert, ed. (New York: Library of America, 1986), 1014 (hereafter cited as Adams, *History*).

17. Brant, *Madison*, 6:302.

18. Ibid., 6:303.

turn to Washington, despite assurances from couriers, refugees, and presidential aides that the British had deserted the capital after their incendiary spree. After almost four days in the saddle, Madison finally talked with the officers of the Baltimore-bound troops; he then wheeled his horse in the direction of the capital, accompanied by Monroe and Rush. Three days after the redcoats had dashed down Pennsylvania Avenue with torches aloft, Madison was back in Washington.

In short order, Madison sent word to his wife that it was safe to return, adding, "I know not where we are in the first instance to hide our heads." The situation was calmer than expected, however, and they soon set up their domestic quarters at their old residence on F Street (now the home of Mrs. Madison's sister, Anna Cutts, and her husband).[19] Nearby, the White House was a charred hulk. Madison, accompanied by Monroe and a few members of his cabinet, rode over the ruined areas, avoiding the main thoroughfares. Gradually the calculated British invasion caused a stir among the returning citizens. How had the invaders known the exact streets to follow to their objectives? Had not Major L'Enfant designed the city to thwart foreign invaders by creating a confusing, mazelike grid? As the city smoldered, the gutted *National Intelligencer* revived to report the rumor explaining British precision: A disaffected former resident had served as a British guide, leading the king's troops straight to their objectives on Capitol Hill and along Pennsylvania Avenue. Were there traitors in their midst?

Another question confronted Madison and his official family. Why had the British bothered to attack the American capital and then pulled out? In Europe the fall of a capital was considered the coup de grace to national pride, signaling the end of a campaign or war. Nothing of the sort occurred in the United States in August 1814. Americans near the city were more angered than frightened, and the incident clearly demonstrated the federal nature of the American government. The states were still in control of day-to-day living, and although Washington was temporarily ablaze, nobody thought of calling off the war. Move the capital? The *National Intelligencer* editor insisted that the idea was preposterous. "It would be kissing the rod an enemy has wielded," he objected.[20]

Washington was left defenseless, but the raiders would not return and the commanders at Baltimore, forearmed by the events at the capital, took heed. Earthworks were hurriedly erected as the British forces returned to their base at Benedict. In fact, the British had retreated from their main ob-

19. James Madison to Dolley P. Madison, 27 August 1814, Madison Papers, DLC; Brant, *Madison,* 6:306–11.
20. Marshall Smelser, *The Democratic Republic, 1801–1815* (New York: Harper & Row, 1968), 27–71; *National Intelligencer,* 2 September 1814.

jective, because Baltimore was now over sixty miles away by water and more than that by land. Admiral Cochrane was relieved that the raid on Washington had been carried out with such happy results, particularly given that he had tried to stop it. Now he was worried about the possibility of a yellow fever epidemic and wanted to depart for the safety of the ocean; but Ross and Cockburn talked the old man into a full-scale attack on Baltimore. Eight days passed as the British commanders argued, giving Baltimore's defenders plenty of time to gather militiamen and shore up harbor defenses. No help came from the federal government because the capital was still reeling from the 24 August disaster, and the state of Maryland bungled by sending the defenders crates that were marked "muskets" but that when opened "were found to contain not muskets, but old government records."[21]

Madison's longtime foe Samuel Smith was about to leave his seat in the Senate, but he retained great local powers and insisted that his militia generalship now made him the local commandant. Repeated calls for militiamen gave General Smith nearly 9,000 well-armed infantrymen, and Winder came from Washington with a column of his own. Winder thought he outranked Smith, but in time he deferred to the senator-general and turned control of 3,185 regulars over to Brigadier General John Stricker of the Baltimore militia. Baltimore dug in and waited.

General Ross decided to send his troops ashore at North Point, roughly fourteen miles below the city of forty thousand (the nation's third largest, after Philadelphia and Boston). Stricker had ordered skirmishers sent out while his men erected more barricades, and as Ross and his men advanced the American sharpshooters opened fire. Ross was hit in the chest and died within moments as the Americans fired a few volleys and retired. Ross's successor halted the attack and ordered an artillery barrage that continued until Stricker's men fell back to the main line of defense.

Admiral Cochrane meanwhile had moved his fleet up to bombard Fort McHenry at the mouth of the bay going into the city's main harbor. On 13 September Cochrane ordered his gunners to commence firing and then a day later dispatched twelve hundred British seamen to attempt a landing for an outflanking movement. The American gunners in Fort McHenry surprised the British with their accuracy, however, keeping the British so far offshore that their cannon made a great deal of noise but did little harm. Of some fifteen hundred British rounds fired, few hit their targets and many burst harmlessly in midair to become immortalized by volunteer artilleryman Francis Scott Key, who witnessed the spectacle from a vessel flying a flag of truce. Key was so impressed by what he saw that his description later became the words to "The Star Spangled Banner": "The rockets red glare . . . gave proof

21. Mahon, *War of 1812*, 3:307–12.

through the night, that the flag was still there." Indeed it was, and at seven o'clock the following morning, the British called off the bombardment.

Rain began to fall as the British land forces prepared to attack the American earthwork defenses, but when news came that Cochrane was unable to silence Fort McHenry, Colonel Arthur Brooke decided to call it quits. During the night, the British army withdrew. When General Smith was told of the retreat, he ordered a half-hearted pursuit but must have heaved a sigh of relief. Baltimore was saved, although in the suburbs British troops had vandalized a few houses and a church or two. *Niles' Weekly Register* exulted in the British withdrawal, claiming that Ross's death was a "Just Dispensation of the Almighty" as recompense for the "rape, robbery, and conflagration" and insisting that the disgraceful events of 24 August had been somewhat avenged.

The departing British felt little remorse at the excesses they had wrought upon the American people. Captain Edward Codrington of the Royal Navy believed that retaliation for the American conduct at York was justified and would help shorten the war. "I do not believe," Codrington wrote his wife, "there is anywhere a more detestable race of people."[22] News of the Baltimore repulse came to Washington along with reports that the British fleet had sailed south and was headed for the Atlantic. For a change, the reports proved to be true. The British fleet under Cochrane hoisted anchor for Halifax on 19 September, leaving a token force that did no further damage and finally left American waters for Jamaica on 14 October 1814.

Weeks before the British finally left the Chesapeake, Dolley Madison had scurried around Washington in search of a substitute for the blackened White House. She found a temporary domicile after Colonel John Taylor offered the first family his Octagon House, which had recently been occupied by the French minister's entourage. A handsome three-story brick structure, the house was almost as roomy as Montpelier and was only two blocks from the White House ruins. While rebuilding of the White House was under way, the Octagon House was the unofficial presidential mansion, until the elegant building was finally overrun with visitors and Mrs. Madison decided it was too cramped for real comfort.

In official Washington, meanwhile, Madison took charge. Citizens were impressed by Madison's spunky order to the cabinet to regroup immediately in a makeshift office on 29 August, even though no one knew whether the British would reappear and the Alexandria merchants were still cringing in fear across the Potomac. The Virginia city was then still technically a part of the Federal District, and to fend off the British incendiaries the local citizens had begged the town council to come to terms with the attackers. An

22. Ibid., 312.

ultimatum from Captain James Gordon (after his little fleet had worked its way up the Potomac, past the ruins of Fort Washington) had brought a rapid response. In short order, the Royal Navy sent men to round up as ransom all naval stores, weapons, gunpowder, and any seaworthy American ships in port. Gordon's men confiscated twenty-one vessels, upon which they loaded what the ships could carry, and burned the rest on shore. The loot was said to include sixteen thousand barrels of flour, one thousand hogsheads of tobacco, one hundred fifty bales of cotton, and casks of wine valued at five thousand dollars.

Americans in neighboring cities thought the Alexandrians had capitulated with too much haste and not a little cowardice, but the deed was done. Gordon spared the city and started back down the Potomac. Commodore Porter, ordered to harass Gordon, moved thirteen cannons into range a few miles below Mount Vernon and waited for Gordon's ships to appear. Gordon was probably surprised to see American resistance after so much retreating, but he returned the fire and sent a short party to silence the American batteries. Commodore Rodgers tried to use fire ships to confuse the British, but his plans miscarried and his three burning vessels fizzled out without inflicting damage. Fewer than two dozen men died on both sides before Gordon's ships finally quit the Potomac. The burning of Washington episode was over, and for all its spectacular effect, this was the last time that British arms would triumph on American soil.

Some finger pointing took place in Washington as the local residents claimed they had shown more courage than their Alexandria neighbors, and the Marylanders strutted after they learned of Baltimore's defenses. The northern congressmen who disliked the climate in Washington thought that this was the time for a fresh start, and they began to discuss a bill that would move the capital "to some more convenient and less dishonored place." Even Congressman Charles Ingersoll, a devoted partisan of Madison's policies, voted for a resolution that seemed to favor his home district (Philadelphia was a primary choice for the new site). Madison was against the whole idea and apparently let it be known that he believed the sooner Congress moved on to real business, the happier everyone would be. Support for the much-amended resolution then dwindled "at every successive vote till finally, by eighty-three to seventy-four, the project was defeated."[23] Local property owners also lobbied in the Patent Office building (the temporary meeting place of Congress) to kill the measure on the ground that they would be ruined. The *National Intelligencer* passed along the confidential word that if the legislation ever passed Congress, Madison would veto any "seat of the government" law.

23. Charles J. Ingersoll, *History of the Second War between the United States of America and Great Britain*, 2 vols. (Philadelphia: Lea & Blanchard, 1845), 2:264–65.

Madison's supporters in Washington were not limited to the cabinet or to government officials. The people generally approved of the president's quick return to the city and his visible presence within hours of the British withdrawal. The sight of the bantam-sized president scurrying hither and yon on his dapple-gray mount drew admiration from onlookers. Monroe in particular thought Madison's sang froid had been vital to the restoration of public confidence. When the *National Intelligencer* reported that "the President . . . was not only active during the engagement which took place with the enemy, but had been exerting himself for two or three days previous" and that "everyone joins in attributing to him the greatest merit," Monroe seconded the accounts. "I am satisfied that if by any casualty the President's return had been delayed 24 hours . . . a degree of degradation would have been exhibited here and elsewhere," the secretary of state observed.[24]

Madison understood the importance of making himself visible to the people. Toward his cabinet members, who had followed him everywhere at a gallop, Madison felt a mutual admiration—for all, that is, except Armstrong. The secretary of war came back from the designated rendezvous at Frederick, Maryland, a chastened man but unwilling to serve as the scapegoat for recent setbacks. Persistent rumors of Armstrong's unfitness swept through the ranks, however, and the president was told that the officers serving with troops left behind at Washington's defenses had vowed that they would rip off their insignia if Armstrong tried to give them orders. Madison confronted Armstrong with his disappointment over the inept performance of the defense forces. The president said that public criticism of Armstrong was "in a great measure rooted in the belief that he had not taken a sufficient interest in the defence of the city, nor promoted measures for it." Armstrong reacted with surprise, said he was the victim of vicious intrigue, and offered to resign.

Looking back on the unpleasant incident some months later, Madison tried to be charitable. As Madison recalled (he had prudently written down his version of their conversation soon after), Armstrong suggested that he be allowed offical leave of absence so that he might visit his family in New York. Obviously this would be the first step toward gracefully easing Armstrong out of the cabinet, and the president approved of the idea. Still Madison made it clear to Armstrong that he had failed his commander in chief by trying to evade responsibility for the fiasco that preceded the torching of Washington. It was obvious that Amrstong had not taken charge, Madison said, "everything done on that subject having been brought forward by myself."[25] Madison was not bragging about his effort but rather was castigating Armstrong for hiding behind a convoluted interpretation of the president's orders.

24. Special broadside, *National Intelligencer*, 30 August 1814; Monroe quoted in Brant, *Madison*, 6:312.

25. Memorandum, [29?] August 1814, in Hunt, *Writings of Madison*, 7:300–304.

Armstrong soon packed his valise and told friends he was going to New York on family business. He tarried in Baltimore, probably talked at length with some of Madison's severest critics, and then on 4 September sent a curt letter of resignation. Madison was relieved, but the incident would not remain private. Nursing his grudge, Armstrong published his side of the story in the bowdlerized version for a Baltimore newspaper. The president, busy on other matters, kept his own counsel concerning Armstrong and again asked Monroe to temporarily assume two cabinet posts. Armstrong's exit from the cabinet, almost as noisy as Robert Smith's, ended forever his slender presidential hopes while making Monroe's nomination more likely.

Amid his contretemps with Armstrong, Madison had listened to his cabinet and issued a presidential proclamation accusing the British invaders of "wanton destruction" of public buildings and records and of violating "the rules of civilized warfare."[26] The proclamation was meant to keep the public calm, to reassure European capitals that the United States had suffered only a temporary setback, and to assert that the damage had been done by brigands. The invasion was all the more reprehensible, Madison said, because it came "at the very moment of negociations for peace, invited by the enemy himself."

As Madison was revising a draft of the proclamation, circumstances in Britain were moving in a more pacific direction than the Washington fiasco indicated. As Dolley Madison pondered the revival of her weekly levees, the British prime minister wrote to an associate, "I wish we could get out of this [American] war: but the point upon which I am most anxious is, that we should not get deeper into it, for I fear we shall feel it a most serious embarrassment some months hence; and it is not a contest in which we are likely to obtain any glory or renown at all commensurate to the inconvenience it will occasion." Lord Sidmouth read the message with satisfaction, for he regarded the fracas in the United States as "almost civil war."[27] Weary of years of war, the British business community was ready for peace and profits; thus pressure on Parliament to negotiate peace seeped into cabinet meetings and made its way across the Channel to the diplomatic quarters in Ghent.

Madison knew nothing of these British political currents as he prepared for the early session of the Thirteenth Congress. The president had some reason to exult, for not only had the Royal Navy abandoned its Chesapeake campaign, but there was good news trickling in from the North. General George Prevost, the governor-general of Canada and commander of the Brit-

26. Rush to Monroe, 28 August 1814, Rush Papers, Historical Society of Pennsylvania; *Niles' Weekly Register*, 10 September 1814.

27. George Pellew, ed., *Life and Correspondence of the Right Honourable Henry Addington, First Viscount Sidmouth*, 3 vols. (London: J. Murray, 1847), 3:121.

ish force aimed at smashing American resistance in upstate New York, had been assuring Americans in the path of his invasion that they had nothing to fear because his battle was against only "the government of the United States, by whom this unjust and unprovoked war has been declared."[28] On 11 September 1814 the British-Canadian forces outnumbered the American land forces at Plattsburgh six to one, whereas on Lake Champlain the Americans, commanded by Captain Thomas Macdonough, had near naval parity with their opponents.

From the decks of his flagship, the twenty-six gun *Saratoga*, Macdonough heard the British guns pound the beleaguered fort but knew that the British had to destroy the American fleet or abandon the campaign. The American commander skillfully maneuvered his flotilla into an impregnable position and then tore the British fleet apart, with becalmed vessels flying the Union Jack taking broadside after broadside. After an intense fight, the British ships were so badly damaged that they, along with the *Saratoga*, had to be scuttled. Lake Champlain was now an American "pond." General Prevost, discouraged by the brisk American defense on shore, called off the siege by what had been "the finest army ever to campaign in America" and limped back to Canada. Although Macdonough was no phrasemaker, his report was dramatic: *The British had been whipped.*

Starved for good news, Americans hailed the victory at Lake Champlain with patriotic hyperbole. "Thus has terminated one of the most formidable expeditions ever fitted out in America," *Niles' Weekly Register* crowed. "If one disgrace can be balanced by another, *Hull's* surrender of *Detroit* is blotted from the catalogue, and the great commander in chief, *Sir George Prevost*, with *Wellington's* 'invincibles,' has carried the mark of dishonor from that miserable old man."[29] Ten days later the glorious news was part of drawing-room conversation in Washington; but at that time, no one in the capital knew that Britain still hoped to win a sizable piece of American real estate to use in the diplomatic bargaining at Ghent.

The Lake Champlain victory took some of the sting out of the British move to control the Maine coast from the Penobscot to New Brunswick. Monroe knew he could do nothing there; so as acting secretary of war he turned his attention southward and warned the governors of Georgia, Kentucky, and Tennessee to be ready for a British incursion from the Gulf of Mexico. Monroe gave General Jackson discretionary orders to prepare for a British landing, probably around New Orleans, and urged the Tennessean to count on 7,500 men from his home state and another 5,000 from Georgia and Kentucky. Governor William C. C. Claiborne in Louisiana was told to also raise

28. *Niles' Weekly Register,* 1 October 1814.
29. Ibid.

a force, just in case. On 28 October 1814 Monroe cautioned Jackson to steer clear of a fight with the Spanish in Florida, but the message did not reach Old Hickory until after he had led his army of militia and volunteers on a detour into West Florida. Warned of the approaching Americans, the Spanish governor at Pensacola ignored British officers who had advised him to erect defenses, and early in November Jackson's forces easily occupied the post with its fine harbor. The outmaneuvered British officers and their Indian allies scurried ahead of the invaders and set up camp on the Apalachicola River. To contain them, Jackson left a subordinate behind at Mobile. Late in November the order went out to Jackson's army for a route-step march to New Orleans.[30] Jackson reached New Orleans on 2 December and found Claiborne's small band of volunteers awaiting his orders.

President Madison took all the news, good and bad, from North and South, in measured stride. After the August invasion, nothing could have been more damaging, and yet as the days passed he realized that the resilience of the "extended republic" exceeded the hopes he had expressed a generation ago. The enormous size of the United States caused the citizenry to discount discouraging news from afar and to exaggerate good tidings close by; so the president knew that pockets of goodwill were everywhere, except perhaps around Boston. Convinced that he had public support, Madison prepared his annual message to the Thirteenth Congress. Madison chose to focus on the peace negotiations but admitted he had no new information. Since Napoleon's downfall, it was public knowledge that the British cabinet had at last revoked the detested Orders in Council, but peace in Europe meant an end to impressment "from American vessels," Madison assumed. Balanced against these favorable developments and the hope for a general peace were reports of recent "increased violence . . . on our Atlantic frontier," which "had more effect in distressing individuals and in dishonoring" the British invaders "than in promoting any object of legitimate warfare." In passing out laurels, Madison singled out General Jackson for his victory over the Creeks at Horseshoe Bend and Captain Macdonough for his triumph at Lake Champlain; the president also praised the fleet of American privateers that had harnassed British ships and thus defied "the incompetency and illegality" of the Royal Navy's blockade of the American coast. Reforms were needed to ease the militia into the regular army in the field, Madison added, and financing the war was not easy. In fact, the president said, the Treasury was down to its last five million dollars, and although more money had to be found, Madison reminded Congress that their constituents were willing to pay the price. It was the old story of the people running ahead of their leaders: "We have seen them everywhere paying their

30. Mahon, *War of 1812*, 350–52.

taxes, direct and indirect, with the greatest promptness and alacrity." Madison concluded his message by promising the nation that his administration would continue to seek "to arrest the effusion of blood and meet our enemy on the ground of justice and reconciliation," working for a peace "on honorable terms."[31] Clearly, the British military forays did not balance, in Madison's mind, with the olive branch waved at Ghent. Because he knew little of what was going on at the negotiating table, Madison chose to give the nation a pep talk and to hope the situation was better than it looked.

Early signals from Congress were not reassuring. Only the Post and Patent Office building had escaped unscathed, and there Congress met. Disgruntled members of both the House and the Senate huddled in makeshift offices while workmen cleared debris from the burned capital. With Henry Clay, the master politician and "wound binder," far away in Ghent, the administration favored Felix Grundy as Clay's successor as House speaker; but instead of complying with this presidential hint the congressmen chose Langdon Cheves, a frequent critic of Madison's policies. Then Congress decided a full-scale investigation of the recent disaster at Washington was in order, and it appointed a committee to inquire into the city's mismanaged defenses. Among the committee's witnesses appeared the former secretary of war, who told congressmen he had been ordered to direct the defense of Washington but was then checked by the president himself. The testimony and report writing went on for months, and like all congressional investigations the result satisfied nobody. Too long to interest the general public, the voluminous document created more heat than light, and Madison resented the misstatements that appeared to have been taken as gospel truth. His secretary, Edward Coles, was particularly offended by Armstrong's testimony. "It was never intended to give the Sec. of War command in the field," Coles vowed, and when Armstrong's statements were discussed by the cabinet, nobody recalled "the representation which he *supposes* he made to them" concerning his countermanded orders.[32] Conceived in a spirit of vengeance, the report absolved everyone of blame.

In fact, Congress seemed more excited about what had happened in Washington than did the rest of the country. A bill promoting the capital's relocation to a more defensible site nearly passed the House; but a Republican coalition mounted enough opposition to prevent a favorable final vote. Perhaps some congressmen believed Madison's hyperbole in the annual message, when he had predicted that the war, far from winding down, was going

31. James D. Richardson, comp., *A Compilation of the Messages and Papers of the Presidents, 1789–1897,* 10 vols. (Washington, D.C.: GPO, 1896–1899), 1:547–51.

32. Stagg, *Mr. Madison's War,* 428–29; E. Coles to J. P. Todd, 3 January 1815, Coles Papers, Princeton University Library.

to become a long struggle with no hope of stopping the Royal Navy should it choose to strike. Finding the men and money to carry on the war seemed all the more difficult when Gallatin and Clay were absent from the national councils.

From his mail Madison found both solace and rumblings of real trouble. A month after the White House was burned, Jefferson wrote a tender note to his successor. "Every reasonable man must be sensible that all you can do is to order, that execution must depend on others, & failures be imputable to them alone," Jefferson observed, "yet I know that when such failures happen they afflict even those who have done everything they could to prevent them. [Not even Washington,] had he been at the helm, could have done better."[33] Looking for a cheerful glimmer, Jefferson thought the Lake Champlain victory demonstrated to the world the myth of British invincibility. "They must now feel a conviction themselves that we can beat them gun to gun, ship to ship, and fleet to fleet." Turning to matters of business, Jefferson noted that the British had burned the Library of Congress, and he hastened to offer his personal library, "now of about 9. or 10,000 vols. which may be delivered to them instantly."

Whatever pleasure Madison derived from his old friend's letter was diluted when Jefferson's offer of his library at a rock-bottom price (twenty-five thousand dollars was mentioned) aroused opposition both in and out of Congress. Madison may have counseled his friends in Congress to leap at the offer, but Federalists denounced Jefferson's gesture as a personal attempt to cheat the taxpayers. And with what mixture of feelings did Madison read Jedidiah Morse's ridicule of the offer? The elder Morse warned Madison against promoting the purchase of Jefferson's library, abounding as it did in "Deistical Books and het [e] rodox Works."[34] Instead, Morse suggested, let each member of Congress buy books worth three dollars, "which is but half a days Pay," inscribe their name on the books, and donate them to the government; the president could set an example by donating the first volume to this library that would not cost the United States a dime.

Madison may have smiled at Morse's outburst, but to Jefferson he was somewhat tentative, knowing how cantankerous some congressmen could be. "I learn that the library Com[mitte]e will report favorably on your proposition to supply the loss of books by Cong[res]s," Madison replied. "It will prove a gain to them, if they have the wisdom to replace it by such a collection as yours."[35] Whether Madison nudged Congress to buy Jefferson's replacement library or not, he doubtless felt satisfied when ten wagons loaded

33. Jefferson to Madison, 24 September 1814, Jefferson Papers, DLC.
34. Morse to Madison, 23 November 1814, Madison Papers, DLC.
35. Madison to Jefferson, 10 October 1814, Madison Papers, DLC.

with 6,487 books arrived in Washington, for as a congressman in 1783 Madison had submitted "a list of books proper for the use of Congress," which was in great part covered by Jefferson's holdings.[36] Congress, Madison must have reasoned, never spent the allotted $23,950 in a better fashion.

Far less satisfying were newspaper reports from New England, where protests evoked by the December 1813 embargo skirted the brink of treason. The Federalists engineering for an ultimatum to the Madison administration were overjoyed, but it took time to shape their defiance in a quasi-legal setting. From South Hadley, Massachusetts, came a town meeting call for a New England convention to consider "the awful crisis" facing the nation; then a flood of petitions to the state legislature complained of undue southern influence in the nation's affairs. With Noah Webster as their spokesman, the petitioners called for constitutional amendments that would give northern states protection against "the future exercise of powers injurious to their commercial interests." Repeal of the embargo was not enough. When the war accelerated during the summer of 1814, the British moved into the Maine District almost unmolested, occupying the port of Castine. A dismayed Governor Strong called up the state militia while pressure was exerted on the lawmakers in Boston for a convention of the New England states to force "from the General Government if possible security against Conscription, taxes & the dangers of invasion."[37]

Madison could not have been unaware of these maneuvers, for they were reported in Federalist newspapers with implicit approbation. In fact, Benjamin Russell's *Columbian Centinel*, the voice of Boston Federalism, told of the printer's flirtation with the enemy. Russell visited a British frigate in midsummer and returned to his office to propose that Madison and his cabinet "should follow the example of Bonaparte, and resign their offices — AS A PEACE OFFERING TO GREAT BRITAIN." Perhaps Russell was only echoing Representative John Low of Maine, who late in 1814 offered a formal resolution that Massachusetts send a delegation to Washington to ask for Madison's resignation. By mid-October 1814 a report recommending a regional convention passed the Bay State legislature, 260 to 90, and twelve delegates were appointed to meet on 15 December 1814 at Hartford, Connecticut, with

---

36. Dumas Malone, *Jefferson and His Time*, 6 vols. (Boston: Little, Brown & Company, 1948–1976), 6:176; William T. Hutchinson et al., eds., *The Papers of James Madison*, 16 vols. (Chicago and Charlottesville: University of Chicago Press and University Press of Virginia, 1962–), 6:63–115.

37. James M. Banner, *To the Hartford Convention: The Federalists and the Origins of Party Politics in Massachusetts, 1789–1815* (New York: Alfred Knopf, 1970), 313, 316.

38. *National Intelligencer*, 13 August 1814.

other New England representatives.[38] Rhode Island and Connecticut joined the movement, but Vermont and New Hampshire balked (although delegates from those states went to Hartford on their own). The ringleaders, on hearing of the attack on Washington, convinced themselves the war was lost and hoped to maneuver Madison into a corner where he would be forced to make concessions to calm an aroused New England. The president's gestures during the summer, including amnesty for deserters, were shoved aside as Federalist leaders used every excuse to blame Madison for the nation's woes.

In tune with their regional leaders, Federalists in Congress publicly held their peace but secretly caucused in a Capitol Hill boardinghouse in mid-October. Led by Senator Rufus King of New York they decided to go along with legislation that would keep the war going but balked at any laws that might force able-bodied citizens to serve in the army. To most Federalists, who drew back in horror from the specter of conscription, this seemed a moderate course. Gouverneur Morris, who claimed to be a "birth-right" Federalist, took a different view. "Any thing like a Pledge by Federalists to carry on this wicked war, strikes a Dagger at my heart," Morris lamented. "What are you to gain by giving Mr. Madison Men and Money?" The Federalists' vendetta against Madison became so personal there was no room for political charity. The president's motives were assumed to be mean, dark, and cruel. Even Madison's State of the Union message to Congress was twisted into part of an evil plot. Federalists claimed that the president sought by his words "to excite the country," when what they yearned for was a speedy end to the conflict, preferably by a negotiated peace that would force Madison to taste some humble pie.[39] Madison must have taken some consolation from the Republican strongholds in Vermont and New Hampshire, which officially rejected invitations to the Federalist gathering scheduled to meet in Hartford. At any rate, he was preoccupied with trying to form a full cabinet while showing the country that his backbone was stiffer than ever.

Madison's opportunity to prove his courage came when word arrived from the American delegation at Ghent. The British had gone to the negotiating table with the harsh terms of a victor: no American fishing or cruising off the Grand Banks, a guaranteed Indian boundary favoring Canadian traders, denial of an American naval force on the Great Lakes, a new border in the upper Northwest that would give more territory to Canada than had the 1783 peace treaty, and confirmation of a British right to navigate the entire Mississippi! The cabinet listened to the British demands with their mouths

39. Ralph Ketcham, *James Madison: A Biography* (New York: Macmillan, 1971), 592; Theodore Dwight, *History of the Hartford Convention* (Boston: Russell, Odiorne & Company, 1833), 310.

agape. Moreover, Madison told Jefferson, "Our ministers [in Ghent] were all present & in perfect harmony of opinion on the arrogance of such demands."[40] Nonetheless, the negotiators' report was bad news indeed, for it now appeared that no real progress had been made at Ghent. The American envoys were prepared to pack and go home. "Nothing can prevent it," Madison added, "but a sudden change in the B[ritish] Cabinet [which is] not likely to happen." In all likelihood the extreme British demands reflected the high-water mark of anti-American attacks carried on by London newspapers through the winter and spring of 1814. As historian Henry Adams noted, "Next to Napoleon, the chief victim of English hatred was Madison." Cartoons displayed in London shop windows depicted a disheveled Madison as Napoleon's lackey: the London *Times* told its readers of Madison's "lunatic ravings"; and the *Morning Post* called the president "a despot in disguise; a miniature imitation" of the French bogeyman himself.[41]

The hostile London newspapers, Napoleon's abdication, and the expectation of successful British campaigns on the Canadian border and in the Chesapeake Bay were circumstances that helped Castlereagh approve the punitive terms. Presumably, if the redcoat army and the Royal Navy did their work well, a final treaty would leave Britain in possession of all territory then occupied (*uti possidetis*), which meant the Union Jack would soon fly over parts of New York, the Maine District coast, and the southern "shoe" of the Canadian border beyond the Great Lakes. Fortunately, the American delegation included a poker player of some renown, Henry Clay. Clay suggested to his colleagues that the British were only bluffing. They rejected the British note and kept talking.

Without knowing whether the peace negotiations were coming apart or not, Madison concentrated on the problem at hand — rebuilding his cabinet. Monroe seemed to thrive in his post at the War Department, which meant the door was open for a strong appointment as Monroe's successor at the State Department. Daniel Tompkins, governor of New York, was Madison's choice, as he sought a northerner not aligned with hostile Republican factions. Secretary of the Navy Jones as well as Secretary of the Treasury Campbell made no secret of the fact that they wanted out of the cabinet; however, Madison persuaded them both to delay their resignations until he could make sure that the State Department was under control. But Tompkins thanked Madison and then explained that he could not accept because he did not want to risk his popularity. Disappointed and a bit angry, Madison accepted Tompkin's excuses and decided to keep Monroe running between the state

40. Madison to Jefferson, 10 October 1814, Madison Papers, DLC.
41. Adams, *History*, 1186–87.

and war offices for a few more months. Rumors of cabinet changes abounded. When Robert Fulton heard that Jones wanted to quit, he threw his hat into the ring for the navy post, but Madison ignored the inventor's hints.[42]

Congress kept busy with its investigation of the August invasion, worried about the puny condition of the treasury, and heard pleas from constituents who feared another British force might be headed for key Atlantic port cities. Mayor DeWitt Clinton and the aldermen of New York, convinced that their harbor would be the next British target, complained to Madison that General Morgan Lewis was unfit for command of the Manhattan defenses. "A full persuasion that he is not equal to the crisis," the New Yorkers contended, compelled them out of "an imperious sense of duty to declare that the public safety requires an immediate change."[43] Madison beat them to the draw by nominating Governor Tompkins, who seemed so eager to stay in New York, to replace Lewis and thereby stifle local criticism.

Madison was calm in the face of the restlessness in his cabinet. Jones ran out of patience and resigned on 19 December 1814. Madison let him vacate the office without naming a successor. Jones was soon followed by Campbell. Even more disquieting was the death, not unexpected, of ailing Elbridge Gerry. The vice-president's coffin was hardly covered with dirt when a rumor circulated of a bold stroke by Madison's enemies in the Senate, who had concocted a plan to place a Federalist next in line to the presidency by making him president pro tem. The rumor proved false, however.[44] A safe Republican was chosen, amid eulogies for the fallen Republican warrior who had been Madison's friend and colleague in the Continental Congress, at the Federal Convention, and in the first two Congresses after April 1789.

Madison appointed Alexander J. Dallas of Pennsylvania to the Treasury post, a choice he could not have made while Michael Leib was a senator from the Keystone State. Madison also made his longtime friend (and former editor of the *National Intelligencer*) Samuel Harrison Smith commissioner of revenue. Jefferson heard of the fiscal difficulties piling up on the president's doorstep and sent Madison an elaborate scheme that called for one hundred forty million dollars in paper money to be issued over seven years; the bonds would be called in and paid off. But in the meantime, the administration could avoid the embarrassment of heavily discounted war loans. "I never did believe you could have gone beyond a 1st. or at most a 2d loan," Jefferson

42. Madison to Tompkins, 28 September and 18 October 1814, Madison Papers, DLC; Robert Fulton to Madison, 5 November 1814, Fulton Papers, Columbia University Library.

43. Corporation of New York to Madison, 14 October 1814, Letters Received by the Secretary of War, National Archives.

44. *Niles' Weekly Register,* 26 November 1814.

admitted.[45] Nobody liked to sell government bonds at bargain prices, least of all Madison, but the president was leery of Jefferson's plan because it invited rampant inflation "and implies a depreciation differing only from the career of the old Continental currency." In short, it was a nightmarish situation that Madison wanted to avoid at all costs. A domestic loan, he thought, "may still be obtained on terms tho' hard, not intolerable," and Madison hoped that "it will not be very long before the money market abroad, will not be entirely shut agst. us."[46]

Military movements on the Canadian border kept Madison on his guard as his wife struggled for a return to normalcy in the capital. On 2 November she resumed her weekly levees, pouring her punch at the Octagon House; but the crowds there soon made her think of seeking larger quarters. Meanwhile, a chastened Congress, still soaked in gloom in its cramped temporary quarters, passed a resolution calling for a national day of "Public Humiliation, and Fasting, and of Praying to Almighty God, for the safety and welfare of these states." Voting money for a larger army as well as trying to raise one were issues that Congress did not want to face. Prayer was cheaper, and although Madison was on principle opposed to religious proclamations, he left his sickbed to sign one that was similar to the congressional appeal to heaven calling for a day of fasting and prayer on November 16.

The truism, "It's always darkest just before the dawn," seemed to apply in Washington that autumn, for the president and his cabinet were ignorant of the shock wave that swept London after it received news of Prevost's retreat and Baltimore's spirited repulse of the Royal Navy. Some British newspapers howled for vengeance; but the London *Morning Chronicle* "openly intimated that the game of war was at an end" at almost the very moment that the American envoys in Ghent rejected Britain's demands.[47] Quietly desperate for a solution to the "American problem," the British cabinet offered the Duke of Wellington command of the redcoat army in Canada; but the duke, while not sidestepping the issue, said that he could not promise "much success there" and firmly undercut any territorial claim by frank talk: "I confess that I think you have no right, from the state of the war, to demand any concession of territory from America."[48] If Wellington saw no justification for more territory and for other demands, Liverpool and Castlereagh had to concede that they had asked for too much.

In Washington the day of fasting and prayer was set for 12 January 1815; but two days after Madison had signed the proclamation a shift in British

45. Jefferson to Madison, 15 October 1814, Jefferson Papers, DLC.
46. Madison to Jefferson, 23 October 1814, Madison Papers, DLC.
47. Quoted in Adams, *History*, 1207.
48. Ibid., 1211–12.

policy showed that the American prayers had already been answered. Britain wanted out of the war. The only remaining issue to be settled was a graceful exit. Across the Atlantic, Madison remained uninformed and thus pessimistic. Whether Madison worried a great deal about appearances is not certain, although he knew he could count on the Republican press, led by the *National Intelligencer*, to make the best out of any agreement that would end the fighting and keep American boundaries and honor intact. There was no point in stressing the impressment issue because it had already been dropped from the negotiations.

As the British public lost interest in the American war, Yankee resolve stiffened. In the Rhode Island legislature the minority that had opposed sending a delegate to the Hartford Convention introduced a resolution denouncing the meeting, but the motion was adjudged improper for "its indecorous language and foul aspersions" and thus was stricken from the record.[49] Crusty John Adams, after hearing from his son at Ghent, wrote Madison the kind of message he loved to receive: "All I can say is that I would continue this War forever, rather than surrender one acre of our Territory, one Iota of the Fisheries . . . or one Sailor impressed from any Merch[an]t Ship." To a fellow Virgininan who had denounced New England foot-dragging Madison sent a cordial note of agreement. "You are not mistaken in viewing the conduct of the Eastern States as the source of our greatest difficulties in carrying on the war," Madison wrote, "as it certainly is the greatest, if not the sole inducement with the Enemy to persevere in it." The citizens of New England "have been brought by their leaders, aided by their priests, under a delusion scarcely exceeded by that recorded in the period of Witchcraft, and the leaders are becoming daily more desperate in the case they make of it. Their object is power."[50]

Power, or lack of it, was much on Madison's mind. Good Republican that he was, Madison was determined not to force a legislative program through Congress, and he was politician enough to realize that with Clay gone and no strong floor leader in the House, effective legislation was unlikely. The president did push Monroe for a military campaign to recapture Maine's ports, but Madison was compelled to continue agonizing over the tedious delays of critical legislation related to the money and manpower needed for the 1815 campaign. The British naval presence in the Gulf of Mexico also raised questions. As the New England delegates gathered in Hartford, Madison confessed that he was running out of patience with the loud-

49. *Niles' Weekly Register*, 26 November 1814.

50. Adams to Madison, 28 November 1814, letter owned by Philip D. Sang, 1961; Madison to Wilson Cary Nicholas, 26 November 1814, Adams Papers, Massachusetts Historical Society.

talking, do-nothing Thirteenth Congress. To former President John Adams, Madison confessed: "I am unwilling to say how much distress in every branch of our affairs is the fruit of their tardiness"; but there was plenty of blame to throw around.[51] A bill from Dallas's desk creating a national bank to help finance the war was going nowhere, as was John C. Calhoun's countermeasure, a money-printing scheme that appalled the administration. Meanwhile, a militia bill was being used as a shuttlecock by the House and Senate until it was finally postponed without a vote.

With Christmas 1814 only a week away, President Madison had regained his health; otherwise he saw little to cheer during the Yuletide season as a third year of war loomed ahead.

51. Madison to John Adams, 17 December 1814, Adams Papers, Massachusetts Historical Society.

9

★ ★ ★ ★ ★

DAWN OF AN ERA,
TWILIGHT OF A PARTY

Fortunately for his peace of mind, President Madison was unaware of the duplicity being practiced by Governor Caleb Strong on the eve of the Hartford Convention. Strong, overreacting to the British invasion of Maine early in September 1814, sent a secret emissary to Halifax to learn first hand from the British commander if a separate peace might be negotiated. Violating federal law if nothing more, Strong tried to learn the alternatives open to Massachusetts if Madison persisted in carrying on the war when further effort seemed (to the Boston High Federalists) useless.[1] Everything was hush-hush as Strong gave oral instructions to a go-between known to Sir John Coape Sherbrooke, who had led the British into Castine from his Halifax station. "The principal object of this message was to ascertain the British attitude toward a separate peace with New England. . . . It appears that the Federal party wishes to ascertain at this early period whether Great Britain would under these circumstances afford them Military assistance to effect their purpose should they stand in need of it," Sir John in the fall of 1814 informed his superiors in London.

The reaction in London indicates how jumpy the British officials had become. Lord Bathurst leaped at the bait and urged Sherbrooke to exploit this proof of American disaffection. By 13 December, when he sent instructions to Sherbrooke, Bathurst knew a peace was about to be signed in Ghent, but he, along with Liverpool and Castlereagh, feared that a cantankerous

1. J. S. Martell, "A Sidelight on Federalist Strategy during the War of 1812," *American Historical Review* 43 (1938): 553–66.

president might reject the package. Betraying some ignorance of the American constitutional system, Liverpool told Castlereagh, "The disposition to separate on the part of the Eastern states may likewise frighten Madison; for if he should refuse to ratify this treaty, we must immediately propose to make a separate peace with them, and we have good reason to believe that they will not be indisposed to listen to such a proposal." Aid and comfort to the enemy? It could easily have reached that point, for Strong was playing a dangerous game.

Spared knowledge of this sordid episode, Madison sought to gather resources for another year of war and was dismayed by reports from Dallas that the Treasury was being rapidly depleted. To ease the sting of republicanism in New England, Madison had persuaded Benjamin W. Crowninshield of Massachusetts to take the secretary of the navy vacancy. Monroe had become preoccupied with the tempest whipped up in the cabinet after the Jackson-led Americans in Florida had taken Pensacola without orders. Monroe was upset and Armstrong called Jackson's Pensacola gambit "ill-judged, . . . an offence to a neutral power" and an unnecessary diversion in view of Jackson's orders to defend New Orleans. Rumors that the British had a force in the Caribbean headed for New Orleans swarmed through capital boardinghouses, and some southerners in Congress raised their eyebrows when it was revealed that Jackson had promised "the free colored inhabitants of Louisiana" equal treatment with white volunteers if they would enlist for the duration of the war.[2] Neither Monroe, Madison, nor anyone else in Washington knew how to handle Jackson. They only knew that he was that rare breed in the American high command: a winner.

Meanwhile, twenty-six delegates from New England met at Hartford on December 1814 with a shared conviction that the peace negotiations in Ghent were going nowhere. Timothy Dwight, elected secretary of the convention, later recalled that the delegates had convened amid rage over Madison's call to the Congress (at the special session) for "more vigorous exertions in carrying on the war, the folly and fruitlessness of which now stared him full in the face." Monroe considered sending an army detachment to Connecticut; but as time passed and nothing alarming took place, he saw no need to panic. Madison's secretary, Edward Coles, turned a watchful eye toward

---

2. J. C. A. Stagg, *Mr. Madison's War: Politics, Diplomacy, and Warfare in the Early American Republic, 1783–1830* (Princeton, N.J.: Princeton University Press, 1983), 490–91; *Niles' Weekly Register,* 3 December 1814; Henry Adams, *History of the United States of America during the Administrations of Thomas Jefferson and James Madison,* vol. 2, *History of the United States of America during the Administrations of James Madison,* Earl N. Harbert, ed. (New York: Library of America, 1986), 1139, 1243 (hereafter cited as Adams, *History*).

Hartford and decided that the *"English* Federalists . . . are pursuing a most extraordinary and disgraceful course." The Hartford delegates, Coles wrote, were meeting "to hatch treason, if New England will support them in it, [and the Yankee dissidents' aim] is to do all injury they can to America, and all the benefit in their power to England."³

Congress moved its schedule up a notch and, finally, on 9 December 1814 the Senate passed a bill creating a national bank. But the vote was close and Madison was soon advised by leading men in his cabinet to veto any patchwork law and shoot for a sounder plan. A militia bill allowing the president to call up forty thousand troops for twelve months of service survived in both houses, but it was full of crippling restrictions. A major limitation was that the soldiers could not be used outside their home state without the consent of their state governor. An additional forty thousand troops might be raised in a volunteer force, but that seemed improbable. Nevertheless, it was all or nothing, and having convinced himself that the peace negotiations were not succeeding, Madison signed the weak law on 27 January 1815. Three days later he vetoed the hodge-podge bank bill.

Nobody in Washington realized, of course, that the war was over. News of the accord at Ghent — signed on Christmas Eve — was still on the high seas. Everybody knew Jackson had stormed into New Orleans in December, declared martial law in the city, and threatened to blow the local authorities to pieces if they tried to thwart him. On 8 January 1815 the unnecessary Battle of New Olreans pitted overconfident Englishmen against the motley American forces. Jackson's artillery raked the British frontal attack, inflicting 2,036 casualties in less than two hours and forcing the enemy to retreat and abandon the whole venture. Only 21 Americans were killed or wounded, making it one of the most lopsided battles in history while creating an instant hero of Old Hickory.⁴ New Orleans was relieved, but because the news did not travel to Washington by pony express, it did not reach the capital until 4 February. "GLORIOUS FROM NEW ORLEANS," the newspapers proclaimed as reports of the victory rushed through Washington like a flood tide. "Glory be to God, that the barbarians have been defeated, and that at *Orleans* the intended plunderers have found their grave!"⁵

While awaiting news from New Orleans, Madison had shared with the nation the report of the Hartford Convention, which had been made public

---

3. Theodore Dwight, *History of the Hartford Convention* (Boston: Russell, Odiorne & Company, 1833), 310; Coles to J. P. Todd, 3 January 1815, Coles Papers, Princeton University Library.

4. Marshall Smelser, *The Democratic Republic, 1801–1815* (New York: Harper & Row, 1968), 278–80.

5. *Niles' Weekly Register,* 11 February 1814.

on 12 January. The New England delegates came out in favor of several constitutional amendments, most of them aimed at the South: eliminating the three-fifths compromise on slave representation); requiring a two-thirds vote in Congress to declare war, to curb commerce, or to admit new states; denying foreign-born citizens eligibility in any federal office; limiting the president to one term; and prohibiting his being from the same state as his predecessor. The anti-Virginia bias of the recommendations must have struck Madison humorously, for he reportedly laughed aloud as he read them.[6]

The president deserved a laugh of two, for he had been under constant pressure for months, and the disaffected Federalists only made life harder. An opponent in Congress read the preliminary dispatches from New Orleans and decided Jackson had already surrendered. A Baltimore newspaper agreed. "Mr. Madison may as well lift the gate and let the flood through," the *Federal Republican* hooted.[7] Thus on the eve of 4 February, the Federalists were convinced Madison was finished. Twenty-four hours later, however, the whole city was in a state of reverie, and presumably Madison joined friends and family in a toast to Jackson — the hero of New Orleans — who had lopped off the head of the British dragon. Ten more days saw the whole complexion of Madison's presidency turn roseate, for more rumors passed through the capital that a peace treaty with Britain had been signed. On 14 February Monroe came to Madison, bearing the official dispatches. The sealed pouches contained confirmation of the rumors racing up and down Pennsylvania Avenue. A Baltimore headline told the whole story: *"Glorious News! Orleans saved and peace concluded."* "The enemy has retired in disgrace from New Orleans, and peace was signed at Ghent on the 24th December, on honorable terms," the *Niles' Weekly Register* proclaimed.[8] "Who would not be an American? Long live the Republic!"

This unexpected good news hit Washington like a thunderclap. A dinner party at the French minister's house broke up when a servant brought in a note for one of the president's intimate friends. The note sent a thrill through the anxious diners as they heard a rumor that a diplomatic dispatch ship had brought confirmation of a settlement at Ghent. The war was over! The president's temporary quarters were said to be abustle, with all the windows lighted by candles in honor of the joyful news. When all the excitement was over, Pennsylvania Senator Jonathan Roberts, who had supported Madison all along, thought he should visit the president to savor the moment.

6. Irving Brant, *James Madison*, 6 vols. (Indianapolis: Bobbs-Merrill Company, 1941–1961), 6:361.

7. Ibid., 6:365.

8. *Niles' Weekly Register*, 11 and 18 February 1815.

I drove to the President's. On arriving there all was still and dark. I found Mr. Madison sitting solitary in his parlor . . . in perfect tranquility, not even a servant in waiting. What a contrast from the scene I had just left. I apologiz'd for my intrusion, stating that I had heard a rumor of Peace, but I apprehended it was incorrect. Take a seat, said he, & I will tell you all I know. . . . I believe there is peace, but we have not as yet the information in such form, as that we can publish it officially. . . . The self command, and greatness of mind, I witness'd on this occasion was in entire accordance with what I have before stated of the Pres[iden]t, when to me things looked so dark. I think it to be regretted that these evidences, of the solidity and Sterling worth of his character, will perhaps find no place in the history of his administration, brilliant as it must ever appear.

The emotional moment passed, and Roberts closed the incident with the notation: "The next morning the news was out."[9]

Whether Madison pinched himself is not recorded — this sudden turn of fortunes had no precedent in American history. Five months earlier the president had looked at a gutted, humiliated city and had heard his leadership denounced by the Federalists. Now they were on the run. The news from Ghent and New Orleans, Federalist Timothy Dwight admitted, had changed everything. As secretary of the Hartford Convention, Dwight had yearned for Madison's intimidation. Between 4 and 14 February Dwight's world was turned topsy-turvy as the peace treaty and military victory provided "a never-failing source of profit to the leaders of the party in power, the public resentment was excited against the opposers of the war, particularly against the New-England States, and the Hartford Convention became the theme of universal calumny and reproach."[10] The Federalists who came to Washington to see Madison squirm were shocked. Harrison Gray Otis, the former congressman and party wheelhorse at Hartford, took offense because Dolley Madison did not invite him to the president's victory celebration. Otis felt constrained to call on Madison, however, and soothed his ego by assuring his wife that when they entered the presidential office "the little pigmy shook in his shoes at our approach."[11]

Madison had not acquired a halo, but his fellow citizens did begin to perceive him as a first-class hero. Among the earliest to congratulate the president was his attorney general, Robert Rush, who from his sickbed told Madison the news of peace came "at a most happy point in time for our interests and

9. Philip S. Klein, ed., "Memoirs of a Senator from Pennsylvania: Jonathan Roberts, 1771–1854," *Pennsylvania Magazine of History and Biography* 62 (1938): 377.
10. Dwight, *History of the Hartford Convention,* 381.
11. Quoted in Robert A. Rutland, *James Madison: The Founding Father* (New York: Macmillan, 1987), 231.

our fame. . . . Your anxious moments, sir, will now be fewer; your labors abridged; your friends, more than ever, gratified; an unmanly opposition more than ever confounded; [and] the nation, in your day, advanced anew in property and glory." Rush did not stretch the truth. The peace treaty called for no territorial changes, no reparations, and no recriminations. There was an amnesty for Indians (on either side), arrangements for boundary questions, and a pledge to end the African slave trade traffic. In additon, all prisoners of war were to be sent home (including the twenty-three Americans the British had shipped to Britain for trial as traitors), and slaves carried away by the British armed forces were to be returned to their American masters. Four joint commissions were established to settle disputes concerning boundries in Passamaquoddy Bay and between the St. Lawrence River and Lake Huron and Lakes Huron and Superior and to establish the source of the St. Croix River and the latitude and longitude of the northernmost point of the Lake of the Woods (an unresolved issue left over from the peace treaty in 1783).[12] There was also an understanding that an Anglo-American commercial treaty would be negotiated as soon as practicable. Impressment, an issue so thorny in 1812, was ignored. The Prince Regent had signed the treaty almost at once. The real Madison, not the curmudgeon of Federalists fancies, sent it to the Senate on 15 February; the Senate hurriedly performed its duty and unanimously ratified the treaty on 16 February. The next day, Madison officially proclaimed the war to be over.

As the president said in his covering letter to Congress, the war "had become a necessary resort, to assert the rights and independence of the nation." Somehow the United States had not been a sovereign nation enjoying all the powers of independence, even after the treaty of 1783. But this nation had twice fought one of the world's great powers, and although the Battle of New Orleans occurred after peace terms had been agreed to, most Americans believed they had trounced the British lion again.

Nobody saw the war and its outcome more perceptively than Albert Gallatin, who had been the key American negotiator. "The war has renewed and reinstated the national feelings and characters which the Revolution had given, and which were daily lessened," he observed. "The people have now more general objects of attachment with which their pride and political opinions are connected. They are more American; they feel and act more as a nation; and I hope the permanency of the Union is thereby better secured."[13] Americans' search for a sense of nationhood was finally over.

12. Rush to Madison, 15 February 1815, Rush Papers, Historical Society of Pennsylvania; Samuel Flagg Bemis, *A Diplomatic History of the United States* (New York: Holt, Rinehart & Winston, 1965), 168–9.

13. Harold Schultz, *James Madison* (New York: Twayne, 1970), 187–88; Gallatin

Gallatin was not alone in discerning a new spirit of confidence pervading the Republic. "Peace has come in a most welcome time," Justice Joseph Story wrote a friend. "Never did a country occupy more lofty ground; we have stood the contest, single-handed, against the conqueror of Europe; and we are at peace, with all out blushing victories thick crowding on us. If I do not much mistake, we shall attain a very high character abroad." Americans had exerted themselves "just enough . . . to get the work done" and had come out of the war feeling that the effort had been worthwhile. Early on, once the "march into Canada" dream had evaporated, the absurd war aims had been curtailed. Thereafter, Americans "fought for respect, not for the fatuous dream of destroying the enemy."[14] From the peace table at Ghent and the battlefield at New Orleans, events confirmed attainment of the nation's primary goal: a respected place in the world community.

Often overlooked in any summation of the significance of the War of 1812 is that the Constitution of 1787 survived intact. Madison surely had wondered himself whether a government planned in peacetime for guiding a peaceful country could survive the rigors of a war that would test every republican institution from personal liberty to heavy taxes for support of a military machine. And would that military establishment dissolve at the end of the war, with all power slipping back into civilian hands in a constitutional way? Madison and the nation now had their answer. However inefficient the means, however misguided the strategy, and however weak the finances, the government constructed by the Constitution had survived and left intact the liberties of the people. The Constitution that worked in peacetime had proved resilient during war, no mean accomplishment. The symbol of the American eagle clutching both olive branches and arrows now stood for something real: international respect, nationhood, and the people's liberties unimpaired. A century would elapse before the United States would again declare war on a major European power. The lesson learned from the War of 1812 was that two great oceans isolated the nation from the bickerings of Asia and Europe; relying on the advice that Washington gave in his Farewell Address, the nation thereafter followed a policy of noninvolvement characterized by both common sense and wisdom gained through experience.

Peace brought a cornucopia of blessings for Madison. Congress was in a jubilant mood. Gone was the urgent need for additional revenues, for more

to Matthew Lyon, 7 May 1816, quoted in Henry Adams, ed., *The Writings of Albert Gallatin*, 3 vols. (New York, 1960), 1:700.

14. Quoted in Robert Wiebe, *The Opening of American Society* (New York: Alfred Knopf, 1984), 189–90.

troop requisitions, and for stringent measures to prevent smuggling in New England. The revived Bank of the United States project, which had Madison's tacit support and Dallas's endorsement, was administered the coup de grace in the House, where it fell one vote short of passage. In late February 1815 Madison notified Congress that the dey of Algiers, angry because his annual tribute from the United States was tardy, had ordered the Stars and Stripes flying from a flagpole cut down as a ceremonial declaration of war. This action came while American seamen still languished in Algerine dungeons, awaiting ransom, and Madison decided it was time to protest with hot lead this kind of international blackmail (which dated from Washington's administration). The president asked Congress to declare "the existence of a state of war between the United States and the Dey and Regency of Algiers."[15] Yankee shipping on the Mediterranean would remain at a standstill until the Barbary pirates were restrained, Madison realized, and he ordered a punitive squadron sent to Algiers that summer, although the American government was still prepared to ransom Yankee captives.

As Congress scurried toward adjournment, Madison decided to rearrange his cabinet and have his nominees confirmed. Probably in the back of Madison's mind was an arrangement that would allow him to take long vacations as he delegated considerable responsibility to various cabinet members. Accordingly, Monroe was shifted from the War Department to the State Department. Crawford would eventually vacate the minister's post at Paris and take over the War Department (after some missed signals that embarrassed Madison and Henry Dearborn). Gallatin was chosen to replace Crawford at Paris, while John Quincy Adams was picked for the ministerial vacancy at London. A much-needed reform law created a board of naval commissioners that would offer the secretary of the navy professional help in overseeing naval installations and keeping the American fleet in a better state of repair. Madison appointed to the board three captains of the line, thus assuring an end to the old policy of leaving logistical naval matters in civilian hands.

When congressmen finally closed their session in a kind of love feast on 3 March 1815, Madison's mind turned at once toward Montpelier. Dolley Madison soon issued packing orders, overjoyed at the prospect of her son's coming home with the American peace team. In a quiet moment Madison reflected on a propaganda piece that his cabinet had been keen to publish two months earlier. Dallas had been assigned the task of writing, for worldwide distribution, an explanation of American grievances and war aims. "It

15. James D. Richardson, comp., *A Compilation of the Messages and Papers of the Presidents, 1789-1897,* 10 vols. (Washington, D.C.: GPO, 1896-1899), 1:554; Madison to dey of Algiers, 12 April 1815, Consular Dispatches, Algiers, National Archives.

was not finished in time for publication," Madison wrote Jefferson as the packing around him proceeded apace, "before the news of peace arrived."[16] The decision made after the news from Ghent arrived was to let the propaganda device drop stillborn from the press. A few copies were preserved and one was sent to Jefferson "to amuse an hour of your leisure." "You will observe," Madison added, "that it was meant for the eye of the British people, and of our own, as well as for that of the neutral world." While Washington still echoed with huzzahs from the official peace celebration, Madison was concerned that the world might forget why the second war of independence had to be fought. In time he allowed a "leaked version" of Dallas's work to find its way into a Philadelphia newspaper.

As Madison was writing the former president, Louis XVIII was making his escape to Ghent and Napoleon was on the trail that would eventually bring him to Waterloo. When news of the French Hundred Days reached Montpelier, Madison was more concerned about Hessian flies than Prussian generals. Monroe, alarmed at Napoleon's daring, recommended that the president recall Congress for a special session to deal with any impending crisis. Madison, however, took the news of the developments in Europe with more composure than Monroe, and Jefferson, writing from his calm mountaintop, was similarly unperturbed. "I sincerely congratulate you on the peace," he told Madison, "and more especially on the eclat with which the war was closed."[17] Jefferson still wanted Britain to acknowledge "the atrocity of impressment" through some formal statement, however: "Without this she must understand that the present is but a truce."

From late March until early June, the Madisons enjoyed a respite on their Virginia plantation, with much coming and going of guests, messengers, neighbors, and kin. Madison carried on his presidential duties by proxy as he listened to the warble of cardinals in the trees behind Montpelier. He learned that the cabinet supported Commodore Decatur's expedition to the Mediterranean and a rendezvous with the Barbary pirates. And, although demobilizing the army provided some headaches, Madison signed orders to cut back on troop strength as disgruntled officers grumbled for special treatment from Congress. The shameless James Wilkinson, whitewashed once again by a court-martial, was finally put out to pasture and reacted with a bitter verbal parting shot at the commander in chief. Madison might have inwardly wondered how so much peacetime energy could be displayed by officers not known for their wartime alacrity.

The novelty of sudden peace finally wore off, and a flood of resolutions

16. Madison to Jefferson, 12 May 1815, Madison Papers, Library of Congress (hereafter cited as DLC).

17. Jefferson to Madison, 23 March 1815, Madison Papers, DLC.

poured in from Republican meetings and town gatherings, fulsome documents that filled the presidential mail pouch. Perhaps the most savored message came from the Boston Republicans, who took the occasion to rub it in on the Federalist opposition and then thank Madison for "maintaining the honor of the American flag against those who had arrogantly assumed the Sovereignty of the Ocean."[18] Private well-wishers also sent a stream of congratulations to Madison, and more than a few added notice of their availability for any vacant public office.

Meanwhile, mighty Britain slowly carried out the treaty terms; the diversion caused by Napoleon's return from Elba was not helpful. Some untangling of wartime captures came to Madison's notice as the British duly evacuated Castine, but he paid more attention to what was heard from Newfoundland, where American fishermen were being harassed. The president was also eager for news that control of Forts Niagara and Malden had been exchanged. Quietly, Gallatin and the American negotiators in London tried to write a commercial treaty with British representatives, but the pace was slow. Newspaper accounts of the mishandled evacuation of 4,700 American seamen held in Dartmoor prison did nothing to assure Americans that Britain was anxious to make bygones into bygones.

Nothing had been heard from the European battlefields when Madison decided to resume his vacation in mid-July 1815. The ports at Baltimore, Charleston, New Orleans, New York, and Boston were clogged with farm produce headed for overseas markets. Madison worried that a resumed European war might jeopardize this new prosperity, but his fears were eased after he learned of Napoleon's defeat at Waterloo. Peace brought the resumption of a slightly luxurious tone to the Madisons' lifestyle. The finest cigars and the best Madeira reappeared on the president's table. Mrs. Madison's fondness for colorful, high-quality textiles from British and European mills found expression in her wardrobe as she prepared for her last year as the presidential hostess. Her friend Mrs. Albert Gallatin was now on watch in Paris, knowing how welcome reports on the latest fashions would be.

If anything demonstrated to the world that the United States was no longer a stepchild in the family of nations now that the war with Britain was over, it was the American flotilla heading for Algiers in the spring of 1815. Facing the Royal Navy, the Americans had been outnumbered by as much as fifty to one, but in going against the Algerine pirates the ten-ship squadron under Decatur's command was "going to pick on somebody their own size."[19] The Americans captured two of the dey's ships, including a forty-four–gun

18. "Address of the Republican Meeting in Boston," 23 February 1815, Madison Papers, DLC.
19. Smelser, *The Democratic Republic*, 312.

frigate, and barely forty-one days after the Yankee ships had cleared New York harbor the dey agreed to stop the piracy, release all captives, and give up the annual tribute payments. Similar treaties were soon recorded at Tunis and Tripoli. The total costs to the United States were one seamen killed in combat and three more killed when a deck gun exploded. The nightmare of embarrassment, ransom, and humiliation at the hands of Muslim potentates was officially ended when a second treaty with the dey of Algiers was ratified late in 1816. Decatur returned to the United States and was toasted by newspapers up and down the coast as the vindicator of American rights. Reading his newspaper in the Montpelier study, Madison must have smiled. Memories of endless cabinet talks about the Algerines, whispers of recrimination, and moments of swallowed pride must have been evoked as the president read of Decatur's triumph. He probably began to make mental notes for his State of the Union message.

Madison kept busy at the writing desk that summer and paid more attention than usual to reports about Monroe's health. Monroe had listened to Jefferson's entreaties some years earlier and purchased a farm, called Highlands, a few miles south of Jefferson's Monticello. Jefferson had pleaded with Madison to move closer so that their tight circle might become even tighter, but Madison resisted on the grounds that his parents' health was poor and Montpelier was not so distant. In the summer of 1815 Monroe returned to Highlands to recuperate from his winter illness. He had been under constant strain since August 1814, and friends who had not seen him since then were shocked at his appearance. Besides the loss of weight, which made him appear haggard, Monroe had fretted over the health of his daughter and was finding it hard to pay his debts. Madison did what he could to ease his friend's burdens, but the president was clearly worried. Monroe had bought another farm in Loudoun County, Virginia, which was little more than an hour's ride from the capital, and he was now torn between trying to make Highlands into a profitable venture and selling it. Madison was a sympathetic listener when the Monroes stopped at Montpelier the first week in October 1815. Napoleon's downfall was now common knowledge; so the president and his top cabinet official could talk in relaxation about the realities of a world in which trade and commerce were dominated by Britain.

Dolley Madison was ready to return to Washington but had been disappointed that her son had missed his ship and was still wandering around in England. Payne Todd had somehow twice missed passage on the *Neptune,* first at Le Havre and then again at Portsmouth; but he had managed to write to his mother and include news of the commercial treaty negotiations in London. After several weeks, Madison received the official version from Gallatin and Clay. The president was somewhat disappointed, however. He had asked Britain to stop discriminating against American goods throughout the British

Empire, but all the American representatives had been able to negotiate was a provision that limited American trading rights to the British Isles and British India. Madison said the treaty was "good as far as it goes," but the agreement fell short of his hopes, particularly since the lifeline trade between the United States and the British West Indies was excluded from the relaxed regulations and Canadian-American trade had not even been addressed.[20] Rather than call a special session of Congress to ratify the "half a loaf" treaty, Madison chose to keep its provisions a secret.

Personal business distracted Madison after he learned of a $6,500 draft charged against him by Baring Brothers, the London bankers. Young Todd had apparently had an informal commission to purchase paintings, statuary, and objets d'art to decorate the stately halls in Montpelier. In the process, he had run up a bill large enough to pay for a Rembrandt if one had been offered. These art selections had been crated and were bound for the United States when Madison learned that Todd had more of an eye for pretty women than he did for somber canvases. Todd's indiscretions cost the president an additional $1,500. Madison ended up paying a total of $8,000. As he signed the check, he probably realized that his stepson needed taming—a chore the president was ill-equipped to handle.

While preparing for his last full year in office, Madison was aware that his cabinet had finally found stability. Dallas had turned out to be a solid replacement for Gallatin, and Monroe, his health returned, took his duties at the State Department as seriously as Madison himself had during his tenure. Crawford, back in town after a visit to Georgia, was in agreement with his chief regarding an altered policy of increased budgets for American defenses.[21] Crowinshield in the Navy Department had also fallen in behind his leader.

As the Fourteenth Congress assembled, Madison was relieved to see that changes there had been for the better. Nothing symbolized these changes more than the Virginia senatorial delegation, for Giles had been replaced by Armistead Mason, who had joined James Barbour in giving the president harmonious home support for the first time. John Randolph was back in the House, but so was Henry Clay, who returned to the Speaker's chair, bursting with energy and full of postwar dreams. Perhaps the change that most pleased Madison was the defeat of Samuel Smith, who had lost his Maryland Senate seat (but did come back to the House). Able William Pinkney, the erstwhile American minister at London as well as attorney general, was a distinctive gain in the House, along with his old friend and onetime brother-in-law, John G. Jackson, now returned from a western Virginia district.

20. Brant, *Madison*, 6:390–92; Stagg, *Mr. Madison's War*, 512.
21. Chase C. Mooney, *William H. Crawford, 1772–1834* (Lexington: University Press of Kentucky, 1974), 79–81.

Scaffolds and masonry kept the first family from moving back to the White House. Mrs. Madison liked the Octagon House, but the servants complained that it was too cramped, so she moved the executive quarters to the well-known Seven Buildings (three blocks west of the presidential mansion on Pennsylvania Avenue). Madison, in a better frame of mind than he had ever known before, sharpened a battery of quills and prepared the draft of his annual report to the nation. The United States was at peace, and although the Washington diplomatic corps was loaded with prima donnas (the Spaniard Chevalier de Onís being among the most obnoxious), Madison was looking at the overall condition of the nation, which made the quibblings in Washington seem inconsequential.

Madison's message to Congress in December 1815 brimmed with optimism. Aware that his fellow citizens would read the message in more than a million parlors, taverns, shops, and offices across the country, the president wanted to kindle pride in the nation's achievements. He took note of Commodore Decatur's expedition to Algiers, which promised "future security for the valuable portion of our commerce," heretofore at the mercy of the Barbary brigands. He revealed the pending commercial treaty with Britain and listed the measures needed to implement the Treaty of Ghent. Then Madison praised the army, which was shrinking because of demobilization, and called on Congress to remember its responsibilities to "the veteran and the invalid."

The difficulties of wartime finance were recognized by Madison, and he was willing to talk about the national debt, which had reached one hundred twenty million dollars. This was the price tag for "the assertion of national rights and independence," and as Madison saw it, the cost was not out of proportion to the inestimable gain. With no national bank in operation, state banks were accommodating the demands of public and private customers; but, Madison added, the time probably had arrived to consider "the probable operation of a national bank."

For all his republican commitment to the militia as the main pillar in the nation's defense, Madison confessed that a drastic change in national priorities was worth risking. A military academy already existed at West Point, but, Madison suggested, now more schools for studying martial arts were needed "in other sections of the Union." The militia system needed to be reorganized to enable the federal government to move promptly and effectively during a crisis, and the navy could not be allowed to fall into disrepair in "an epoch which calls for the constant vigilance of all governments." Thus the penny-pinching gunboat policy of Jefferson's presidency was abandoned without a whimper of protest. Nor were there raised eyebrows when the clerk read Madison's suggestion that a protective tariff be enacted to help "enterprising citizens" whose interests required a buffer "against occasional competitions from abroad."

Madison also addressed the rising clamor from the western territories for better roads and canals. Surely Clay must have perked up and looked around to see how his colleagues reacted as they heard Madison declare that highways and waterways would promote prosperity and help to bind more tightly the cords of the Union. The states had started these projects and, the president added, "the General Government is the more urged to similar undertakings." Betraying his suspicion that the Constitution as it then stood would not countenance national expenditures for local purposes, the president suggested that a judicious amendment would remedy "any defect of constitutional authority." And while he was at it, the president even suggested federal support for "a national seminary of learning within the District of Columbia," founded under "the patronage of Congress . . . as a nursery of enlightened preceptors, and as a central resort of youth and genius from every part of their country."[22]

There was something in Madison's message for everybody except the old Republicans, who hated taxes, hated debt, and wanted the "general welfare" clause of the Constitution squeezed dry. As more than one historian has mentioned, this was not the Madison of 1789 speaking to the nation. This president had decided that the war had exposed the shortcomings of a nickel-and-dime democracy, and he was anxious to hail reforms in national defense, banking, transportation, and education. Madison was not trying to stand time-honored Republican doctrine on its head, but he realized that the country had gone far beyond that struggling Republic of 1787. Then a national debt of sixty million dollars loomed like a mountain; now a debt twice that size seemed little more than a hillock.

When the official figures were calculated in 1815, the total cost of the war was said to be $68,783,122 (one day's cost for the United States government in World War II was twice that amount).[23] Most of the money came

22. Richardson, *Messages of the Presidents*, 1:562–58.

23. *American State Papers: Documents, Legislative and Executive*, 38 vols. [Finance] (Washington, D.C.: Gales & Seaton, 1832–1861), 2:839–40, 887. This is the official figure from the Treasury Department and is therefore the cost as calculated by contemporaries. In *The War of 1812* (Gainesville: University Presses of Florida, 1972), John K. Mahon states that the war cost the United States $105 million (p. 385). Still more enlarged is the sum of $158 million given in *Historical Statistics of the United States*, 2 vols. (Washington, D.C.: GPO, 1975), 2:1140 — the original cost was $93 million, with $65 million added through interest on war loans and veterans' benefits. Considering that the national debt was extinguished by 1834 and that veterans' and widows' pensions were a congressional bonanza created after the Civil War, I am inclined to stick by the 1816 statement. I am indebted to J. C. A. Stagg for his help in sorting the evidence on this matter.

from various war loans so that a precedent was established for fighting wars with borrowed money. Part of the loan for the Louisiana Purchase was still on the books (and would not be paid off until 1823) because sales of public lands in the West and South had never met expectations. A General Land Office established by Congress in April 1812 as a bureau of the Treasury Department was meant to serve settlers and funnel money into the federal coffers. But less-than-careful surveys, lax administration, and loose credit terms worked against an efficient system or a dependable source of revenue. By the time surveyors were paid, agents' commissions settled, and other expenses handled, the government often came out on the losing end of the bargain. During the war, most surveying was suspended or carried on haphazardly; thus Treasury records in 1815 showed that settlers owed over three million dollars on their claims. President Madison, like Congress, was inclined to look the other way, for no prudent politician wanted to see legitimate settlers of the western lands jailed for debt, even though the laws of many states permitted this "court of last resort."

Although Madison's political hide had grown a lot thicker during the war years, he heard little criticism of his postwar program. But like every president since Washington, he had critics and they accused him of inconsistency. Strict constructionists such as John Randolph believed that the loose constitutional construction implied in the president's message represented an about-face for one of the founders of the Republican party: The determined opponent of the Bank of the United States in 1790 was now ready to talk business about a new charter. Somewhat surprised, Randolph said that Madison's proposals proved that the president "out-Hamiltons Alexander Hamilton" and he accused Madison of abandoning the venerated Republican principles of 1798.[24]

Ignoring the critics and taking its cue from the president, the Senate approved the "half a loaf" commercial treaty with Britain, leaving the ironing out of details to the chief executive. A tax bill and a protective tariff lumbered through committees to floor debate before becoming laws. Moving slowly, the House gave signs of a favorable attitude toward the national university Madison had recommended, but the bright beginning turned dark as the sluggish committee did its work by turns until the whole scheme was wrecked.

The chartering of the Bank of the United States was something else. Hard money had disappeared from sight as the exigencies of war led to printing-press money; now sixty-eight million dollars in currency was circulating. "There is no money but paper money," Calhoun told the House, "and that

24. Quoted in Ralph Ketcham, *James Madison: A Biography* (New York: Macmillan, 1971), 603.

money is beyond the control of Congress." Creating the new national bank was no longer a constitutional issue; rather, the nation now needed a regulated currency of uniform value.[25] As congressmen and senators lined up on either side of the issue, the division, basically following geographic loyalties, revealed how things had fundamentally changed. The southern and western states wanted the Bank, whereas the traditional money men of New England opposed it. The proposed twenty-five–year charter left the government holding one-fifth of the stock, promised a $1.5 million bonus to the federal government early in the Bank's career, and gave the president power to appoint five directors (subject to Senate approval). Madison may have been slightly disappointed that the Virginia House delegation voted against the Bank, 11 to 10, but the whole package passed comfortably and Madison signed the charter on 10 April 1816. In short order, Madison nominated five Republicans for the board of directors. When the Bank's doors swung open in January 1817, another Republican would be its president.

Chartering the Bank was the main business of the Fourteenth Congress, although other matters were discussed at the presidential dinner table and at Mrs. Madison's Wednesday afternoon levees. Most of the time, Madison was all business, but he did listen to William Thornton (head of the Patent Office) talk about horses, especially after Madison had joined him in acquiring a purebred stud as an investment. (Next to money, horses formed the most important topic of conversation in Washington boardinghouses and in the corridors of Congress.) After anxious debate, congressmen voted to end the old $6 per day salary rule and gave themselves an annual paycheck of $1,500. Although it seemed like a good idea, some lawmakers had signed their political death warrants when they voted for this bill.[26] Madison signed the bill into law, his own $25,000 salary left untouched.

Another bill appropriating $100,000 for a westward extension of the Cumberland Road also gained presidential approval without a quibble. If this was pork-barrel legislation favored by Clay and his friends, Madison was not ready to fight over the constitutional issue he had raised in his annual message. Farmer that he was, Madison knew how vital passable roads were for the commodities produced beyond the Appalachian Mountains. His constitutional conscience, touchy at times, was not terribly disturbed. Besides, Madison owed Clay a favor or two.

Congress had already spent $60,000 on the Cumberland Road, but in truth the so-called National Turnpike in 1815 was little more than a wide cowpath and had not yet reached Wheeling, in western Virginia. The na-

25. Bray Hammond, *Banks and Politics in America from the Revolution to the Civil War* (Princeton, N.J.: Princeton University Press, 1957), 235.
26. Adams, *History*, 1273–76.

tion's canal system was in no better shape, as fewer than one hundred miles had been finished by 1815, and the waterways that were in operating condition were "neither profitable nor useful."[27] A rider on horseback could, with fortitude, travel from the Maine District all the way to Georgia; but roadside accommodations were miserable in most places, and the highways were dusty in the summer, muddy in the winter, and always serpentine. Thus the traveler went "at a pace which would have provoked unfavorable comment in the world of Augustus Caesar." Wise Americans took to the coastal waterways when possible, for even though the Atlantic and its bays were sometimes risky places to venture, the trips were on vessels far cleaner and more comfortable than anything provided by four-legged animals.

Horsepower moved Americans west and south, however. The rise in cotton demand caused the pattern of settlement to swerve south and increase once the war ended. The army was still under orders to remove settlers who squatted on lands belonging to Indians, and trouble soon developed in the southeast where, technically, millions of acres belonged to the Creeks, Cherokees, Chickasaws, and Choctaws. General Andrew Jackson was unsympathetic to the Indian's charges that they had been misled or even defrauded at earlier treaty powwows, and his sentiments echoed those of thousands of pioneers from the Carolinas and Tennessee who were seeking new lands. An order from the War Department calling for the ouster of illegal settlers from Indian lands and the destruction of their buildings drew the settlers' wrath; in at least one instance, they burned in effigy the bureaucrat who had signed the order.[28]

Reports in the spring of 1815 of defiant squatters moving into the lands of the southern Indian tribes soon captured Madison's attention. Peace medals bearing Madison's likeness had been distributed to the chiefs at treaty ceremonials where government officials had grandly promised to honor the agreements, but impatient, law-breaking white men nevertheless slipped into the inviting wilderness ahead of government surveyors and land office officials. Madison signed a proclamation ordering federal officials to remove "uninformed or evil-disposed persons" who squatted on public lands where the titles were still under negotiation. The president gave these squatters until 10 March 1816 to vacate their premises.[29] Nothing much happened except that some visiting Cherokee tribesmen came to Washington to complain about the way their lands were being invaded. General Jackson was in Washington at the time and he urged Madison to ignore the chieftains. Instead, through interpreters, Madison promised the Indians that he would give orders to pro-

27. George Dangerfield, "The Awakening of American Nationalism, *1815–1828* (New York: Harper & Row, 1965), 17.
28. Mooney, *Crawford*, 85.
29. Richardson, *Messages of the Presidents*, 1:572–73.

tect their rights, although he also negotiated a deal to allow a military road from the East coast to New Orleans to pass through their hunting grounds. To make good on his promise, Madison passed word to the Indian commissioner for the region — General Andrew Jackson himself — ordering him to suspend further treaty negotiations for Indian lands unless they were conducted "upon principles consistent with their ideas of justice and right."[30] The sentiment was proper, but Madison already knew how Jackson felt about Indians and their rights. He must have realized that his demand would go unheeded. Meanwhile, citizens in Tecumseh's old stomping grounds along the Wabash were authorized to prepare for statehood.

After the Battle of Tippecanoe in 1811 the Indians vacated enough land in the Old Northwest to encourage settlement of the Indiana Territory. News of war in the East took a long time to reach the peaceable settlements of Jeffersonville and Vincennes and the busy little village of Madison on the Ohio River. In Ohio, where all Indian titles had been extinguished, the population jumped from 230,000 in 1810 to 400,000 by 1815. Citizens seeking cheaper lands moved on to Indiana for a piece of the public domain. In 1810, only 24,520 citizens called the Indiana Territory their home, but a census ordered by the territorial legislature in 1815 showed 63,897 souls were residents. Thereafter, pressure for statehood rose as town promoters hoped to secure the capital at Madison or at the rival village of Croydon. Republicans in the territorial government, most of them appointed by Madison, were more interested in the scramble for seats in Congress than in the petty politics of "capital grabbing."

Congress was sympathetic when petitions for statehood from the Indiana territorial legislature arrived in Washington early in 1816. Except for a handful of New England congressmen who opposed the admission of any western state, there was no impediment to quick passage of an enabling act. Madison signed the approved bill on 19 April 1816. A convention to write a constitution was called for June, and within eighteen days the Indiana delegates had prepared a bill of rights and constitution. Their whirlwind session had cost taxpayers a mere $3,076. In most western territories a faction would emerge to insist that statehood always costs more money than it is worth; thus in Indiana the Vincennes *Western Sun* appealed to voters to block the statehood drive because it would mean higher taxes. Statehood enthusiasts were undeterred, however.[31] Before the year was out, an admission bill would be passed, creating the eighteenth state in the Republic. So far as we know, President Madison was not disappointed that the river town bearing his name lost to Croydon in the scramble for a capital site.

30. Quoted in Brant, *Madison*, 6:401; Mooney, *Crawford*, 83–84.
31. R. Carlyle Buley, *The Old Northwest: Pioneer Period, 1815–1840*, 2 vols. (Bloomington: Indiana University Press, 1983), 1:69, 74.

Meanwhile, the president had other things on his mind. Monroe had regained his health and, although Madison appears to have been very discreet, everybody in Washington who read the *National Intelligencer* assumed the president favored his old friend and fellow Virginian as his successor. Only one other man in Madison's cabinet, William H. Crawford, had any pretensions to the office. Crawford was forty-four and had served in the Senate and as minister in France, but even he figured that he had plenty of time for presidential service. Clay, Calhoun, and Webster were still young men enjoying the House atmosphere, not yet hopelessly infected with presidential fevers. As in Madison's case in two earlier campaign years, a caucus was called in early March 1816 to choose the Republican standard bearer for 1816, but it was so poorly attended that it had to be rescheduled. Madison apparently never lifted a finger or discussed the caucus with party leaders. When the second caucus met on 16 March, Monroe beat Crawford by nine votes. Daniel Tompkins, the forlorn hope of New York Republicans, was an also-ran. Hearing of Monroe's nomination, Madison realized he had fewer than twelve months left in office, and he determined to make them memorably pleasant.

There was some unfinished business after Congress adjourned in April, but it did not prevent the Madisons from slipping away before the heat and humidity of summer settled on Washington. The arrival of Sir Charles Bagot, the newly accredited British minister, proved a boon. Sir Charles had not come to stir up trouble. Following encouraging talks with the Englishman, Madison instructed Monroe to write to John Quincy Adams to propose friendly discussions with Lord Castlereagh regarding armed vessels on the Great Lakes. Bagot wanted a package deal tying the unsettled American fishing rights off Newfoundland with the inland waterways, but Madison pressed for settling one issue at a time. "There is no connection between the two," Madison explained, and it was time to move before the British remilitarized on Lake Erie. "What seems expedient," Madison added, "is 1. that no increase of existing armaments should take place. 2. that existing armaments be laid up. 3. that revenue Cutters if allowed at all be reduced to the minimum of size and force."[32] Months would pass before the British came around to Madison's view, but the upshot was that before the president left office an informal agreement to limit armaments on the border lakes to four harmless revenue cutters had been struck. Although the final pact demilitarizing the Great Lakes would not be ratified until after Madison had left office, it was on his initiative that the once-heated issue cooled down.

The calendar showed 5 June 1816, but Washington was cool and wet when the Madisons departed for their summer vacation. No war clouds,

32. Madison to Monroe, 11 July 1816, Monroe Papers, DLC.

only the dark billows of a heavy downpour, hovered over the city. The rebuilt Capitol was rising and looked sturdier than the old sandstone structure Congress had used before the fire. The president's house was not to be occupied again during Madison's tenure, but the roof was up and the walls were whitewashed. The capital's roads were muddy when it rained and dusty when the sun shone, but even Sir Charles confessed that Washington was not the hick town he had imagined.

Once back at Montpelier, the Madisons could have used some of the rain that fell in torrents as they departed. The thermometer had stayed in the seventies for longer than anyone could remember, but the rains finally stopped. Under a cloudless sky, a host of guests descended on Montpelier for a traditional Fourth of July meal. The picnic—although Mrs. Madison did not call it that—kept nearly ninety hungry guests swarming in the Montpelier kitchen. The diners were all men except for the first lady, the president's mother, and two other women in Dolley Madison's entourage. Madison had an extra room prepared for his aged mother, who despite several lifelong afflictions, would live into her ninety-ninth year. The tempo of life at Montpelier suited the temperaments of valetudinarians.

Messengers from Washington kept Madison informed of affairs in the various departments, particularly the State Office, where faithful clerks carried on after Monroe went on his vacation. Madison became his own troubleshooter when several diplomats in Washington became indignant. Before he departed, Monroe had a run-in with the French minister, who took umbrage of remarks made at Baltimore's Fourth of July celebration. The Frenchman heard reports of the slight to his sovereign lord, Louis XVIII, after he had visited Montpelier, where the president outdid himself to make Hyde de Neuville at home. Back in Washington, the French envoy learned of an insulting Fourth of July remark made by the Baltimore postmaster (who alluded to Louis as "an imbecile tyrant"), and he sent his private secretary to demand the exuberant Republican's dismissal. Madison managed to deflect the minister's wrath until the incident blew over. In another incident, the president heard that the Russians were upset over a gross indiscretion by an imperial miscreant in Philadelphia. Madison subsequently sent his private secretary on a quick mission to placate the tsar.[33] Long accustomed to the slow and mysterious ways of international diplomacy, Madison figured that the passage of time would heal most of these petty wounds. He was right. What concerned him more directly was the lack of rain that had nearly ruined the

33. Brant, *Madison*, 6:407–9; Madison to Edward Coles, 7 July 1816, Coles Papers, Chicago Historical Society. Madison explained to Coles that he would be paid six dollars a day for the mission, "the outward & return passage provided by the public; the expences on shore borne by the party himself."

Montpelier corn crop. Then, in September, the skies opened, bringing a flood that drowned the shriveled corn and damaged the pitiful tobacco crop. Madison wrote down 1816 as a bad year in his crop-accounts book.

Weather aside, the last summer vacation of Madison's presidency was memorable. He did not return to Washington until 9 October, making his four-month absence from the capital probably the longest vacation ever taken by a president. Some northern states had already voted on the presidential electors, and within a few weeks it was apparent that Monroe would easily outdistance the Federalists' token candidate, Rufus King. The calm on international waters provided a respite from executive decisions, and most of the gossip in Washington concerned speculation on who would serve under the new president rather than who would cast their lot with the outgoing chief magistrate. Surely Madison and Monroe talked about cabinet choices. In October 1816 the long-suffering Dallas insisted that he had served too long as secretary of the Treasury and he resigned. The vacancy was offered to Gallatin, but no amount of wooing could convince him to return to his former job. Crawford was shuffled out of the War Department to the Treasury. Ambitious men wanted to be free to fill Monroe's shoes in the State Department, but Crawford was a patient man.

Madison looked at the unfinished business of the nation as he drafted his final State of the Union message. The message, delivered on 3 December 1816, was not downright dull, but one had to read between the lines to catch the president's drift. There were old grievances still unredressed, such as Britain's restraints on American trade with the British West Indies. Furthermore, the dey of Algiers was trying to renege on his promise to leave American shipping alone; but Madison said the United States was ready to teach him another lesson in international manners "should he renew his warfare on our commerce." The Indian tribes were serene, but the militia system needed drastic overhauling, and no uniform standard for weights and measures had been adopted. Madison's pet project for a national university had not moved forward, and he urged that something be done for edudation as well as for "a comprehensive system of roads and canals." Violations of the prohibition against importing slaves needed looking into, Madison noted, and the federal judicial system deserved attention, particularly the practice of sending Supreme Court justices on the annual circuit, which had outlived its usefulness. The office of the attorney general also needed budgetary help from Congress, so that the nation's chief lawyer could become a full-time employee. (The money seemed to be there because there was a surplus of nine million dollars in the Treasury for the first time in years.) With the newly chartered Bank of the United States about to launch its operations, there was also the hope that the much-needed "uniform medium of exchange" would soon exist to ease the problems attending the nation's rickety currency structure.

Finally, Madison mentioned his coming retirement. He observed that "the American people [had] reached in safety and success their fortieth year as an independent nation," and a generation had passed with the Constitution as the nation's organic law. The Constitution had weathered good times and bad, but more important, it embodied a "reconcilement of public strength with individual liberty." Moreover, the nation's westward movement proved that the Constitution was flexible enough to be adapted for territorial expansion "without losing its vital energies." In his summation of constitutional blessings, Madison noted how the personal rights of citizens were protected while providing them with a government capable of promoting "peace on earth and good will to man."[34] Attentive congressmen must have thought that the message was part sermon, part history, and all optimism.

Soon the Washington social season was in high gear. Madison broke his own custom of avoiding parties at foreign ministries during the Christmas holidays and attended an entertainment at the French envoy's quarters. Onlookers noted how the president seemed to enjoy himself, and although 4 March was a few months away, he was already unburdening himself and looking more relaxed.

Bad weather early in 1817 kept the harbors closed and made Washington residents shiver. The snows that fell and then usually melted in a few days lingered on, and Madison noticed that the thermometer rose from "4 above 0" on 14 February to "6 1/2" the following morning.[35] "The severe weather," he told Jefferson, "unites with the winding up of my public business, in retarding the preparations during the session of Congress." The whiplash effect of the higher salaries act caught up with the House, and a new compensation bill set the clock (and salaries) back. A bill retaliating against Britain's commercial restrictions — the kind of bill Madison had unsuccessfully sought in the First Congress twenty-seven years earlier — was finally passed. The law simply imposed "on foreign vessels the same restrictions and prohibitions which were imposed by foreign nations in America."[36] The chief target, of course, was Britain's Navigation Acts. How Madison must have relished signing a bill like the one he favored in 1790!

Meanwhile, Jefferson had a bee in his bonnet and had written from Monticello, urging Madison to pay him a visit once he was resettled on his Virginia farm. The Virginia legislature in 1816 had taken the first steps toward creating a state university, and Jefferson was anxious to sustain the momentum. A board of visitors for Central College at Charlottesville was appointed by Governor Wilson Cary Nicholas, and his commissions went to Jefferson along

34. Richardson, *Messages of the Presidents*, 1:573–80.
35. Madison to Jefferson, 15 February 1817, Madison Papers, DLC.
36. Adams, *History*, 1281.

with those for James Madison and James Monroe. Jefferson received notice of his appointment and during the winter suggested that the board get busy the next spring. Madison promised to attend the first meeting.

Another testimonial, a farewell salutation from the Virginia legislature, came to Madison's office a few days before he was to leave the presidency. In acknowledging the legislators' gesture, Madison took pains to justify the recently concluded war with Britain and to say that the alternative had been "a prostration of the national character and of the national rights."[37] "Through the remaining days of a life hitherto employed with little intermission in the public services, which you so much overvalue," Madison concluded, "my heart will cherish the affectionate sentiments which the representatives of my native State have addressed to me."

Before Madison could take final leave of his official chores, he was handed Henry Clay's bonus bill. In the 1816 charter for the Bank of the United States, care had been taken to see that Congress was left with $1.5 million to use as it saw fit—a so-called bonus. Clay had subsequently drafted a bill that took the windfall and appropriated the money for internal improvements — roads and canals — to stimulate commerce and "render more easy and less expensive the means . . . for the common defense." Nobody in Clay's office seemed to have considered that the president was not yet over his earlier, acute case of strict constructionism.[38] From newspaper accounts and office gossip Madison learned of a bill "to compass by law only an authority over roads & Canals." Had he not warned that a constitutional amendment would be proper if federal funds would be needed for domestic improvements? Had he been too lenient when he did not flinch at the earlier one hundred thousand dollar appropriation for roads? Calhoun thought that the general-welfare clause covered such matters; however, when faced with the bill on his desk during the dying moments of his presidency, Madison decided it was time to teach the nation a lesson in constitutionalism.

On his last day in office, Madison dropped his bombshell. The bonus bill, he said, failed to take into account the fact that Congress had enumerated powers under section eight of the first article of the Constitution, "and it does not appear that the power proposed to be exercised in the bill is among the enumerated powers, or that it falls by any just interpretation within the power to make the laws necessary and proper" for carrying other constitutional powers into execution. Madison had no law degree, but he was trying

37. Dumas Malone, *Jefferson and His Time*, 6 vols. (Boston: Little, Brown & Company, 1948–1976), 6:250; Madison to the Virginia General Assembly, 1 March 1817, Henry E. Huntington Library, San Marino, Calif.

38. Merrill Peterson, *The Great Triumvirate: Webster, Clay, and Calhoun* (New York: Oxford University Press, 1987), 79–80.

to tell the lawyers in the Republican Congress that they had not done their homework. He had said before, and he repeated now, his claim that the general-welfare clause was not intended to become a Pandora's box for loosely drafted legislation "embracing every object and act within the purview of a legislative trust." Furthermore, Madison emphasized, a loose construction of the general-welfare clause would prevent the national judiciary from "guarding the boundary between the legislative powers of the General and State governments, inasmuch as questions relating to the general welfare . . . are unsusceptible of judicial cognizance and decision."[39] Madison hinted that a constitutional amendment was the only proper way to provide for federally funded roads and canals.

Clay was shocked by the president's reaction to his pet bill. When warned that Madison had constitutional qualms, Clay beseeched him to leave the bill untouched. During the alloted ten-day span, Monroe would take office and the new president could sign it into law. Madison relished the opportunity too much, however, to duck the issue. From his position as Speaker, Clay called for passage of the bill over Madison's veto. The sparring over the bonus bill was not full of such invectives as had been hurled during the bank charter debate, and Clay's chagrin did not take a vindictive course. He was simply surprised at Madison's demurral; besides, he thought he had the votes to overturn the president's dissent. A showdown vote proved otherwise, however; and Madison's veto was sustained, a fact he learned after he was safely in retirement.

In all likelihood, Madison had decided to use his last day in office to remind the nation that the Constitution was a document of checks and balances. His predecessors had used the veto power sparingly (Jefferson avoided the issue completely); but Madison thought it was time to say that the Constitution was not a blank check for Congress to fill in as it wished. In rejecting the bonus bill — as in his previous vetoes of the Bank or the gift of land for a church — Madison wanted to establish a presidential precedent of constitutional stewardship.[40] Unlike Tyler, whose vetoes would benumb and confuse the nation, Madison wanted to propound consistent constitutional principles. He reminded his party and the nation in general that even though the legislative branch controlled the governmental purse strings, a president could anticipate constitutional questions early on and either protect the Supreme

39. Richardson, *Messages of the Presidents*, 1:584–85.

40. Madison's early vetoes included one bill incorporating a church in the Federal District and another giving public lands to a Baptist church in Mississippi (see p. 77). In both cases, Madison based his veto on the First Amendment clause prohibiting the establishment of any church or religion by Congress. (See Rutland, *Madison: The Founding Father*, 238).

Court from infringement of its powers or spare the justices from unnecessary labor. Several of Madison's vetoes, particularly on the Bank issue, saw the president splitting hairs, but in his rejection of the bonus bill Madison followed a line of reasoning that was part of the Republican party's creed. What Madison used as a threat, Andrew Jackson would later turn into an art.

Dolley Madison, too, had important things on her mind. Trunks and crates filled the Madisons' rented quarters. Servants had to be reminded that everything was going by wagon or boat and therefore must be packed carefully for the hundred-mile journey to Montpelier. The slaves bustled, unaware of currents then moving elsewhere that would involve their master as head of the American Colonization Society chartered to send free blacks to an African refuge. At the moment, Madison probably worried more about the foul weather in Washington. After watching Monroe take the oath of office, Madison began sorting his papers, carefully arranging his personal letters so that they could be returned to Virginia in good order. Cabinet officers always left their official papers in the government's possession; but starting with Washington, every president had considered his presidential correspondence as personal and had taken it home. Madison must have anticipated the leisure to look over the mounds of paper, and he was surely aware of how valuable the notes he had made at the Philadelphia convention in 1787 had become. Madison mulled over the idea of a posthumous publication. For one thing, only a handful of the fifty-five delegates were still alive, and public interest in the proceedings was bound to be rekindled on the thirtieth anniversary (in 1817) of the main event.

When the sun appeared on 6 April all the crates had been packed, so the Madisons decided it was time to go. They were probably escorted by a host of friends as they took a carriage to the steamboat landing on the Potomac. The vessel bound for the Aquia Creek dock churned the water, and the former president and his lady probably looked on Mount Vernon as they glided past the red-roofed mansion. A well-wisher who accompanied the Madisons noted how relaxed Madison seemed: "During the Voyage he was as playful as a child; [he] talked and jested with everybody on board, and reminded me of a school boy on a long vacation."[41] The fireplaces at Montpelier crackled their welcome as the Madisons arrived and climbed the front steps. James Madison had been serving the people since the spring of 1776. Now he was retired, for good.

No American, not even the redoubtable Washington, participated so directly in the formation of the American Union. In the Virginia Convention

41. Quoted in ibid., 239.

of 1776, the Continental Congress, the Philadelphia Convention of 1787, the Congresses from 1789 to 1797, and his eight years as secretary of state, Madison helped in making fundamental decisions about the political structure of the new nation. He was often in the lead in the decision-making process, and each step in his career is a well-known story, a part of a national heritage of selfless public service. Similarly, we have seen how Henry Adams set the tone for a harsh judgment of Madison's presidency by a long recitation of "executive weaknesses" and mismanagement. Generation after generation of American historians accepted Adams's judgment. For example, one of the most widely adopted college textbooks in American history recently described Madison as a president who "inspired little affection and no enthusiasm." The authors admitted Madison wrote diplomatic notes that were logical, but condemned Madison's lack of a working relationship with Congress. Worst of all, these authors told thousands of collegiate Americans that "Madison was stubborn to the point of stupidity."[42] Little wonder that generations of Americans have placed Madison in the questionable company of Grant, Harding, and Hoover.

On the other hand, Henry Adams admitted (in his final chapter) that "until 1815 nothing in the future of the American Union was regarded as settled." Consider the facts and the probabilities. The facts are that the United States went to war to assert its neutral rights in world commerce and that it was not the last time an American president would insist that "free ships made free goods." Furthermore, in Madison's last year as president the United States was no longer a third-class power — it came of age during his presidency. As to the probabilities, it seems unlikely that the Monroe Doctrine could have been promulgated and accepted by the great powers without the British-American cooperation that Madison inaugurated in 1816. Historians writing in the century since Adams's 1889 tour de force have not stressed this positive side of Madison's presidency. Madison's contemporaries were more magnanimous, and his loyal cabinet members left testimonials to Madison's abilities, which the best (Rush, Dallas, and Monroe) lauded.

Surely it is not fair to judge a man by the shrillness of his enemies' attacks. Even John Randolph muted his criticism during Madison's last year in office. But the judgment that must stand alone is that of the elder statesman John Adams. On the eve of Madison's departure, Adams wrote Jefferson that he was sorry the president and Mrs. Madison had no children of their own: "I pitty our good Brother Madison. You and I have had Children and Grand Children and great Grand Children. . . . I pitty him the more, because, notwithstanding a thousand faults and blunders, his Administra-

42. Samuel E. Morison et al., *A Concise History of the American Republic,* 2 vols. (New York: Oxford University Press, 1977), 1:160.

tion has acquired more glory, and established more Union, than all three Predecessors, Washington, Adams and Jefferson put together."[43]

If thoughtful Americans (those who buy and read books, attend lectures on the same night a popular television program is shown, and avoid "theme parks" as a point of honor) can be excused for their indifference to Madison's presidency, the general public is also guilty of the normative apathy or indifference. Historians have found the Civil War to be a veritable gold mine when it comes to writing chronologies and biographies, but historical literature on the War of 1812 and its prelude is relatively sparse; indeed, this period was all but ignored until recently, when excellent books on the subject were produced by Harry Coles, Reginald Horsman, John K. Mahon, and J. A. C. Stagg. Popular history on the War of 1812 has been written even more infrequently, and Walter Lord's *The Dawn's Early Light* (1972) never made the bestseller's list—which was probably fortunate, because it portrays President Madison as a small man riding a big horse in comic-opera fashion.

Perhaps the burning of Washington permanently seared the American psyche. As historian Paul H. Smith noted, "For most Americans, the failure to defend Washington is probably a symbol for how [badly] the war was managed, and no amount of information on Madison's actual achievements will balance that one fact."[44] The war began with American leaders immersed in a sea of misconceptions about the power of the Yankee militiaman, the weakness of Canadian defenses, and the ability of American generals. Absurd beliefs led to embarrassing debacles. If Madison's name is forever linked only to the burning capital of 1814, then we do the man an injustice. A perceived sense of failure affects history indelibly. Small wonder that Madison was not in contention when Gutzon Borglum began to outline his Black Hills monument of great presidents.

Owing to the excessive popularity of the presidential office and its holder in the twentieth century, Madison's reputation as a first executive has hinged on the conduct of the war (dismal), the fall of Washington (a tragedy), and the sudden change of fortunes provided by events in Ghent and New Orleans (a miracle, perhaps two miracles). In any event, the historical profession has not held aloof from snap judgments but rather has abetted the weakness inherent in popularity . Its is obvious that Madison was not in the same league with the most popular presidents of this century—for example, Wilson, Hoover, Franklin D. Roosevelt, Eisenhower, Nixon, and Reagan. Consider

43. Adams, *History*, 1331; Lester Cappon, ed., *The Adams-Jefferson Letters*, 2 vols. (Chapel Hill: University of North Carolina Press, 1959), 2:508.
44. Paul H. Smith to author, 11 April 1988.

that few presidents were as popular as Harding in the months before his death. What were a president's contributions to the national welfare *before* he entered the White House?

Although it may be true that "a poor politician usually makes a bad President," this judgment on Madison is manifestly wide of the mark. Madison was one of the cofounders of the Republican party, a role he accepted and cultivated by writing essays, corresponding with leading public men all over the nation, and working with key political figures (including John Beckley, Thomas Ritchie, Gallatin, and Gerry). Madison's report of 1800 on civil liberties (particularly freedom of the press) became part of the democratic creed that helped carry the election of 1800. As president he called on congressmen and senators for advice and paid much (perhaps too much) attention to their directions. Working with Macon, Clay, and the moderate wing of the Senate Republicans, Madison helped shape the legislation that did not prevent the outbreak of war but did give the nation a foreign policy that appeared to be consistent with the national interest as these men saw it.

As we have seen, Jefferson's following in the Congress eroded during his second term until it nearly vanished, whereas Madison's stock rose in Congress late in his second term, enabling him to encourage the enactment of major proposals. Jefferson is deemed a most successful president, yet in 1808 the vital Bank of the United States was tottering, the embargo was a disaster, and his last appointments were insultingly rejected by the Senate. When Madison headed for retirement, the Bank was being restored with vigor, the nation had won major concessions at the peace table, and his designated successor could glide into an office where there was so little rancor that the nation subsequently experienced an era of good feeling. These are not mean accomplishments, and certainly not, the actions of a stupid leader. Yet too often the Henry Adams–oracle, textbook critique cited earlier has been the picture of Madison fixed in the public's imagination.

Familiarity breeds content. After working on Madison's papers and writing about his public career for more than a generation, I find no difficulty in accepting President Madison at face value. He was a Republican of the old-fashioned model by the time Andrew Jackson became president in 1829, but in Madison's mind the nation needed more than ever some perspective on the problems besetting the Republic. Most of them could be solved with money, it seemed, but several could not. After fifty years of worrying about slavery and its effects on the national psyche, Madison had no clearer idea of a solution than he expressed when his bonded servant Billey begged not to be sent back to Virginia in 1783. In particular cases, Madison was eager to do the right thing, but a broad, far-reaching, and terribly expensive solution to the slavery problem was beyond Madison's grasp.

To a large degree, then, Madison's reputation is a victim of the much-publicized capture of Washington in August 1814 and the burning of public buildings by British marines. We have seen that it was only a tactical victory and had no real effect on the outcome of the war because the Republic was still a loose-jointed federation that was not mortally wounded when its capital fell (unlike, say, Paris in 1940 or Berlin in 1945). But instead of the War of 1812 being the wrong war against the wrong nation at the wrong time, it was, rather, a war that the United States could fight against a major power without losing and thus emerge with its self-respect. This explains why the War of 1812 was not "the unnecessary war" so many critical historians have proclaimed it to be while admitting in the next breath that the "United States was never again denied the treatment due an independent nation."[45]

What one needs to remember about Madison's administration is that it was the penultimate tie of the Revolution with the presidency. From Washington through Monroe, each president represented a link with the ideals of 1776 and, more specifically, with the gentry class that had fostered and fought the great battles from 1775 onward. Whether nurtured near the Braintree Common or at a Blue Ridge foothill plantation, the American leaders born between 1720 and 1758 represent a flowering era of men trained to accept responsibility as legislators, vestrymen, and militia colonels. (The perfect example was Washington's career, which combined all three roles.) Madison knew the pressures of public life from 1776 onward, but only as a lawmaker, cabinet officer, and president. Nearly all of these men believed they had a duty to perform by going into the public arena, and although most of them openly complained about the burdens the bore, they secretly loved the power they exercised. They could all agree that leadership must devolve on what Jefferson once called "the thinking part of the nation." The concern for numbers, which started in Andrew Jackson's day and which now mesmerizes pollsters, was foreign to these men: "Gentlemen calculated majorities and minorities by counting their own heads, not the people." Secure in the knowledge that the best ideas and guidance came from the top of the heap, not the bottom, Madison and his generation had only a short time during which they were in full control. When Andrew Jackson's star blazed, the quiet revolution led by a generation of shy, thoughtful, well-educated Americans was over. For better or worse (and historians are not always good judges), the numbers game began in 1828 and has never ended.

Politically, the nation was headed for an era of calm simply because the Federalist party had committed suicide. The defiance spouted in Boston and Hartford rankled the rank-and-file Federalists, who loved the nation and distrusted Britain; so by the war's end the hard-line Federalists were on the defensive in their home precincts. Monroe was prepared to go a step further

45. Morison et al., *Concise History of the American Republic*, 1:170.

than the forgiving Republicans and declare political partisanship passé, thus giving full meaning to Jefferson's plea in his first inaugural for a party encompassing all creeds. Yet something was missing as Madison in early 1817 began to contemplate his retirement from public life. In a sense, "the lost world of Thomas Jefferson" had also become the lost world of James Madison, for the nation was on the threshold of a monumental crisis as Missourians prepared for statehood under a black cloud.

The foundation of Madison's political credo was "union," and for thirty years he had watched and sometimes maneuvered as compromises skirted a showdown over the slavery issue. As he clung to the notion of an African safety valve, Madison moved in a direction that the American majority declined to follow.[46] More practical men would soon prevail in national councils, and the one whom Madison somewhat distrusted—Andrew Jackson—was one of the few who adhered to Madison's old-fasioned idea that all differences must be forgotten when the Union was threatened. In most other areas, however, Jackson's presidency broke so much new ground and changed the face of American politics so dramatically that James Madison's political world had essentially disappeared by 1836. The French observer, Alexis de Tocqueville, was among the first to recognize the vast gulf between Jefferson-Madison political realities and those prevailing after Jackson's two terms. The Virginia dynasty faded before the onslaught of a more common majority—not well-born, well-bred, or well-educated, but still a majority.

Despite his many contributions to the creation of this nation, Madison the president may not be the kind of leader that proud Americans like to remember. But the man has not been forgotten. A survey of place names for American rivers, cities, towns, and counties shows that Madison leads his contemporaries Jefferson and Hamilton by a considerable margin.[47] Fifty-three geographical entities bear Madison's name, as opposed to forty-seven for Jefferson and forty-seven for Hamilton.

Such figures in themselves mean little, except as an eponymous indication of the esteem in which citizens held Madison from the time of his presidency until late in the nineteenth century, when most of the country was settled and the few remaining unnamed localities leaned toward the likes of Washington, Franklin, Lincoln, Grant, or Cleveland. Once a year, however, on 16 March a Marine guard of honor dutifully fires a salute over Madison's grave in the family cemetery at Montpelier. The tombstone merely notes a

46. For Madison's retirement years, see Drew R. McCoy, *The Last of the Fathers: James Madison and the Republican Legacy* (New York: Cambridge University Press, 1989).

47. I am indebted to C. B. Wood of Princeton, New Jersey, for this geographical observation.

place of burial. Modesty prevailed when Madison chose only a simple marker, with no litany of his accomplishments. None of the presidents from the generation of the Founding Fathers was a pyramid builder. Utmost simplicity was in keeping with their idea of true republicanism.

James Madison's life was spent in a land rich with natural resources. Thick forests of hardwood and pine provided building materials for ships, farmhouses, mansions, furniture, wagons, and a thousand other items used in daily life as well as for fuel in furnaces and fireplaces. Flowing rivers and streams furnished the power to run mills that ground grain and turned cotton into cloth. The fertility of virgin lands in the Midwest and newer South was a magnet that drew settlers toward even more promising lands farther West. Such words as "unemployment," "homelessness," and "poverty line" were not in the American lexicon during Madison's time. But it was the preservation of American liberty, the gains of the American Revolution carried forward in the Constitution, rather than economic well-being that remained Madison's chief concern.

As president, Madison labored — as he had when he first entered the Continental Congress in 1789 — to maintain that spark of freedom he had first seen lit in 1775. His first duty as president, he believed, was to maintain the Union, for national unity was essential if liberty's flame was to keep burning. When he left the White House in 1817 Madison knew his long career as a public servant had ended. As his carriage passed through the green piedmont, Madison probably reflected on the richness of the land, on the optimism that pervaded the nation, and, most important, on the comforting truth that the Union was again firmly in place. When the outlines of Montepelier took shape in the dimmed vision of the former president, it must have been one of the happiest moments of his life.

BIBLIOGRAPHICAL ESSAY

PRIMARY SOURCES

The Papers of James Madison in the Library of Congress contain over twenty-two thousand separate documents and are the main source for any serious work on the fourth president. Much of the material consists of Madison's drafts or letters to or from his friends and political associates as well as his wife. Important material is also found in letters received from complete strangers or from Republican societies that wished to express esteem for the president. Madison treasured these outbursts of party support and always answered them, usually in his own handwriting. Madison's letters to and from Jefferson are found in either the Madison Papers or the Thomas Jefferson Papers in the Library of Congress manuscript collection and at scattered depositories in Princeton, New Jersey; Boston; and Charlottesville, Virginia. Other vital correspondence is located in the James Monroe Papers, Library of Congress; Albert Gallatin Papers, New-York Historical Society; Richard Rush Papers, Historical Society of Pennsylvania; and William Thornton Papers, Library of Congress. Most of these documents are available on microfilm or in printed editions; in a few cases (for example, Jefferson and Gallatin) both versions are extant. An exception is the Samuel L. Mitchill Papers at the Museum of the City of New York Library.

Printed documentary editions of all the main Founding Fathers are now available, although some are incomplete. The modern edition of Madison's complete writings is William T. Hutchinson et al., eds., *The Papers of James Madison*, 16 vols. (Chicago and Charlottesville: University of Chicago Press and University Press of Virginia, 1962–), including one volume of the presidential series already published and a second on the way (1989). Earlier printed sources of Madison's writings, useful for supplementary purposes, are William C. Rives and Philip R. Fendall, eds., *Letters and Other Writings of James Madison*, 4 vols. (Philadelphia: J. B. Lippincott & Company,

1865); and Gaillard Hunt, ed., *The Writings of James Madison*, 9 vols. (New York: G. P. Putnam's Sons, 1900–1910). Of greatest importance for Madison scholars is Julian C. Boyd et al., eds., *The Papers of Thomas Jefferson*, 24 vols. (Princeton, N.J.: Princeton University Press, 1950–). Also indispensable for the period 1809–1816 is Clarence Carter, ed., *The Territorial Papers of the United States*, 28 vols. (Washington, D.C.: GPO, 1934–1975), which contains Madison's executive correspondence with territorial governors and other frontier officials.

Printed documentary collections of secondary figures include John Quincy Adams, *Memoirs*, 12 vols., Charles F. Adams, ed. (Philadelphia: J.B. Lippincott & Company, 1874–1877); *The Diary of William Bentley* (Salem, Mass.: n.p., 1905–1914); Lyman H. Butterfield, ed., *Letters of Benjamin Rush*, 2 vols. (Princeton, N.J.: Princeton University Press, 1951); "The Letters of Samuel Taggart," American Antiquarian Society *Proceedings* 33 (1923); Bernard Mayo, ed., "Instructions to the British Ministers to the United States, 1791–1812," *American Historical Association Annual Report for 1936*, 3 vols. (Washington, D.C.: Da Capo, 1971); Winfield Scott, *Memoirs*, 2 vols. (New York: Sheldon & Company, 1864); and James Wilkinson, *Memoirs of My Own Times*, 3 vols. (Philadelphia: Abraham Small, 1816).

Newspapers or weekly journals relevant to the Madison presidency range from the pro-Madison *Niles' Weekly Register* (Baltimore), the *National Intelligencer* (Washington, D.C.), and the *Enquirer* (Richmond), to the opposition's *Columbian Centinel* (Boston). All are available on microform or microfilm; a facsimile reprint of *Niles'* is a godsend to any nearsighted researcher.

Important speeches given during the Eleventh through Fourteenth Congresses are found in Joseph Gales, comp., *Annals of Congress, 1789–1824*, 42 vols. (Washington, D.C.: Gales and Seaton, 1834–1856). Committee reports are printed in the *House Executive Documents* or the *House Miscellaneous Documents* for the particular session. Two other invaluable works are *American State Papers: Documents, Legislative and Executive* [Finance, Indian Affairs, and so on], 38 vols. (Washington, D.C.: Gales & Seaton, 1832–1861); and James D. Richardson, comp., *A Compilation of the Messages and Papers of the Presidents, 1789–1897*, 10 vols. (Washington, D.C.: GPO, 1896–1899). Any scholar who overlooks Noble Cunningham, Jr., ed., *Circular Letters of Congressmen to Their Constituents, 1789–1829*, 3 vols. (Chapel Hill: University of North Carolina Press, 1978), is missing an important source of the political byplay during Madison's presidency.

SECONDARY SOURCES

Biographical Accounts

Some day James Madison will attract a biographer of the stature of the late Dumas Malone, whose six-volume work, *Thomas Jefferson and His Time* (Boston: Little, Brown & Company, 1948–1976), will long stand as a model for historians and an intellectual monument to Jefferson. With the passage of a generation, Irving Brant's labor of love, *James Madison*, 6 vols. (Indianapolis: Bobbs-Merrill Company, 1941–1961), seems too narrow in focus and perhaps too apologetic about Madison's shortcomings. Brant was a newspaperman and a New Deal Democrat (both admirable traits in my eyes); but his use of evidence, his footnoting, and his indexing left professional historians uneasy. One is far better off using Ralph Ketcham's sensible one-volume *James Madison: A Biography* (New York: Macmillan, 1971), for a good overview of Madison's life and career. Somewhat less detailed but still useful are Harold Schultz, *James Madison* (New York: Twayne, 1970), and my two books, *James Madison and the Search for Nationhood* (Washington, D.C.: Library of Congress, 1981) and *James Madison: The Founding Father* (New York: Macmillan, 1987).

Madison the president owed much to Madison the Federal Convention delegate. The most readable, authentic account of Madison's role at the Philadelphia meeting is in Clinton Rossiter, *1787: The Grand Convention* (New York: Macmillan, 1966). Adrienne Koch's *Jefferson and Madison: The Great Collaboration* (New York: Alfred Knopf, 1950) is an affectionate portrait written by an intensely partisan Jeffersonian. Similarly, Koch's *James Madison's Advice to My Country* (Princeton, N.J.: Princeton University Press, 1966) tells of Madison's preoccupation with the future of the Union. No survey of the field would be complete without mentioning Merrill D. Peterson, ed., *James Madison: A Biography in His Own Words*, 2 vols. (New York: Newsweek Books, 1974), which is a skillful weaving of narrative and selections from Madison's principal papers.

Although a fresher biography of Vice-President George Clinton is needed, E. W. Spaulding's *His Excellency George Clinton* (New York: Macmillan, 1938) will do for now. George A. Billias's *Elbridge Gerry: Founding Father and Republican Statesman* (New York: McGraw-Hill, 1976) is reliable and readable. Madison's cabinet affords no rich field for biography, but the main figures have been adequately covered. Harry Ammon's *James Monroe: The Quest for National Identity* (New York: McGraw-Hill, 1971) remains the best standard account. Henry Adams's affectionate portrait, *Life of Albert Gallatin* (Philadelphia: J. B. Lippincott & Company, 1879), has not been surpassed by modern scholarship. The up-and-down career of the man who might have succeeded Madison as president is well told in Chase C. Mooney, *William H. Crawford, 1772–1834* (Lexington: University Press of Kentucky, 1974). There is merit in J. H. Powell, *Richard Rush: Republican Diplomat, 1780–1859* (Philadelphia: University of Pennsylvania Press, 1943); and Raymond Walters, Jr., *Alexander James Dallas* (Philadelphia: University of Pennsylvania Press, 1943). C. Edward Skeen's *John Armstrong, Jr., 1758–1843: A Biography* (Syracuse, N.Y.: Syracuse University Press, 1981) is a rather generous view of the subject's ambitions and accomplishments. Glyndon G. Van Deusen's *The Life of Henry Clay* (Boston: Little, Brown & Company, 1937) has not been superseded by later scholarship.

There is something about unpleasant men's careers that drives biographers away. Assessments of William Branch Giles and Michael Leib are buried in obscurity; but one of the Invincibles has been treated with respect in Frank Cassell's perceptive *Merchant Congressman in the Young Republic: Samuel Smith of Maryland, 1752–1839* (Madison: University of Wisconsin Press, 1971). Old as it is, Henry Adams's *John Randolph of Roanoke* (New York: Houghton, Mifflin & Company, 1882) is the best book on this strange man.

Biographies of the military and naval heroes and scapegoats of the War of 1812 abound. Fresher approaches are needed, but there is much to be said for Freeman Cleaves, *Old Tippecanoe: William Henry Harrison* (New York: C. Scribner's Sons, 1939); A. D. H. Smith, *Old Fuss and Feathers: The Life of Winfield Scott* (New York: Greystone Press, 1937); Thomas R. Hay and M. R. Werner, *The Admirable Trumpeter: A Biography of General James Wilkinson* (Garden City, N.Y.: Doubleday, Doran & Company, 1941); E. M. Barrows, *The Great Commodore: The Exploits of Matthew Galbraith Perry* (Indianapolis: Bobbs-Merrill Company, 1935); and Hulbert Footner, *Sailor of Fortune: The Life and Adventures of Commodore Barney, U.S.N.* (New York: Harper & Brothers, 1940). So many books on Andrew Jackson are available that it is a matter of narrowing the choice. I like Robert V. Remini's *Andrew Jackson and the Course of American Empire*, 2 vols. (New York: Harper & Row, 1977–1981), for its overall balance.

Dolley Madison is such an appealing figure it is unfortunate that she left so few records. Thus handicapped, her biographers have had to rely upon information supplied by Margaret Bayard Smith, *The First Forty Years of Washington Society*, Gaillard Hunt, ed. (New York: G. P. Putnam's Sons, 1906), to fill in the gaps. Mrs. Madison's social life and her duties as hostess are adequately covered in Conover Hunt, ed., *Dolley and the "Great Little Madison"* (Washington, D.C.: American Institute of Architects Foundation, 1977); Ethel S. Arnett's *Mrs. James Madison: The Incomparable Dolley* (Greensboro, N.C.: Piedmont Press, 1972) also emphasizes the social aspects of the first lady's life. Details concerning Mrs. Madison's efforts to transform the executive mansion into a showplace are found in Margaret B. Kapthor's "Benjamin Latrobe and Dolley Madison Decorate the White House, 1800–1811," *United States National Museum Bulletin* 241 (1965). Virginia Moore's *The Madisons* (New York: Macmillan, 1979) relates matters in Dolley Madison's private life that are not found anywhere else.

The War of 1812

Special studies dealing with Madison and the War of 1812 constitute a growing body of literature. The best detailed account published in recent times is John K. Mahon, *The War of 1812* (Gainesville: University Presses of Florida, 1972), a thoroughly researched narrative that has become the standard by which other efforts are judged. Henry Adams's *The War of 1812*, Henry A. DeWeerd, ed. (Washington, D.C.: Infantry Journal, 1944), is a reprint of Adams's chapters detailing the war in his magnum opus. Donald R. Hickey's *The War of 1812: A Forgotten Conflict* (Urbana: University of Illinois Press, 1989) explores the military, diplomatic, and domestic history of the war. Francis F. Beirne's *The War of 1812* (Hamden, Conn.: Archon Books, 1965) is skillfully written, detailed, and inclined to regard the war as a mistake from start to finish. Harry L. Coles's *The War of 1812* (Chicago: University of Chicago Press, 1971) is a splendid, brief account. J. Mackay Hitsman's *The Incredible War of 1812: A Military History* (Toronto: University of Toronto Press, 1965) gives a Canadian vantage point; Reginald Horsman's *The War of 1812* (Gainesville: University Presses of Florida, 1972) and J. C. A. Stagg's *Mr. Madison's War: Politics, Diplomacy, and Warfare in the Early American Republic, 1783–1830* (Princeton, N.J.: Princeton University Press, 1983) are soundly researched, carefully detailed, and perceptively written. Glenn Tucker's *Poltroons and Patriots*, 2 vols. (Indianapolis: Bobbs-Merrill Company, 1954) is based on newspaper sources and is easy to read. For naval warfare, Alfred T. Mahan's *Sea Power in Its Relation to the War of 1812*, 2 vols. (Westport, Conn.: Greenwood Press, 1968), was started while Roosevelt was a Harvard undergraduate and finished some years later; it is fun to read for the author's display of naval tactics and his bouncy style. Indeed, for sheer readability C. S. Forester's *The Age of Fighting Sail: The Story of the Naval War of 1812* (New York: Doubleday, 1956) is in a class by itself. Howard I. Chapelle's *The History of the American Sailing Navy: The Ships and Their Development* (New York: Norton, 1949) is a general history with important material on events from 1812 to 1815. George Coggeshall's *History of the American Privateers and Letters-of-Marque* (New York: By author, 1856) is difficult to find; but William B. Crane's *Men of Marque: A History of Private Armed Vessels Out of Baltimore during the War of 1812* (New York: W. W. Norton & Company, 1940) is accessible and gives an overview of the period. C. H. J. Snider, in *Under the Red Jack: Privateers of the Maritime Provinces of Canada in the War of 1812* (Toronto: Musson Book Company, 1928), tells the story from the Canadian side of the border. The reader should also see Edward Eckert, *The Navy Department in the War of 1812* (Gainesville: University Presses of Florida, 1973).

Regional and specific (battles, individuals, towns, and so on) studies on the War of 1812 are plentiful. These include Alec R. Gilpin, *The War of 1812 in the Old Northwest* (East Lansing: Michigan State University Press, 1958), a thorough study of the region around the Great Lakes, most of it prepared from primary sources. Jane L. de Grummond's *The Baratarians and the Battle of New Orleans* (Baton Rouge: Louisiana State University Press, 1961) focuses on Andrew Jackson's role, with some attention to the controversial Jean La Fitte, and is far less detailed than Robin Reilly's *The British at the Gates: The New Orleans Campaign in the War of 1812* (New York: Putnam, 1974), which provides a wealth of information and an excellent map of the battle area. Other detailed studies include W. S. Brown, *The Amphibious Campaign for West Florida and Louisiana, 1814–1815* (University: University of Alabama Press, 1969); Frank L. Owsley, Jr., *Struggle for the Gulf Borderlands: The Creek War and the Battle of New Orleans, 1812–1815* (Gainesville: University Presses of Florida, 1981); and Samuel Carter III, *Blaze of Glory: The Fight for New Orleans, 1814–1815* (New York: St. Martin's Press, 1971). Allan S. Everest's *The War of 1812 in the Champlain Valley* (Syracuse, N.Y.: Syracuse University Press, 1981) is a detailed account of actions in the crucial theater of the war; Robert B. McAfee's *The History of the Late War in the Western Country* (Lexington, Ky.: Worsley & Smith, 1816) is a contemporary account of the transmontane war; Victor A. Sapio, in *Pennsylvania and the War of 1812* (Lexington: University Press of Kentucky, 1970), tells how citizens of the Keystone State reacted to and conducted the war as it touched them; and Morris Zaslow, ed., *The Defended Border: Upper Canada and the War of 1812* (Toronto: Macmillan Company of Canada, 1964), is a collection of important articles and contains a useful bibliography. For this book I used T. Harry Williams, *The History of American Wars from 1745 to 1918* (Baton Rouge: Louisiana State University Press, 1981), as a reliable study.

Among the most helpful scholarly articles on the War of 1812, one must list older works of merit along with more recent contributions. The most useful include Lawrence D. Cress, "'Cool and Serious Reflection': Federalist Attitudes toward the War of 1812," *Journal of the Early Republic* 7 (1987); Louis M. Hacker, "Western Land Hunger and the War of 1812," *Mississippi Valley Historical Review* 10 (1924); Donald R. Hickey, "American Trade Restrictions during the War of 1812," *Journal of American History* 68 (1981); Lawrence S. Kaplan, "France and Madison's Decision for War, 1812," *Journal of American History* 50 (1964); Julius W. Pratt, "Western Aims in the War of 1812," *Journal of American History* 12 (1925); Norman K. Risjord, "1812: Conservatives, War Hawks, and the Nation's Honor," *William and Mary Quarterly* 18 (1961); Abbott Smith, "Mr. Madison's War," *Political Science Quarterly* 57 (1942); J. C. A. Stagg, "Enlisted Men in the United States Army, 1812–1815," *William and Mary Quarterly* 43 (1986); George F. G. Stanley, "The Indians in the War of 1812," *Canadian Historical Review* 31 (1950); George R. Taylor, "Prices in the Mississippi Valley Preceding the War of 1812," *Journal of Economic and Business History* 3 (1930/31); and Joseph G. Tregle, Jr., "Andrew Jackson and the Continuing Battle of New Orleans," *Journal of the Early Republic* 1 (1981). Madison's concept of his role as commander in chief is assessed in Harry L. Coles, "From Peaceable Coercion to Balanced Forces, 1807–1815," in Kenneth J. Hagan and William R. Roberts, eds., *Against All Enemies: Interpretations of American Military History from Colonial Times to the Present* (Westport, Conn.: Greenwood Press, 1986). Important too is Marcus Cunliffe, "Madison (1812–1815)," in E. R. May, ed., *The Ultimate Decision: The President as Commander-in-Chief* (New York: G. Braziller, 1960). Various interpretations of the war are discussed in Don Higginbotham, "The Early American Way of War: Reconnaissance and Appraisal," *William and Mary Quarterly* 44 (1987).

For the political backdrop of the war, the choices range from the recollections of a contemporary congressman to diligent modern scholars. Important for its "insider's" view is Charles J. Ingersoll's *History of the Second War between the United States of America and Great Britain*, 2 vols. (Philadelphia: Lea & Blanchard, 1845). Roger H. Brown, in *The Republic in Peril: 1812* (New York: Columbia University Press, 1964), discusses the Republicans and their ideological opposition to the Federalist party. Steven Watts, in *The Republic Reborn: War and the Making of Liberal America, 1790–1820* (Baltimore: Johns Hopkins University Press, 1987), gives an interpretation of the problems traditional Republicans faced during the war. George Rogers Taylor, ed., in *The War of 1812: Past Justifications and Present Interpretations* (Westport, Conn.: Greenwood Press, 1980), provides speeches and reports from the Congress from 1811 to 1812 and excellent interpretive articles (some of which are cited earlier in this essay) by Taylor, A. L. Burt, Margaret K. Latimer, Julius W. Pratt, and Norman K. Risjord. Collections of pertinent documents leading to the war include Bradford Perkins's *The Causes of the War of 1812: National Honor or National Interest?* (New York: Krieger, 1962), and Robert A. Rutland's *Madison's Alternative: The Jeffersonian Republicans and the Coming of War, 1805–1812* (Philadelphia: Lippincott, 1975). The role of the militia as an ideological concept is discussed in Lawrence D. Cress, *Citizen in Arms: The Army and Militia in American Society to the War of 1812* (Chapel Hill: University of North Carolina Press, 1982).

Where does this leave Henry Adams's two-volume work entitled *History of the United States of America during the Administrations of Thomas Jefferson and James Madison*, reissued in 1986 in a superb edition by the Library of America? From my earlier comments, it must be clear that I think Adams was far too harsh on Madison as chief executive and that I believe Adams excessively influenced historians from his time to our own, until the repetitions of "executive weakness," "incompetency," and "government by proclamation" created an unfavorable public impression that is still hard to dispel. A book of 1,417 pages that goes into a second printing soon after it is reissued (after it was first published almost a century earlier) cannot be lightly dismissed, and the quality of Adams's research set a high standard; still, I continue to think that Adams's personal disappointment with the course of American history colored much of his thinking about Jefferson and Madison. The book deserves to be read, but at times with more than a grain of salt.

The City of Washington

There is a great deal of literature on the capital and the White House, but most of it was prepared for tourists. Of value to the scholar are William Seal, *The President's House*, 2 vols. (Washington, D.C.: White House Historical Association, 1986), and Amy La Follette Jensen, *The White House and Its Thirty-two Families* (New York: McGraw-Hill, 1958). The standard reference work on Washington is still W. B. Bryan's *A History of the National Capital*, 2 vols. (New York: Macmillan, 1914–1916); Constance McLaughlin Green's *Washington: Village and Capital, 1800–1878* (Princeton, N.J.: Princeton University Press, 1962) is also outstanding. Valuable details regarding the early history of the White House, Capitol, and other public buildings can also be found in Talbot Hamlin, *Benjamin Henry Latrobe* (New York: Oxford University Press, 1955) — Latrobe was the official superintendent for the construction of major public structures in the capital during the Madison administration.

The Diplomatic Front

Two superb monographs on the diplomacy preceding and following the outbreak of war are available in Bradford Perkins, *Prologue to War: England and the United States, 1805–1812* (Berkeley: University of California Press, 1963) and *Castlereagh and Adams: England and the United States, 1812–1823* (Berkeley: University of California Press, 1964) — both volumes are full of solid information and remarkable insights. Still worth examining is Alfred L. Burt's *The United States, Great Britain, and British North America from the Revolution to the Establishment of Peace after the War of 1812* (New Haven, Conn.: Yale University Press, 1940), a landmark study of Republican efforts to avoid war. For Franco-American diplomacy of the era, see Clifford L. Egan, *Neither Peace nor War: Franco-American Relations, 1803–1812* (Baton Rouge: Louisiana State University Press, 1983).

Madison's Florida policy has provoked harsh criticism from several regional historians, the most outspoken of whom is Joseph Burkholder Smith. The title of Smith's book — *The Plot to Steal Florida: James Madison's Phony War* (New York: Arbor House, 1983) — makes his viewpoint clear, and the narrative presents the author's belief that Madison was a mendacious chief executive and "the father of covert-action operations." Madison's use of his executive powers in the Florida venture is also treated critically, although in a more scholarly fashion, in Isaac J. Cox, *The West Florida Controversy, 1798–1813* (Baltimore: Johns Hopkins Press, 1918); Cox, "The Border Mission of General George Mathews," *Mississippi Valley Historical Review* 12 (1925): 303–33; Julius W. Pratt, *Expansionists of 1812* (New York: Macmillan, 1925); and Rembert W. Patrick, *Florida Fiasco: Rampant Rebels on the Georgia-Florida Border, 1810–1815* (Athens: University of Georgia Press, 1954).

The British viewpoint comes through in Francis James Jackson's correspondence, published in Lady Jackson, ed., *The Bath Archives: The Diaries and Letters of Sir George Jackson*, 2 vols. (London: R. Bentley & Sons, 1873); and Sir Augustus John Foster, *Jeffersonian America: Notes on the United States of America, Collected in the Years 1805-6-7 and 11-12*, Richard B. Davis, ed. (Westport, Conn.: Greenwood Press, 1980).

Articles on Robert Smith (by Charles C. Tansill) and James Monroe (by Julius W. Pratt) in Samuel Flagg Bemis, ed., *The American Secretaries of State and Their Diplomacy*, 17 vols. (New York: A. Knopf, 1927-1967), are controversial. Tansill blamed Gallatin for Robert Smith's downfall, whereas Pratt is extremely critical of Monroe's handling of the East Florida episode. Daniel G. Land, in *Foreign Policy in the Early Republic* (Baton Rouge: Louisiana State University Press, 1985), sweeps across the critical period, 1805 to 1812, with broad strokes. The impressment issue cut across several categories but was chiefly a diplomatic problem. James F. Zimmerman treats this subject definitively in *Impressment of American Seamen* (New York: Columbia University Press, 1925).

Domestic Affairs

Much of Henry Adams's work relates to the internal politics of the United States during Madison's administration, but nearly always within the context of a wartime situation. The rise of the caucus system and its part in Madison's selection as the Republican presidential nominee is covered in two articles in Arthur M. Schlesinger, Jr., and Fred Israel, eds., *History of American Presidential Elections, 1789–1968*, 4 vols. (New York: Chelsea House, 1971). In the first volume, "The Election of 1808" is related skillfully by Irving Brant, and Norman K. Risjord gives helpful details in his "The Election of 1812" account. For the day-to-day running of the federal government, see Leonard D. White, *The Jeffersonians: A Study in Administrative History, 1801-1829* (New York: Macmillan, 1951).

Politics in Washington forms the core of James S. Young's *The Washington Community, 1800-1828* (New York: Columbia Univeristy Press, 1966), which tells of the role played by "boardinghouse" factions in the Congresses that convened during the Madison administration. James M. Banner, in *To the Hartford Convention: The Federalists and the Origins of Party Politics in Massachusetts, 1789-1815* (New York: Alfred A. Knopf, 1970), gives the rationale behind the Federalists' drive to present Madison with an ultimatum to his war policy and gives details of the domestic maneuverings behind this extraordinary assemblage. M. J. Heale's *The Presidential Quest: Candidates and Images in American Political Culture, 1787–1852* (New York: Longman, 1982) is valuable for its look into an era when vigorous politicking was still considered the height of bad taste. Ralph Ketcham, in *Presidents above Party: The First American Presidency, 1789–1829* (Chapel Hill: University of North Carolina Press, 1984), presents an insightful view of the constitutional office and how its earliest holders perceived their responsibilities. Madison comes off well.

Economic factors during Madison's presidency are covered thoroughly in Curtis P. Nettels, *The Emergence of a National Economy, 1775–1815* (New York: Holt, Rinehart and Winston, 1962); and in Lewis C. Gray, *History of Agriculture in the Southern United States to 1860*, 2 vols. (Washington, D.C.: Carnegie Institution, 1941). Economic concerns are among the diverse interests treated in George Dangerfield, *The Awakening of American Nationalism, 1815–1828* (New York: Harper & Row, 1965). Dangerfield's other important book, *The Era of Good Feeling* (New York: Harcourt, Brace, 1952), picks up the story and is worth study because of its presentation of diplomacy, national and local politics, and economic patterns in an expanding nation. Drew McCoy, in *The Elusive Republic: Political Economy in Jeffersonian America* (Chapel Hill: University of North Carolina Press, 1980), covers more than the economic forces at work during the Jefferson and Madison administrations. To understand more on the chartering of the Bank of the United States, consult Bray Hammond, *Banks and Politics in America from the Revolution to the Civil War* (Princeton, N.J.: Princeton University Press, 1957). For a complete study of public land policies, see Malcolm J. Rohrbough's *The Land Office Business: The Settlement and Administration of the Public Lands, 1789–1837* (New York: Oxford University Press, 1968).

Our views of early nineteenth-century Indian policies continue to alter. A good starting point is Reginald Horsman, *Expansion and American Indian Policy, 1783–1812* (East Lansing: Michigan State University Press, 1967), along with Francis P. Prucha, *American Indian Policy in the Formative Years: The Indian Trade and Intercourse Acts, 1790–1834* (Lincoln: University of Nebraska Press, 1970). In his search for a just course of action in dealing with the tribes, Madison was pulled in several directions, as the careers of Crawford and Jackson reveal.

Regional political matters affected Madison's administration through strong personalities. The outstanding work on Clay, Calhoun, and Webster is Merrill Peterson's *The Great Triumvirate: Webster, Clay, and Calhoun* (New York: Oxford University Press, 1987), a work particularly useful for uncovering the motives of these ambitious, powerful men. For local struggles and factions in the important states of New York and Pennsylvania, the best accounts are presented in De Alva S. Alexander, *A Political History of the State of New York, 1774–1882*, 4 vols. (New York: H. Holt & Company, 1906–1923); and Sanford W. Higginbotham, *Keystone in the Democratic Arch: Pennsylvania Politics, 1800–1816* (Harrisburg: Pennsylvania Historical Commission, 1952). For the transmontane region, R. Carlyle Buley's *The Old Northwest: Pioneer Period, 1815–1840*, 2 vols. (Bloomington: Indiana University Press, 1983), is an excellent source.

Constitutionalism as an issue during Madison's presidency is handled well in Melvin I. Urofsky, *A March of Liberty: A Constitutional History of the United States*

(New York: Alfred A. Knopf, 1988), particularly Chapter 10. Specialists may want to consult the Holmes Device volume on the Supreme Court during this period, written by George L. Haskins, and Herbert A. Johnson, *Foundations of Power, 1801–1815* (New York: Macmillan, 1981). Madison's dealings with the Supreme Court are covered in Henry J. Abraham, *Justices and Presidents: A Political History of Appointments to the Supreme Court* (New York: Oxford University Press, 1985). For Madison's declining years, when he relished the role of elder statesman, see Drew McCoy, *James Madison: Last of the Fathers* (New York: Cambridge University Press, 1989).

Finally, two important items relevant to Madison deserve mention, for they give us Madison's own explanation for certain events and actions in his long career. These are Madison's "Autobiography," edited by Douglas Adair, *William and Mary Quarterly* 2 (1945), and Madison's "Detached Memorandum," edited by Elizabeth Fleet, *William and Mary Quarterly* 3 (1946). The *William and Mary Quarterly* has also recently published significant articles on Madison by Joyce Appleby, Lance Banning, Drew McCoy, Robert Shalhope, and Gordon Wood that deal with the president's ideas on republicanism and constitutionalism in their broadest forms.

INDEX

	DATE DUE	
NOV 0 6 2004		